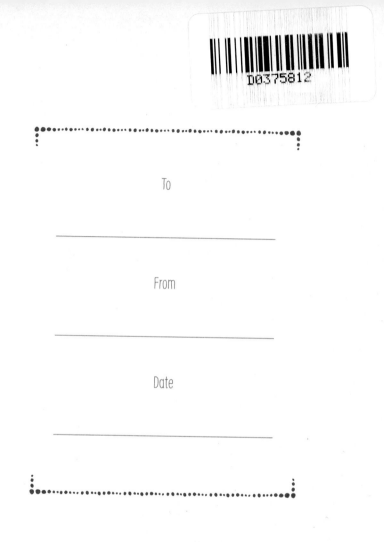

To

_____

From

_____

Date

_____

365 Devotions
for Hope

Karen Whiting

Edited by Christina Zimmerman

365 Devotions for Hope

Copyright © 2015 by Zondervan

Requests for information should be addressed to:
Zondervan, 3900 Sparks Dr., SE, Grand Rapids, MI 49546

ISBN 978-0-3103-5962-3
ISBN 978-0-3106-3183-5 (custom)

Printed in the United States

19 20 21 22 23/LSC/ 18 17 16 15 14 13 12 11 10 9 8 7 6 5 4 3 2 1

Introduction

Norman Vincent Peale was not always an optimist, but he always had hope. He practiced hope, looking for it in each situation he encountered, offering it to others along the way, and seeking it to provide a permanently happy spirit.

We can do that too. We can practice hope no matter what our circumstances are and no matter what life is like for us at this very moment. Hebrews 11:1 reminds us that faith gives us confident assurance that what we hope for is going to happen. It is the evidence of things we cannot yet see.

You have every reason for hope, every reason to have a happy spirit. As you read through the pages of this book, may you be reminded of the ways that having a hopeful heart strengthens and renews you. May you see new possibilities for each area of your life and continue to walk in faith.

With the rising of each morning sun, may your spirits be lifted high, carried along on the wings of hope.

In hope and joy,
Karen Moore

JANUARY

•••••••••••••••••••••••

He who is not everyday conquering some
fear has not learned the secret of life.

—Ralph Waldo Emerson

The Door to Hope

"I am the door. If anyone enters by me, he will be saved and will go in and out and find pasture."

—John 10:9 ESV

Today marks the beginning of a new year. It is an open door to many possibilities. An open door looks inviting and beckons you to walk through and discover what is inside. You hope that when you open the door, what you find will be bigger and better than anything you could have imagined. You hope that what you find will not confine you like a closet.

Jesus said, "I am the door" (John 10:9 ESV). Jesus is the door through which all must enter to receive eternal life, and for those who enter, He becomes so much more. Just imagine that you are standing on a threshold with Jesus, looking at the world and all of its possibilities. These possibilities are bigger than life. More amazingly, Jesus is with you to protect you through the storms of life. Though a storm may come, it cannot break apart your dreams. Jesus promised to keep you safe. With Him all things are possible. With Jesus there is hope for today and tomorrow. He is the door by which you should enter if you want an extraordinary, secure, and hope-filled year.

Lord God, thank You for Jesus. He is the door to my dreams and my life. He is my hope for today and tomorrow. In Jesus' name I pray, Amen.

Hope in Purpose Fulfilled

The Lord will fulfill his purpose for me.

—Psalm 138:8 ESV

God created the world. He made the mighty sun that warms the earth and the powerful oceans, including all the creatures that inhabit the oceans, both small and great. Everything that God has made has a purpose. Take the seashells for example. Have you ever strolled along a beach looking for seashells? You catch a glimmer of a seashell's color in the sparkling grains of sand and stoop to pick it up. Seashells come in many shapes and colors: some are brown; some are tan; some are white, and all have distinctive patterns. Each beautifully designed shell once served as a home for a little sea creature. Though the sea creature has moved on, the empty shell, having fulfilled its purpose, is left behind. It is a small reminder of God as Creator and His purpose fulfilled.

Sometimes we get caught up in the busyness of life—jobs, bills, relationships, and family. These can become distractions that take our eyes away from God, who created each of us for a purpose, just as He created the tiny seashells. Everything God has made has a purpose, which He will fulfill in His time. Rest in this amazing truth, and allow it to give you hope.

Heavenly Father, thank You for creating me for a purpose. I will rest in the hope that You will fulfill my purpose in Your time. Amen.

Hope in God's Plans

As for you, you meant evil against me, but God meant it for good.
—Genesis 50:20 ESV

The book of Genesis reveals that God gave Joseph dreams and a vision to do great things. Joseph knew that God had a plan for him. However, being sold into slavery by his brothers did not seem to fit the plan. Joseph came to realize that the plans of his brothers were for harm. But although it was meant for harm, God turned everything around for Joseph's good. God knew ahead of time what would happen, and He had already devised a plan to make Joseph a ruler in Egypt.

Are you stressed because your life seems out of sorts? Are you currently in the midst of a hopeless situation? Remember that God always has a plan, even when the unexpected happens or when things go wrong. God took care of Joseph when his brothers wanted to get rid of him. He used their actions to fulfill a plan that He had ordained. Their actions became tools in His hands to fulfill His purpose for Joseph. If God did that for Joseph, He will certainly do the same for you. He ordered your steps a long time ago and will keep you in His plan, even when others intend to harm you or when circumstances become difficult. Joseph never lost hope, nor should you. Remain faithful to God, and determine to pursue His will. Remember that God is in control.

Dear God, thank You that You know all about me and can use any situation for good. Amen.

A Legacy of Hope

Commit to the Lord whatever you do, and he will establish your plans.

—Proverbs 16:3

There's a story from China about people who strive to make long-term plans that will last for six hundred years. The reason for this is that they want their dreams to go beyond the first person who makes the initial plan. They want to build a legacy and a lasting future.

The Israelites suffered greatly at the hands of their enemies. They were defeated in battle and were carried away to live in another country where they remained for more than seventy years. But while they were in exile, God gave the prophet Jeremiah a prophecy of hope. He told the people that God had good plans for their future. God wanted the Israelites to know that His plans for them were not just for one day. He planned to build for them a legacy and a lasting future.

Dreaming big with long-range plans is a good idea, no matter what you are currently experiencing. Real hope looks to places, people, and ideas in the future that are yet to be seen. You can experience an abundance of hope, knowing that in spite of your current condition, God has a plan to build a legacy and lasting future for you.

Dear God, thank You that You have a plan for my future. I will always trust in Your care for me. In Jesus' name I pray, Amen.

One Act of Courage

In God, whose word I praise—in God I trust and am not afraid.

—Psalm 56:4

Are you afraid? You are not alone. Fear is a natural human emotion. Few people boast about not being afraid of anything. If they say they have no fear, then we should question their ability to stand in the face of fear. It is just not realistic to have no fear.

Consider King David. He was no stranger to fear. David had enemies who sought to annihilate not only him but also his kingdom. But David overcame his fear because he knew he was not alone. In verse 1 of Psalm 27, he said, "The LORD is my light and my salvation—whom shall I fear?" Through a rhetorical question, David demonstrated his awareness that God protected him.

Overcoming fear did not happen all at once for King David. It was a process that grew out of his everyday walk with God. He understood that God was not against him. He had faith and hope in God's ability to sustain him. So in a time of fear, place your hope in the One who can sustain you. If necessary, meditate on David's words, and hide them in your heart. As a child of God, there is no need to fear.

Dear God, my Father, You are my strength during times of trouble. Therefore, I will not fear. Thank You for Your protection day by day as I walk with You. In Jesus' name I pray, Amen.

Biblical Strategy

"On the seventh day, march around the city seven times, with the priests blowing the trumpets."

—Joshua 6:4

Throughout the history of Israel, many battles have been fought and won. Joshua led the Israelite army in many of those battles, but the most renowned is the Battle of Jericho. According to the book of Joshua, the battle strategy involved marching around the city of Jericho, blowing trumpets, and shouting. It was a strategy that God had given to Joshua, and it was a strategy that worked.

A believer's strategy for the future should begin with God. Take Him into consideration in your decisions. Also, when strategizing your future, be sure to be flexible in how you are going to accomplish your goals. Flexibility in planning is important because God may lead you in a different direction or there may be unexpected challenges along the way.

Do not be overcome by unexpected and discouraging circumstances. You simply need a new strategy so you can refocus and rebuild. Trust God, believe in yourself, and then step out and develop a new approach. Keep in mind that God uses seemingly impossible situations to make His glory known. Have faith in His plan as He guides you forward. And always, no matter what, maintain a clear picture of your future and your hope.

Dear God, thank You for Your wisdom and guidance. Help me to always begin with You. In Jesus' name, I pray, Amen.

Celebrate Growth in Hope

He who began a good work in you will carry it on to completion until the day of Christ Jesus.

—Philippians 1:6

Celebrate the uniqueness of your hope. Just as each snowflake is different, your hope is uniquely your own. We cannot see the difference of each snowflake with our eyes, but it is there just the same. We cannot see the uniqueness of hope, but it is also there. What makes each person's hope unique? Like a snowflake, your hope is patterned with your unique design. If you are in Christ, then celebrate your uniqueness in God. He is the One who created the hope that is within you, and He is not finished yet. God promises to complete what He has begun in you. This promise from God is a hopeful and unwavering word even in the face of sin.

Just as a snowflake exists in the midst of other snowflakes, you are never alone or insignificant. When seen together, snowflakes are a vision of beauty that transforms the landscape and blankets the earth. With other believers you will grow to be a vision of loveliness. You are bound by love to those with whom you live and fellowship. So celebrate your unique hope, and together with others celebrate the work that God has done and will continue to do. Trust that the hope that is within you is a process that God will complete.

Father in heaven, thank You that You are creating a hope within me and in others around me. Amen.

Fighting for Hope

Praise be to the LORD my Rock, who trains my hands for war, my fingers for battle.

—Psalm 144:1

The alarm clock blares as a new morning dawns. You do not know what will happen throughout the day, but God does. The one thing that you can be sure of is that at some point in your day or maybe even throughout the day you will struggle to maintain your hope in God. This is normal for believers. How do you fight this feeling? First, you must own up to this struggle, or else you may grow sluggish and negligent in your fight for hope. Second, use the hope that God has placed within you. Moment by moment, hope will help you to love others by responding to evil with good. Hope will keep you going when you are faced with physical issues like sickness. Hope will strengthen you to deal with emotional stresses.

Each day when that alarm clock wakes you from sleep, allow it to be a reminder to begin with a prayer that God will refresh your hope and strengthen you for the day's journey. Choose to move forward enthusiastically in the Lord, and prepare yourself to fight for your hope.

Lord, thank You for strengthening my hope day by day. When I call on You in prayer, You will be with me to deliver me, honor me, and strengthen my hope. I can spend my day with the assurance that it will end in victory because of You. Amen.

Faithful Hope

"Well done, good and faithful servant."

—Matthew 25:21 ESV

A major responsibility to the hope that we have within us is that we can simply be faithful to the responsibilities that God has given us. Jesus told a parable to illustrate this. A master who was about to embark on a long trip entrusted his money to his servants. When he returned, he praised and rewarded the two servants who invested his money but punished the servant who hid the money. In the same way, God entrusts us with time, abilities, resources, and relationships. His expectation is that we will be faithful in employing them for the good of His kingdom.

You will be faced with many opportunities to prove your faithfulness each day. How should you respond when faced with these opportunities? Be sure that you honor God in all you do and measure your response by what impacts God's kingdom. The person who has no heart for the kingdom of God will be punished. But those who are faithful will be rewarded. As you carry out your day-to-day responsibilities, remember that you must remain faithful in all that you do. Then you will honor God and continue to build on your foundation of hope.

Dear Lord, strengthen me to be faithful to all You have given me to do. In Jesus' name I pray, Amen.

Hope for the Future

"For the revelation awaits an appointed time; it speaks of the end and will not prove false."

—Habakkuk 2:3

You may have a vision for publishing a book, launching a new invention, or opening your own business. Whatever your dream may be, it is going to take time. And when you speak of your dream, do not speak of it in ordinary terms of hope. Do not say that you hope to do this or that you hope to do that. Instead, be confident in your vision, and trust that God has placed this desire in your heart. Do not become discouraged as Habakkuk did when God's plans for the Israelites did not happen quickly. God told Habakkuk to be patient because what He promised would occur.

As you trust and wait on God to make your dream a reality, take the time to allow Him to fully form the vision. Let this confidence in God strengthen you to overcome obstacles along the way and inspire you not to give up on your vision. Trust that in the end God will fulfill what He has placed in your heart. Expect it. Exercise your God-given hope, which is not just a desire for something good to happen. Exercising your hope means you have great expectations for God to fulfill your dream in the future according to His will.

Heavenly Father, I will hold fast to the hope for the future that You have given me. In Jesus' name I pray, Amen.

Diligent Hope

We want each of you to show this same diligence to the very end, so that what you hope for may be fully realized.

—Hebrews 6:11

Be warned: some who hope will not endure to the end. Perseverance is difficult because of the stresses and strains of everyday life. However, consistency will not be overlooked by God. He sees those who fully realize hope and work to maintain it. Now what does hope being fully realized mean? It means hope that is fully assured. It is hope that is confident and certain. This hope is not wishful thinking or finger-crossing hope. Because of your fully realized hope, you gave to those on the margins; you showed love to those who were downcast, and you helped those who could not help themselves. Your hope is not a temporary experience but is a display of your godliness.

Though sometimes you may become discouraged, the writer of the book of Hebrews encouraged you to press on. God has not forgotten you. So with the same excitement that you have shown in the past, continue to have assured hope to the end. The zeal that you demonstrated in the past will carry you through. Nothing in life is more important than this. Keep your hope alive.

Dear God, help me to keep Your hope alive. When I am discouraged, give me strength to press on until the end. In Jesus' name I pray, Amen.

Overcoming Fear

In God I trust and am not afraid. What can man do to me?

—Psalm 56:11

Life can be filled with many fears. Remember the fear you had as a child learning to ride a bicycle. The only way you overcame that fear was to trust that your mom or dad would not let you fall. Kneepads, training wheels, and a helmet helped too. The psalmist wrote about the awesome power of trust for when you are afraid. He knew and understood the power of God; therefore, no matter what happened, his hope was not destroyed. The Bible has warned us that the days of darkness will be many. We will suffer and experience difficulties. But you know what? It is during those times when you should activate your hope by placing your trust in God. Complete and total trust in God is the key to overcoming fear. When you trust God, giving into fear is not an option. Trusting God is turning to Him even in the darkest times and trusting Him to make things right.

Are you fearful? Know that God is good, and He loves you. Conquer your fears by connecting with God through prayer. Then with hope-infused anticipation, look forward to what is coming.

God, my Father, You are my strength and my hope. Thank You for always being with me. In Jesus' name I pray, Amen.

Encouraging Friends

"Greater love has no one than this: to lay down one's life for one's friends."

—John 15:13

Treasure friends who encourage you, for they are precious gems. You can confidently share your dreams and hopes with a true friend. A true friend can be rare, but when friendship is proven, it must be treasured and kept safe. Real friends believe in you. They listen and cheer you on as you pursue your dreams. They share your pain at each failed step, share your joy at each moment of progress, and celebrate your triumphs. True friends love at all times. There is nothing you can say or do that will diminish the love of a friend who loves unconditionally. If you make a mistake, rest assured that your friend will show constant affection toward you and be honest with you because of the love you share.

The greatest love is when a friend lays down his or her life for you. This is the way that God loves us. God laid down His life through His Son, Jesus Christ, so that we could be saved. Now, that is true friendship! What is more, anyone may become His friend by trusting in Him as one's personal Savior, being born again, and receiving new life in Him.

Heavenly Father, You are love itself. Thank You for the gift of Your Son, Jesus, who laid down His life for me. That is true friendship. In Jesus' name I pray, Amen.

Being a Friend

Do not forsake your friend.

—Proverbs 27:10

One of the greatest friendships in the Bible was that of David and Jonathan. When Jonathan's father, King Saul, tried to kill David, Jonathan protected him. Even though Jonathan faced death, he remained loyal to David. Loyalty is one of the prerequisites for being a friend. Loyalty is a selfless feature of love. To be loyal, you cannot live for yourself. Loyal people not only stand by their friends, they also are willing to suffer for them.

Friends are people who bring hope to your spirit. Choose to be a real friend who stays in touch, listens, hugs, laughs, invests time in the relationship, and believes in your friend's dream. Friends are indispensable in this life. There is something special about being a friend to someone you can confide in, tell your troubles to, and share your life with. In turn, your friend can do the same for you. Be a friend by encouraging your friends to pursue their dreams. Hope with them, and celebrate their triumphs. Rejoice in the hope that is found in being a true friend.

Dear God, friends are a precious gift from You. Thank You for my friends. Help me to be the kind of friend that my friends need me to be, one who loves selflessly and bears the pains of others. Bless my friends with health, prosperity, life, and love. In Jesus' name I pray, Amen.

Hope in Marriage

Above all, love each other deeply.

—1 Peter 4:8

Togetherness is sweet when it is with a beloved spouse. Doing special things with each other such as eating, sharing a joke, and chatting about the day are little ways of intertwining your lives. You can also share hopes, make plans together to reach common and individual goals, and support each other in pursuing your dreams. At your wedding you and your spouse promised to be there for one another for a lifetime. Your wedding vow is a declaration of security, trust, and hope. The foundation of your hope in marriage should be the truth of God's Word. God reveals true values in His Word that will strengthen both of you, provide solutions to issues, and build the love that is between you. Not being plugged into the Bible can dangerously cause the hope and security of a marriage to weaken.

If you are married, be thankful that you have someone to depend on and who is committed to building your marriage relationship on a foundation of God's Word. If you are not, keep in your heart all the hopes you have for a future someone. Do not be afraid to celebrate the lasting marriages of friends and family. They are a testament to fulfilled dreams.

Heavenly Father, I pray that You will bless me to be a spouse who cherishes marriage and seeks to build it from the solid foundation of Your Word. In Jesus' name I pray, Amen.

Know Thyself

Do not think of yourself more highly than you ought.

—Romans 12:3

Knowing yourself should be something that happens naturally, but this is not always the case. Even though our experiences help to shape us into who we are, this does not mean that we necessarily know who we are. Many do not know what they are passionate about or what they want from life. The process of knowing yourself does not have to be difficult. Begin with the understanding that God made you special and different from any other person on earth. Then with that understanding accept yourself. Know your strengths and weaknesses. Be kind to yourself, especially regarding your weaknesses. Be thankful that you can always improve in areas where you are lacking. Use your strengths with humility so that you do not become arrogant. Base your worth in God, the One who made you. In Him we are capable of completing valuable work that is godly.

Ask God to help you discover more about yourself, your motivations, your personality, and what brings you joy. Evaluate yourself, asking what really interests you, what makes you laugh, and what memories you cherish. Rejoice at what you find. Let your capabilities and positive character traits give you confidence to act upon your hopes.

Dear God, my Creator, help me to discover my true self, the one whom You made me to be. And may I always be true to who I am in You. In Jesus' name I pray, Amen.

Hope Makes You Stronger

Be joyful in hope, patient in affliction, faithful in prayer.

—Romans 12:12

Most of us have endured devastating trials in our lives. We have been devastated by financial loss, heartbreak, loss of loved ones, and other troubled times. Many of these stories are reported on television on a daily basis. And yet, time after time, the resilience of those who are facing adversity shines through. The main reason many of us do not buckle under the weight of our circumstances is because of the hope that is in our hearts. Characteristically, just like faith, hope is strengthened by adversity. The experience of having gone through something difficult toughens our resolve so that we believe we are going to be okay. In verse 12 of Romans 12, Paul tried to help us understand that going through difficult times was no excuse to abandon hope. We should remain joyful in hope as we wait in anticipation for God's promises to be fulfilled, with the greatest promise being heaven.

When you experience difficulty, you have a choice. One option is to hide in a dark place away from the world, or you can face the adversity head on, knowing that you are not alone. God is there. Just reach out to Him in prayer. The hope that He has placed in your heart will see you through. And the next time you endure a trial, your hope will be stronger.

Dear God, thank You for hope that is strengthened through every trial. Amen.

The Heart of Home

My people will live in peaceful dwelling places, in secure homes, in undisturbed places of rest.

—Isaiah 32:18

Home is a condition of the heart that focuses on love for one's family. God ordained the family in the home as an institution of trust and hope. Yet trouble is at the doorsteps and in the homes of many families today. Alienation often exists between husband and wife, between parents and children, or among brothers and sisters. What instruction does God's Word provide to help us keep hope alive in our homes? First, take a stand for God. In spite of criticism from outsiders, families must commit to God and be willing to follow through on that commitment.

Second, make your home a place where the love of God dwells. Be intentional about how you relate with each other. In your family, choose to be fully present. Share hugs and smiles, and look into your loved ones eyes when you are sharing thoughts. Avoid checking text messages or thinking about your to-do list during meals or during family times. The things you share with each other will remain when you have parted. When you spend time with your family and allow your hearts to connect, your hope and love will be kindled.

Heavenly Father, I pray for peace to dwell in my home, and I ask that my loved ones will experience the joy of Your love and respond in obedience to Your will for our family. In Jesus' name I pray, Amen.

Home Builders

Unless the LORD builds the house, the builders labor in vain.

—Psalm 127:1

If home is the place where your heart resides, then home-making is your greatest career and goal. Homemaking is the art of changing a home into a haven, a place to reenergize and relax. You will be nourished by love, joy, and hope when you reside within the space where your heart longs to stay. A homemaker in every sense of the name is also a home builder. Home builders work hard and long to accomplish goals within the home. But according to the psalmist, the home builder labors in vain if the goals for the family are not God's goals. When we try to build a home and a family without the Lord, our efforts will ultimately fail.

When building a home, you must seek the Lord's will and depend not on your own strength, but know that success lies only with God. Do not trust in the world and its ungodly standards, and do not build your home on gold, silver, or precious stones and metals. These things will not survive eternity. Instead, spend time seeking God through prayer before you begin to build. Pray that He will be with you as you build your home and use you to help build His kingdom. As a home builder there is no better way to nurture hope and love in your home.

Lord, our God, everything that is good has its beginning in You. Establish our home, and bless us with peace and love as we do Your will. In Jesus' name I pray, Amen.

Believe in Goodness

We have an advocate with the Father—Jesus Christ.

—1 John 2:1

A Jewish girl named Anne Frank and her family hid from Nazis during the Holocaust. Many people helped this family by supplying them with food and other resources. Despite the evil that surrounded her and though she lived for two years in a cramped apartment, hope remained alive in Anne's heart because she believed in the goodness of life and others.

When life is difficult, find strength in your hope. Like Anne, seek goodness in others. Notice those who reach out to provide for you and protect you. Respond with faith and trust instead of building walls that keep out others. Look for loving people with whom you can build relationships, as their goodness will fuel your hopes. Also, when people need your help, do not hesitate to give them a hand. God rewards our good works when we sacrifice for others with humble spirits. Just as Jesus is our Advocate and is pleading our case to the Father, we should stand in the gap for others. Our actions add value to their lives and to our own lives as well.

Dear God, thank You that Jesus is my Advocate. His love helps me to love others. May I always be willing to be an advocate like Christ. In His name I pray, Amen.

Carefree Times

"Therefore do not worry about tomorrow, for tomorrow will worry about itself. Each day has enough trouble of its own."

—Matthew 6:34

Do you take time to escape from your everyday life and spend it with loved ones and friends? All your worries can wait. The break will allow you to recover from the cares of your life and refresh your hope. If you cannot escape for a weekend retreat, plan a little getaway such as a night out with a friend for coffee or a movie. Even tea for two at home provides an opportunity to celebrate life and offers a break from worries. Speaking of worries, Jesus taught us that we should not worry. Most of our worries are about situations that will never happen. We fret about the future based on what we have today. But Jesus assures us that God will provide just as He provides for birds and flowers.

This lesson should not be hidden from others. Share it so that your loved ones can relax and trust God too. Invite a friend who is facing a difficult situation to join you, and bless that person with a joyful interlude. Let go, trust God, and look at the amusing side of life. Laughter and joy today make facing tomorrow a little easier. Trusting in God brings hope for carefree days.

Father, help me to trust You instead of worrying about days that have yet to come. In Jesus' name I pray, Amen.

Sharing Our Adventures

Make my joy complete by being like-minded, having the same love,
being one in spirit and of one mind.

—Philippians 2:2

New experiences, both tragic and unexpected pleasures, add dimension to our lives. When we bring them home and share stories of our adventures, our loved ones become a part of those adventures too. When we share our adventures with others, they are enlivened, and their hope is strengthened. Paul warned that Christians should not be selfish and should work for unity, even as it relates to our experiences. What has blessed you will certainly bless others. And when you invite them to share in your experiences, you esteem them to feel important.

Connecting people with our joys and sorrows defines unity and is a way we can share with others. We grow together through sharing, but we can grow apart if we remain silent among our loved ones. When we share our adventures, we are looking out not only for our own interests but for the interests of others as well. Sharing our life stories with one another lets others into our lives and helps us to understand each other better. The reward of sharing life's beautiful adventures is that you get to know others more intimately and share in the hopes that connect you.

Dear God, my Father, thank You for friends, family, and others with whom I share life. Help me to unselfishly share all of the blessings with which You have blessed me, even those stories of blessed adventures. In Jesus' name I pray, Amen.

Forgiveness Brings Hope

"If you hold anything against anyone, forgive them."

—Mark 11:25

Rocks piled into long, low walls dot a countryside. They keep cows from crossing but are not high or strong enough for much else. Each spring neighbors mend the walls that storms have toppled. The walls enhance the beauty of the country scene. However, the walls we sometimes build have a different purpose. We build walls that keep friends away from us. These walls go up because of misunderstandings, hurtful words and actions, or neglect. These grievances are reflected in the thoughts of Robert Frost's poem "Mending Wall." In it the speaker asks the reader to consider whether building a wall keeps something in or keeps something out. The speaker says, "'Good fences make good neighbors.'" Sometimes these walls are built because of offenses made against one another. The Bible clearly provides instruction on how you should respond to another's wrongdoing against you—forgive.

Ask yourself whether you have put up walls between you and someone else. Is it time to seek forgiveness to mend the relationship? Be quick to forgive. By doing so, you prevent your lack of forgiveness from damaging hope.

Dear God, forgive me that I am sometimes slow to extend forgiveness to others. Help me to take down any walls I have built, so that I can develop godly relationships. In Jesus' name I pray, Amen.

In Spite of Betrayal

Jesus asked him, "Judas, are you betraying the Son of Man with a kiss?"

—Luke 22:48

*L*osing a friend can be painful, especially when it is the result of betrayal. Betrayal causes disappointment as the expectations or hope that you had in someone else is diminished. It can be such a great sorrow that only time and an act of forgiveness will bring healing. Jesus looked at Judas and questioned him about a kiss that signaled deception. A kiss usually communicates affection, but Judas' gesture toward Jesus was his betrayal. Judas's deceptive heart was revealed in an instant and launched a conspiracy that resulted in the death of our Savior.

But all was not lost; Jesus rose from the dead and met on several occasions with His disciples and others. He shared new life and new hope through the good news of His resurrection. Though He never mentioned Judas, it is clear by His teachings that Jesus must have forgiven him. In spite of Judas's betrayal, hope has changed the world and continues to exist. Even today it continues to impact every area of our lives. Recognize its power in your life, and allow it to undergird the hope you have in others.

Dear God, thank You for the hope You have provided through the resurrection of Jesus. Help me to forgive as Jesus did and to grow stronger, in spite of betrayal. In His name I pray, Amen.

Make Friends, Not Frenemies

Wounds from a friend can be trusted, but an enemy multiplies kisses.
—Proverbs 27:6

Actions reveal who truly loves you. People who pretend to care but hurt you or jealously compete with you are called *frenemies* in pop culture. Their deceptive care and concern can be your downfall. But you do not need them and can let go of such relationships. In the book of Proverbs, King Solomon gave sound advice to his son about this type of friendship. He implied that an enemy under the guise of being a friend may do everything right but has an ulterior motive. This enemy selfishly seeks to take something you have, hurt you, or worse, destroy your hope. Do not allow this to happen. Solomon advised that you learn to recognize your frenemies and seek out friends who have your best interests at heart.

Real friends will be honest with you even though the truth may hurt. Real friends also encourage you to reach your goals, commiserate with you over disappointments, and want to spend quality time with you. Genuine friends are truly happy with no display of jealousy when you succeed. Be thankful when a friend responds with joy over your good news or hugs you when you share bad news. Furthermore, you should work at being the kind of friend you want to find. There is always room for more real friends.

Dear Father, thank You for the real friends You have brought into my life. Help me to be a real friend too. In Jesus' name I pray, Amen.

The Gift of Time

A time to love.

—Ecclesiastes 3:8

A pretty surprise package with a bow sparkles with hope and love. This unexpected gift reminds you that someone cared enough to send you something special. However, do you know what matters more? Time and attention. But busyness has overtaken our lives and has affected the time we spend with those we love. Not only has our time with one another been impacted, but also our time with God has diminished. The responsibilities of our lives have pushed our relationship with people and God to the bottom of the proverbial pile. How can we dig our way out? Solomon made a discovery that can help us deal with this issue. He took his readers on a journey as he sought to discover the meaning of life. He discovered that everything in life, including his responsibilities, was futile except his relationship with God.

It is quite clear that God desires quality time with His children. It is our relationship with Him that should cause us to focus on people, whom He loves, and not responsibilities. The love we share does not need a bow and pretty wrapping. A phone call, a coffee break, or any time with others can meet the needs of our hearts. Hope is renewed whenever you make time to be with people. Choose to connect with someone, and be the gift of time and hope that someone needs today.

Dear Father, help me to make time with others and with You a priority. Amen.

Just Around the Corner

In their hearts humans plan their course, but the LORD establishes their steps.

—Proverbs 16:9

If you enjoy drinking Coke, then you have Dr. John S. Pemberton to thank. Dr. Pemberton was a pharmacist in Atlanta who indirectly created this popular recreational drink. Using coca leaf, kola nut, and damiana in the original formula, he had intended to provide a product that replaced morphine. However, Pemberton's French Wine Coca, as he called it, was soon altered, and the name changed to Coca-Cola. Though serendipitous in nature, unintentional discoveries are never surprises to God.

God creates serendipitous meetings as well. While the apostle Philip was enjoying a successful preaching ministry in Samaria, God redirected him to a desert road. There he met and witnessed to an Ethiopian eunuch, whose life was changed forever because the eunuch became a Christian that day. Every day each person you meet brings an opportunity for something wonderful and unexpected. It may happen with someone you have just met, or it could be a person you have known for a long time. If you allow God to direct your steps and you stay alert for these opportunities, every day will be adventurous. You also may be the serendipitous hope that someone else needs.

Dear Lord, thank You for being my guide even during serendipitous moments. It is a true adventure to be led by You. Amen.

Optimistic Hope

Surely your goodness and love will follow me all the days of my life.
—Psalm 23:6

Living in hope means you know good things are going to come your way. You have a sense of optimism about your future, your life, and yourself. On a partly cloudy day, do you see dark clouds and the possibility of rain, or do you see dark clouds and the sun that shines behind the clouds? If it does rain, do you see the rain as an intrusion to your schedule or as a blessing that waters the plants and trees? Choosing to be optimistic means that you see a glass of water as half full instead of half empty because you know that God is in control, and it is He who sends good things your way. Because God has promised to protect and guide us through life, we can be optimistic about the good things that are ahead.

Therefore, in all things, look for positive outcomes. You cannot always control what you will face, but your attitude is yours. If you choose to view problems negatively, they will wear you down and leave you hopeless. But if you choose to view problems optimistically, they will always be for your good and will empower you for the future. Surely goodness will follow you, so you should keep an optimistic view.

Dear God, thank You that according to Your Word, goodness will follow me. Help me to remain focused on that truth no matter what happens. Amen.

Fuel Your Dream

Moses saw that though the bush was on fire it did not burn up.

—Exodus 3:2

Sitting in front of a warm, glowing fire is lovely, especially on a cold day. To keep that fire going, though, you constantly have to add wood or some type of fuel. Unlike the burning bush that Moses saw, fire needs fuel. God was the source of Moses' fire, but what can fuel the fire of your dreams? God can give you the fuel you need to live the life He wants for you. Your desires can be the fuel you need to achieve your dreams. If you would like a better home, keep that in focus as you save to purchase that house or to improve the one in which you live. If you dream of a new career, let your desire be the burning motivation that drives you to study, add new skills, and actively check job listings. If you hope people around you will treat you better, then fuel those relationships with love and acts of kindness.

A fire does not burn without fuel. Thoughtfully consider your hopes and dreams, and give them the fuel needed to achieve these goals. Through fuel, focused work, and obedience to God, your dreams can become a reality.

Dear Father, thank You for the dreams that are in my heart. Strengthen my desires so that day by day my dreams will be fueled and will become a reality. In Jesus' name I pray, Amen.

Working Toward Goals

Whatever you do, work at it with all your heart, as working for the Lord, not for human masters.

—Colossians 3:23

A little bird pecks at the dirt to dig up a worm or scratches the ground in search of seed. The bird flits here and there, finding pieces of string, twigs, and other material for a nest. These are layered together to create a soft bed. The bird steadfastly works to accomplish its goals, which are to provide a means for life and survival for itself and other birds that depend on it.

To make our goals come true, we need to work steadfastly toward them. Little by little, we should labor toward success, and as Paul advised the Colossians, we should work at whatever we do with all our hearts as if we are working for the Lord. If working toward your goals becomes a drudgery, remember for whom you are working. You are working for the Lord. Remember, too, the part that God plays. He is by your side as your guide, strength, and resource. We may find help with other resources and teachers, and we may invest our own time and efforts, but also look to God. If you hope to fulfill a dream, then believe it is worth the work and remember that you are working for the Lord.

Dear God, my Father, may You be pleased with the work that I have completed in order to accomplish my goals. Thank You for supplying all the resources I need. In Jesus' name I pray, Amen.

Imagineering

"Therefore I tell you, whatever you ask for in prayer, believe that you have received it, and it will be yours."

—Mark 11:24

Walt Disney had amazing dreams that came true, and his dreams continue to bless people of all ages. To make his dreams a reality, he combined the science of engineering with imagination, which is referred to as *Imagineering*. Our imagination is a wonderful gift from God. It is a function of the mind and a part of the soul. When we place what we imagine about our dreams under the Spirit's control, God releases a supernatural force. Jesus said if you believe that your prayers have been received, then what you pray, what you dream, will be yours. But do not miss the key to receiving this type of response in prayer. Make sure that what you are praying for is a dream that is rooted in the heart of God.

Your dreams grow out of your imagination. You imagine that what you believe will happen. It is a cycle: your imagination feeds what you believe, and what you believe causes your imagination to grow. Just be sure that what you imagine is what God wills for you. His will in your life is the hope necessary for making your dreams a reality.

Dear God, my Father, thank You for the gift of imagination. I pray that all that I imagine will be according to Your will so that the blessing of my dreams will be realized. In Jesus' name I pray, Amen.

FEBRUARY

The February sunshine steeps your boughs and
tints the buds and swells the leaves within.

——William C. Bryant

Unlimited Hope

I pray that from his glorious, unlimited resources he will empower you with inner strength through his Spirit.

—Ephesians 3:16 NLT

Do you like to dream big? No dream is too big for God. He has unlimited hope to make dreams come true. If you think your dream is too big, then ask God for His help. He can help you to achieve your hopes and will cause them to multiply more than you could ever imagine. Perhaps your dream is to accomplish something noble. You may want to help a poor neighbor but are not sure how. God will help you find the way. Your hope to help one person might cause you to organize a clothing drive at your church for a local shelter. What began as a small dream to help one person can become a big dream that helps many. With God's help you have the power to think big and touch the lives of many people.

A. B. Simpson offered encouragement by saying, "Our God has boundless resources. The only limit is in us. Our asking, our thinking, our praying are too small. Our expectations are too limited." Dream big with big expectations that God will provide unlimited hope. Paul said that God has unlimited resources at His disposal and will use those resources for you. All you have to do is ask Him. Let prayer propel your dreams forward as you listen for God's direction.

Dear Father, I ask in Jesus' name that You will empower me by Your unlimited resources to accomplish the dreams of my heart. Amen.

Waiting Expectantly

Listen to my voice in the morning, LORD. Each morning I bring my requests to you and wait expectantly.

—Psalm 5:3 NLT

When you pray, expect God to listen and respond. Your hope is that He will answer your prayer as you have prayed. However, He knows what you need and will wisely provide what you need each day. Therefore, when you pray, you should wait. When you make the decision to wait on God, you may find some impatience that floats to the top because He does not respond according to our timing. However, in waiting your eyes will be opened to His sovereign will, and you will learn that the sooner you trust His will, the sooner your expectations will be realized.

Waiting on God takes patience that is intertwined with hope. It teaches you that you can depend on Him to work on your behalf. You can afford to wait on God because only by His power are your prayers answered. After you pray, begin looking for His response. This is what the psalmist called "wait[ing] expectantly" (Psalm 5:3 NLT). God always answers prayer. God knows the future, and His future contains the best for you. He loves you and knows the right time to bless you with an answer. Trust that the wait will be worth it.

Dear Lord God, I trust that You will bless me with an answer to my prayers. And if the answer does not come right away, I will wait expectantly for Your response. In Jesus' name I pray, Amen.

Dominoes

*Jesus said, "If you hold to my teaching, you are really my disciples.
Then you will know the truth, and the truth will set you free."*

—John 8:31–32

Dominoes is an old game that was designed to be played on a flat surface. However, many children have found it entertaining to set up the dominoes one after another in an upright position. Once the dominoes are all set, the first domino is toppled to trigger a chain reaction that sends the others tumbling one by one until each has fallen. This is called a domino effect.

Domino effects are found repeatedly in the Bible, helping the reader to understand that certain actions have certain consequences. Consider John 8:32. Jesus told His disciples that they would be set free if they set into motion the domino effect of holding to His teaching.

Domino effects govern your dreams. The reality of your dream is the result of a chain reaction. The reaction may begin with a little desire that starts within your heart and mind. Lining up the steps needed to realize the dream is like setting up a row of dominoes. Along the way you will find joy in hopes and expectations as you overcome challenges and continually build the chain. When plans are initiated, each step triggers a wonderful reaction to make your hopes and expectations come alive. Give thanks to God each time your carefully laid plans fall into place just the way you hope.

Dear God, thank You for each step along the way to making my hopes and dreams real. Amen.

Unfolding Expectations

"Each day has enough trouble of its own."

—Matthew 6:34

When you look back over the days that have passed, you may see times of pain and grief that you never expected. But you will also see times of joy and blessings that you never anticipated as well. Your review of those days may cause you to realize that it was best that those days unfolded one at a time. You can trust all your tomorrows to God. But today has the opportunity for living and enjoying present moments. Today your hope is alive and is all you can handle. Jesus said the troubles that we experience are only for that day. Tomorrow has not come so we do not know what it will bring. The strength that you have is for today and not tomorrow.

Between the soft lights of dawn with the newness of the morning dew and the setting of the sun with its glorious colors, there is enough time to fill with work, pleasure, cares, and dreams. Enjoy every moment to the fullest. You cannot make time move any faster, so do not try to rush it, and do not waste time worrying about tomorrow. Relish the glorious moment-by-moment unfolding of today.

Dear God, thank You for today. Bless me to live to the fullest, and help me to let tomorrow take care of itself. Amen.

Zero Expectations

"But love your enemies, do good to them, and lend to them without expecting to get anything back."

—Luke 6:35

Performing acts of kindness or a loving deed without expecting anything in return can give you a great sense of freedom. When you give up your desire to receive something and instead focus on giving, you will be filled with a great sense of joy. God's kindness and love serve as the ultimate example of giving without any expectations. He loved us so much that He sacrificially gave up His one and only Son, Jesus Christ, so that we may receive eternal life. What did God receive for what He gave? Nothing. Many people refuse to receive the precious gift that God has given, but God continues to love them in spite of their response to Him.

Extend love and kindness from your heart without measure. Allow God to use you to bring hope to someone today through an act of kindness. That person can be a friend or an enemy. If an enemy, your act of kindness will not be easy for you. But act in obedience to Christ. Let the gift be as free as a breeze, with no expectations. Everyone involved will be blessed with joy, and most of all God will see and smile.

Dear God, You are my example for loving others without expecting anything in return. Help me to cling to this way of loving others so that Your joy will be multiplied in our hearts. In Jesus' name I pray, Amen.

Doglike Hopes

Always give yourselves fully to the work of the Lord, because you know that your labor in the Lord is not in vain.

—1 Corinthians 15:58

Dogs make wonderful pets. Most are faithful and loyal companions. Their connection with their owners can run deeper than many human relationships. Wagging their tails signals joy and happiness. They delight in a pat on the head or a tiny morsel of food, which they gobble up and then wait expectantly for more. Dogs never tire of hoping for something good from their masters' hands. They spend a good amount of time moving from one thing to the next without looking back. Dogs commit to finding their next adventure. Their tenacity is a trait that demonstrates how to pursue hope beyond discouragement.

Your heart is filled with hope and with the expectation that good things will come. Rejoice when your expectations are met. When your expectations are unmet, it is natural to grieve the loss, but you must move doggedly beyond your loss so that you may seek and discover new hopes. This is what Paul meant when he said that we are to "give [ourselves] fully to the work of the Lord" (1 Corinthians 15:58). Give yourself fully to the pursuit of new hopes. Before too long you will dream afresh and be strengthened for days ahead.

Dear God, today I give myself fully to the hopes of my heart. And when my expectations are not met, strengthen me to pursue new hopes. In Jesus' name I pray, Amen.

Overcoming Disappointment

Naaman went away angry.

—2 Kings 5:11

In the book of 2 Kings, Naaman, a commander of the army of the king of Aram, became ill with leprosy. The Bible reveals Naaman to be a great man who was highly regarded because the Lord had shown to him great favor in battle. One day the servant of his wife told Naaman that the prophet Elisha could heal him, so Naaman followed the advice of his servant and went to see the prophet. But Elisha wounded Naaman's pride. The prophet told Naaman by messenger to dip in the Jordan River seven times. Naaman was disappointed that the prophet Elisha did not stand before him personally and heal him. He allowed pride to dampen his hope for a cure.

If you have allowed pride get in the way of your expectations and your hopes, thinking that your way of reaching your goals is the only way, then you must do what Naaman did. After his servants encouraged him to follow Elisha's orders, he humbly accepted the prophet's method for his healing, which was God's way, and he was healed. When Naaman changed his attitude, not only was his hope for a healing fulfilled, but his heart was changed too. If you are disappointed because your expectations have not been met, check your pride and follow God's plan.

Dear God, help me to look to You when I am faced with disappointment so I can see the fulfillment of my hopes. In Jesus' name I pray, Amen.

Young in Hope

Abraham and Sarah were already very old, and Sarah was past the age of childbearing.

—Genesis 18:11

Grandma Moses, who began painting late in her life, is known for remarkable works of art. Age was not an obstacle for her. She did not allow the years that had gone by to dictate what she could accomplish in the future and stop her from learning new things. It is amazing to see people retire from a lifelong career and begin something new. They are living out a dream that may have been buried years earlier. The new freedom of time has allowed them to follow their dreams.

Like Grandma Moses, Abraham and Sarah were advanced in years when their dream of having a child was fulfilled. Sarah was barren and no longer within childbearing years. Time and age had seemingly stolen her dream. So at first she did not believe it was possible to conceive, but both Abraham and Sarah discovered that God could defy the laws of nature to make their dream a reality. If you have tucked away a dream in your heart for years, this may be the day to pursue it. The calendar moves onward, but that is no reason to stop dreaming and hoping. And if time causes your hopes to become stale, remember the power of God. It is He who can make all things new. Just continue to believe and have faith that your hopes will come true.

Dear God, through the passage of time I pray that my heart will remain strong and young in hope. In Jesus' name I pray, Amen.

Sparkles in the Darkness

"I will make your descendants as numerous as the stars in the sky."

—Genesis 26:4

When your vision grows dim and everything seems to go wrong, take time to step outside on a clear night and gaze at the stars. Allow them to be sparkling reminders that there are glimmers of hope in the darkness. Our world could not exist without stars. They are always in the sky and serve as a source of energy and light. Most are small and shine their brightest at night. God used stars to strengthen Isaac's hope. He promised that Isaac's descendants would be as numerous as the stars in the sky. This was a difficult promise to grasp since Isaac and his step brother, Ishmael, were the only children of their father, Abraham. He probably asked in his heart how he could possibly have so many relatives. So God used the vastness of the stars in heaven to help Isaac connect his hopes to the promise.

Pastor Charles Spurgeon once said, "Hope itself is like a star—not to be seen in the sunshine of prosperity, and only to be discovered in the night of adversity." Look for glimmers of hope in the darkness of failed attempts when you are reaching for your dreams. Your dreams glitter with new possibilities and beckon you to try again. In the darkness of failure, follow the tiny lights of hope to move forward.

Dear God, thank You for the stars that shine in the night. May they continually remind me of my hope for the future. In Jesus' name I pray, Amen.

Grasping Hope

Hold on to what is good.

—1 Thessalonians 5:21

When you reach the end of your rope, tie a knot in it and hang on." This quote has been misattributed to Benjamin Franklin and Presidents Jefferson, Lincoln, F. D. Roosevelt, and Theodore Roosevelt. Though its origin is unclear, its meaning has been consistent. If you have ever tried to climb a rope, you know that it is impossible unless the rope is knotted in various places. Or if you have played a game of tug of war, you know that unless the rope is knotted on your side, you will not win. In both cases the rope will be difficult to hold on to.

A knot redefines the function of a rope. A rope may be used for one reason or another, but when it has a knot, its purpose changes. The knot becomes the strength of the rope because at that point, the rope almost never breaks. The believers in Thessalonica were listening to many doctrines, some of which were false. Paul wanted them to hold on to sound doctrine and let no person take it away. Sound doctrine was profitable for living a life of hope. Make sure that you define a few knots in your hope. They can be inspirational truths or motivational statements that you have heard along the way. Then when you begin to slip, hold on to those knots so you can continue on your journey to dreams fulfilled.

Dear God, bless me with good solid knots that I can hold on to when my hope begins to slip. Amen.

Forward with Motivation

The righteous cry out, and the LORD hears them; he delivers them from all their troubles.

—Psalm 34:17

Martin Luther King, Jr. made many inspirational and moving speeches during a time when the attitudes of some in the United States needed to be redefined. The most famous of those speeches was his "I Have a Dream" speech. This speech, which included words like *prosperity*, *faith*, and *hope*, motivated people of all races not to cave in to the disparity across the land. He shaped the dreams of the masses and motivated them to fight for that dream.

Sometimes dreams fade or begin to die. When this happens, it is the moment to fight. Begin by writing down the dream that seems to be evaporating and all the reasons you want it to come true. Then motivate yourself. To motivate yourself, talk with someone who can inspire you, read the Bible for words of inspiration, or have a heart-to-heart talk with God in prayer. God is only a prayer away. Through prayer God will hear you and strengthen you. This alone should be all the motivation necessary to keep moving forward.

Dear God, You are my help when my dreams begin to fade. Thank You for the inspiration I receive when I call out Your name. Thank You for hearing me when I pray. In Jesus' name I pray, Amen.

Courageous Growth

"Be strong and courageous."

—Deuteronomy 31:6

Robert Graetz was a minister who, though he was white, supported the efforts of African Americans during the Montgomery, Alabama, bus boycotts. He and his family were threatened by those who opposed integration, and twice bombs went off in his yard. He never gave up his support, even though he and his family faced very real danger. As a sign of hope, he planted a tree in the crater where a bomb had been ignited. That tree lasted a long time and before it died was a symbol hope. This act and his reaction to indifference turned many hearts toward his dream of bringing peace to the community.

In the midst of adversity or evil that is caused by others, look for good soil on which to plant a dream. Even the rockiest foundation can become rich soil that will nurture the growth of your dreams, if you allow God to begin a transformation in your life. Like Joshua, "be strong and courageous," for God loves you and will not fail you (Deuteronomy 31:6). Remember the people you want to serve, and forgive those who try to cause harm. Your courage will inspire like-minded people who will help to grow your dream.

Dear God, thank You for courageous people who fight to help others realize their dreams. Help me to be the kind of person who inspires others as well. In Jesus' name I pray, Amen.

Clinging to Hope

Gideon replied, "But how can I save Israel? My clan is the weakest in Manasseh, and I am the least in my family."

—Judges 6:15

In the Old Testament, God called a farmer named Gideon to be a warrior and rescue the Israelites from the hands of their enemies. However, Gideon doubted himself and did not think God could use him. He tested God three times before he would believe. Self-doubt and listening to negative voices can dash your hopes, especially if you replay them in your mind. The words can tease and taunt you over and over again. Clinging to your hope and faith in yourself is a choice that will keep your dreams alive.

God revived Gideon's hope not only in himself but in God, and God humored him by providing three signs to show Gideon that He would be with him. Through Gideon, God led the Israelites to victory. Surround yourself with positive reminders to hope in the Word of God, and display mottos, benefits, and reasons for your dream. These will become voices of faith that will cheer you on as you dare to believe and strive to turn your hopes into reality. If a doubt creeps in, face it and declare it unworthy of your time. Let your faith in your hope leave doubts behind.

Dear God, thank You for the victory You give when I trust in You and cling to my hope. Amen.

The Light of Hope

"Whoever can be trusted with very little can also be trusted with much."

—Luke 16:10

One candle gives off light that dispels the darkness as the flame flickers and burns. The light can be passed to spark the glow of another candle and add more light. Irish writer Oliver Goldsmith once said, "Hope, like the gleaming taper's light, adorns and cheers our way; and still, as darker grows the night, emits a brighter ray." Goldsmith had only a small light of hope when he left school. He was unsuccessful in his studies of medicine. While in London, Goldsmith had little money to support himself. So he put to use his light of hope, which were his writing skills along with other odd jobs. He went on to successfully write essays, poems, novels, and plays in the 1700s.

It is often the ordinary, little things that brighten a day and bring hope. A smile, kind word, or the sun peeking through a cloud brings hope when your day has been darkened with sadness, pain, or tragedy. But God has given you a little light of hope through a skill or other gift. Begin to use it when the days are dark, and God will cause your hope to glow and grow. He will also use you to light the candles of others.

Dear Lord, thank You for the light of hope You have given me. Amen.

Reshaped with Hope

Yet you, LORD, are our Father. We are the clay, you are the potter;
we are all the work of your hand.

—Isaiah 64:8

In the Bible, God has often been referred to as a potter, and we are referred to as clay. It is a powerful metaphor that helps us understand our relationship to God. A potter is a person who makes earthenware from clay. The process can be grueling as the clay is spun and heated at high temperatures. Sometimes the pottery is broken while it is being shaped. But a cracked or broken piece of pottery can be reused to make items stronger. Potters grind broken pieces into grog and then add the grog to soft clay to strengthen the mixture. The clay is still flexible but stronger because of the tiny broken particles. The right balance is needed before the potter slaps the clay on the wheel and shapes it into a beautiful bowl, jar, or other ware.

When hope seems dashed and dreams shattered, trust that God will recycle the brokenness. He will take the shattered pieces, add the soft newness of hope, and help you to reshape your dreams. Like the grog-infused clay, let the bits of past failures make your next attempt stronger.

Dear Father, even though dreams are sometimes shattered, I can trust that You will reshape my hope. Amen.

Strength from Crisis

The righteous person may have many troubles, but the LORD delivers him from them all.

—Psalm 34:19

President John F. Kennedy once said, "The Chinese use two brush strokes to write the word *crisis*. One brush stroke stands for danger; the other for opportunity. In a crisis, be aware of the danger—but recognize the opportunity." The Chinese use brush strokes that paint words with deeper meanings. Known for its beauty, grace, and history, the technique for this type of writing dates back to the time of the Yellow Emperor, which was at least four thousand years ago. Using this technique, the word *crisis* combines images of danger and opportunity. Everyone will experience a crisis at one time or another. In a crisis you face dangers, disappointments, or losses, but when you overcome the problems, you will find the hope of new opportunities. That hope comes from the knowledge that God will help you in a time of trouble, and He promises to deliver you.

Let a crisis bring out the best in you. It allows you to become courageous and an overcomer. You will learn from new experiences that may be painful. As you focus on solutions, which come from God, you will discover you are stronger than you thought. Believe that blessings will come from a crisis.

Dear God, thank You for new opportunities that are born in a crisis. Allow me to face them courageously because You are with me. Amen.

Living Wide

"For God so loved the world."

—John 3:16

Stepping out of a safe and comfortable place to act upon dreams takes courage. True stories of people who took big risks to achieve their dreams can give us encouragement. Their stories are reminders that the journey is exciting and makes you feel alive. Taking risks to reach your goals is sometimes referred to as "living wide." When you live wide, you are ready to feel and even fail, but the journey is worth it. Consider Rosa Parks who stood firm against a legal system that denied her the right to sit in the front of a city bus. Or consider our first president, George Washington, who crossed a river in the bitter cold to keep this country from falling into the hands of British soldiers. They took risks and succeeded. They lived wide. But there is One who took the biggest risk in all of history. God loved us so much that He gave up His Son and risked whether or not sinful mankind would love Him back. God lived wide so that you could have hope, and He wants you to live wide too.

Living wide is a risk, but it allows for opportunities to meet new people and experience more of life. Living wide is what so many people in history did before they fulfilled their dreams. Living wide will fuel your hope.

Dear God, thank You for taking a risk for me. Give me the courage to live wide as You do. Amen.

Choosing Joyful Hope

Wearing a linen ephod, David was dancing before the LORD with all his might.

—2 Samuel 6:14

It is a joy to get up each day when you like what you do. On one occasion David danced before the Lord with all his might. He was excited and overjoyed because he was bringing the ark of the Lord back to Jerusalem after it had been in the land of the Philistines. Bringing home the ark was a job that brought David great joy because the presence of the Lord was in the ark, and where the Lord dwelled, many blessings occurred. David found joy in that task.

Discover joy in your current job and learn to love it, or find a new job that you will love. Match your passions and hope to your job. As you imagine your ideal career, look for ways to develop needed skills, and set goals to obtain a job you will love. When opportunities arise, apply for a job that matches your desires and skills. With persistence, you will find it; then rejoice and praise God when you find the perfect match. Like David, you too can find joy and hope in work that fills you with hope and that pleases the Lord.

Dear God, praise You for the joy and blessings that unfold when we love our work. Amen.

Hope Through Failure

I can do all things through him who strengthens me.

—Philippians 4:13 ESV

Was Thomas A. Edison a failure? Edison tried and failed many times with his inventions, but each time he learned what not to do again. Edison could have easily been considered one of the biggest failures in history. He tried many ways to improve the lightbulb, and most others would have just quit. But he finally found a way to create a long-lasting, widely successful incandescent lightbulb.

Was the apostle Paul a failure? No, but he could have been. Paul persecuted followers of Christ and had watched and approved when the Jews stoned Stephen to death. Yet he later established many first-century churches. Paul had been flogged and left for dead, imprisoned, shipwrecked, in danger at sea, attacked by fellow Jews, and deprived of food and sleep (2 Corinthians 11:23–28). Yet Paul became a successful missionary to the Gentiles, shining Christ's light so that they could come to Christ.

Let failure become your teacher. Be ready to persist, and let your hope inspire you to keep going. Like Paul, we can be used by God to do the work that is required of us.

Dear God, I have failed many times, but like Paul and Edison, help me to persist so that my failures will turn into successes and my hope will thrive. In Jesus' name I pray, Amen.

Hope in Time

He has made everything beautiful in its time.

—Ecclesiastes 3:11

Have you ever looked at your life or at a situation and thought you had made a mess of everything? Did you feel as though there was no way the complete mess could ever be anything more or better? You may have felt hopeless during these times. Even though you might look at parts of your life as ugly or shameful, God can make all things work together for your good and His glory.

Because you can only see bits and pieces of the whole picture, there might be times when you cannot imagine anything beautiful coming out of your life or out of an ugly situation. But the God of hope is making all things beautiful in His time. When you trust your Creator with your life, He will give you the peace and hope you long for, and He will show you bit by bit how He makes all things beautiful. You'll see how He can make beauty from ashes.

The Bible calls you to have steadfast faith during times of trail and pain. When your life feels like a mess, place your hope in this truth: God will make everything beautiful.

Dear Father, thank You for giving me the hope that you can and will make something beautiful out of my messes and for showing me the beauty You have made in my life and in the world. Amen.

Unseen Hope

What is seen is temporary, but what is unseen is eternal.
—2 Corinthians 4:18

On a frigid wintery day as you bundle up to stay warm, you may dream about warm summer days of walking along the beach or sitting in the sun and reading a book. You may be miserable, and you may shiver now and then, but it will not be long before those sunny days arrive again. Paul taught that our hope is in the unseen. He had experienced a life of hardship, suffering, and persecution and was eventually martyred. But Paul had his sights on eternity because he recognized that what he was going through was not all there was to life. He recognized that he would one day live in a better place. He would spend eternity with God.

Your main hope when things are dismal should be on what God has for you in the future. This hope lets you believe in what is unseen. An image in your mind can draw your thoughts from current circumstances and transport you mentally to another time and place. It helps you to discover the joy of believing in future possibilities. If you are shivering with doubts and fears, know that this season will pass. Know, too, that God has a place for you in glory that outshines every dark moment.

Dear Father, though the days are sometimes dark, I look forward to the future You have for me. It is an unseen hope. Amen.

Supper Hopes

"If anyone hears my voice and opens the door, I will come in and eat with that person, and they with me."

—Revelation 3:20

Walking into a candy store reveals the variety in life's unending supply of sweetness. Although an overindulgence of candy is not good for you because it can supply your body with a large amount of sugars and fats, there are good reasons to eat chocolate. Dark chocolate contains potassium, copper, and magnesium. These are good for your body. Chocolate helps lower blood pressure that spikes when you worry or feel a bit hopeless. The cocoa also helps blood flow to the brain and improves thinking. These benefits of chocolate cause one to wonder whether it will be served at the Lord's banquet table. The book of Revelation speaks of His sitting down to eat with anyone who opens the door and invites Him in. The meal will not be a quick snack but will be the main meal of the day.

After a long day, a meal with loved ones is important. It is what you hope for. And after a long, difficult life, a meal with Jesus is what you have prayed for. Whether chocolate is on the table will not matter because of whom you will be dining with. It will be a blessing to eat with your Lord.

Dear God, thank You for Jesus, who has extended an invitation to all to supper. I accept His invitation. Amen.

A Child's Giggle Inspires Hope

He will yet fill your mouth with laughter and your lips with shouts of joy.

—Job 8:21

A child's laugh is spontaneous and delightful. The pure joy in a child can refresh your spirit and make you feel young and hopeful, but Job had nothing to laugh about. Almost everything that he loved and cherished was taken from him. Yet one of his friends gave him sound advice and tried to lift Job's spirit. In verse 20 of Job 8, his friend Bildad said, "Surely God does not reject one who is blameless or strengthen the hands of evildoers." Then he told Job that God would fill his mouth with laughter. Laughter is a spontaneous reaction to something that is perceived as funny or enjoyable. It is necessary when disappointments arrive and hope is shattered. Laughter in the face of difficulty reveals strength and hope for better days. It helps you to get in touch with the joy that is buried deep within your soul.

Let a toddler inspire you to laugh and see the world with fresh eyes. You may find yourself laughing and smiling at little wonders. Laughter ignites the hope of joy and helps you take life a little less seriously. Consider keeping a photo of a laughing child nearby or of a picture that brings about your smile to rekindle your hope.

Lord, help me laugh like a child and find the humor in the midst of pain and trouble. Amen.

Daffodil Shoots amid the Snow

The winter is past; the rains are over and gone. Flowers appear on the earth.

—Song of Songs 2:11–12

Spotting the first flower sprout in spring when snow still litters the ground is a joyful sight. Luscious green leaves pop through the frozen ground to signal coming changes. Some early buds even bloom while snow still falls. Spring is God's handiwork. He is the One who changes the seasons and makes the flowers grow. Meteorologists define spring as that time when the axis of the earth increasingly tilts toward the sun. The snow melts. The rains begins. Daylight rapidly increases, and the temperature rises. This is what causes the growth of flowers and other plant life.

Daffodils and crocus are among the first flowers that bloom with signs of new life. Rejoice at signs of life, and think of them as a reminder that change is always possible for you. A walk in a garden that will soon spring forth with flowers may prepare your heart to build new dreams and hopes. Chances for personal and spiritual growth are coming, just as the flowers burst from the earth and rise toward the sun. Return to the garden once the flowers bloom to rekindle your hope among the bright colors.

Dear Father, Your springtime handiwork is a revelation of life yet to be lived. Thank You for spring and the hope it brings. Amen.

The Good Book

*"Keep this Book of the Law always on your lips; meditate on it day
and night, so that you may be careful to do everything written in it."*
—Joshua 1:8

Being deep in the pages of a good book allows you to leave the worries of the world and enter a place that captures your heart and your mind. The greatest book ever written is the Bible. It is a collection of narratives, poems, laws, history, and wise sayings that were written throughout a period of approximately 1,600 years. Various authors, approximately forty in all, wrote its contents. The Bible has been widely regarded as the bestselling book of all time. There are several benefits and blessings for reading the Bible. Mainly, since the Bible is actually God's words, you learn what God requires of you. The Bible helps you to grow spiritually and to strengthen your relationship with God. It should definitely be added to your reading list.

When you sit and read, the hours can slip by unnoticed. When the book is good, it is difficult to put it down and return to daily tasks. If a good book ends in a way that delights you and gives you hope, be sure to lend it to a friend. And be sure to pass along a Bible. Reading God's Word not only gives you hope but also will strengthen your life.

Dear God, thank You for the Bible, which is Your message to me. May I read it for life and strength. Amen.

A Welcome Mat

"If the home is deserving, let your peace rest on it."

—Matthew 10:13

A friendly welcome starts with a wreath or cheery mat at the door. It beckons you to enter and find hope within. The words and decorations we place at the entrance of our homes greet each person. Does your doormat reach out with hope to invite people inside? When Jesus sent His disciples out to minister among the Jews, He gave them instructions on how to enter a home. If the household welcomed the disciples, they were to let their blessings rest on the home and those who lived there. Jesus sent them forth to "heal the sick, raise the dead, cleanse those who have leprosy, drive out demons," and to save souls (Matthew 10:8). But if there was no welcome for the disciples at the home, they were to take their blessings with them. What a difference a welcome can make.

A mat provides a spot to wipe off the weariness and muck of the world. The word *welcome* on the mat instills in visitors a hope for goodwill and blessing. But it is also what visitors see when leaving. It gives them a sign of hope that they can return and be refreshed once more. A welcome mat at your door may be just the hopeful message that your visitors need.

Dear Lord, use me as a source of hope who welcomes others not only to my home but to Your kingdom as well. Amen.

Sunrise

His coming is as brilliant as the sunrise.

—Habakkuk 3:4 NLT

The sun peeks up over the eastern horizon and signals the start of a new day. The sky fills with beautiful colors as light replaces darkness. The colors, which are softer than sunset, gently stir your senses. In the Old Testament, a sunrise represented God's power and presence rising among His people, the Israelites, when they were in despair. The prophet Habakkuk used the sunrise as an analogy to depict how God would rescue them from their enemies. This analogy was part of Habakkuk's praise to God for His help. But first the Israelites had to endure discipline for turning away from their hope in God. Their repentant hearts would revive their hope for the dawning of a new day when God would appear in His glory and all the powers of heaven and earth would be shaken as God's people returned to Him.

With the sunrise comes a brand new day. Take time to look out and take pleasure in the natural beauty of creation, and reflect on the power of God. Morning is a time to regroup and pray for what you hope the day will bring. Each morning is a gift of more time to start again to work toward your dream and hope that you will move a little closer to its realization.

Dear God my Lord, thank You for the sunrise that ushers in a new opportunity to hope again. Amen.

Sunset

Do not let the sun go down while you are still angry.

—Ephesians 4:26

William the Conqueror made a law that people were to put out fires and candles at the close of the day. The bell would ring in all the cities and towns throughout England to indicate the curfew, which was set for 8:00 p.m. *Curfew* comes from the French term that means "cover the fire." William the Conqueror made this law because British nobles had rebelled against him while he was away on an occasion, causing him to make severe laws. As William the Conqueror had the fires put out at sunset, we should make sure that our conscience is cleansed of animosity and evil passion toward another person. Paul encouraged the believers in Ephesus to do this so that they would not sin against God.

Sunset is a good time to evaluate your conscience to determine whether or not you are holding a grudge against someone else. If you are, forgive that person as God leads so that you can begin the new day fresh. Sunset also allows time to rest from the day and holds the promise that a new day will follow. As the light fades, so should anger, frustration, and hurt, while you let love and forgiveness settle the day. And rest in hope that tomorrow will come more kindly.

Dear God, help me to forgive anyone with whom I hold a grudge. Let my love for others at the end of the day reflect Yours. Amen.

MARCH

· •·•··•·•··•·· • ·•··•·•···

*"Then you should say what you mean," the
March Hare went on. "I do," Alice hastily
replied; "at least—at least I mean what I
say—that's the same thing, you know."*

—Lewis Carroll

Invitation to Tea

She was always doing good and helping the poor.

—Acts 9:36

Tea with a friend fulfills the need for closeness and warmth. Even sipping tea alone and letting the curls of steam rise up to your face brings warmth and soothes your throat. It is a moment of quiet reflection. Making toast with a little jam and brewing tea transforms a table into a place of comfort and nourishment. Whether a large tea party or tea for two, it brightens any day and draws friends close to share their hopes and encourage one another.

An invitation to tea is an act of kindness such as Dorcas had shown to the people of Joppa. She did not have a tea party but made robes and clothes for the widows. When Dorcas died, all the widows wept, and the apostle Peter's disciples sent for him. When Peter arrived, the people showed him the clothing that Dorcas had made. This kind and gentle lady was sorely missed. But Peter did not despair. He prayed and raised Dorcas back to life. She was once again able to serve and give hope to others. Does your life include invitations to tea and acts of kindness? Who will speak of your kindness when you are no longer here?

Dear Father, give me a heart of kindness and the opportunity to show that kindness to others. Amen.

Glow, Little Stick

He did what was right in the eyes of the LORD and followed completely the ways of his father David, not turning aside to the right or to the left.

—2 Kings 22:2

Have you ever used a glow stick? When you bend the flexible exterior container that holds a solution, it breaks the fragile inside container that holds another solution. Both chemicals react to make it glow. Children enjoy the dazzling light that shines in the dark. A glow stick only lasts for a short time, like the blush on your cheek when you receive a compliment. Compliments are kind words that open your heart and create hope, and the hope within you glows like a light for all to see.

Many compliments were written about Josiah. Josiah had a reputation for doing what was right during his reign as king of Judah. The Bible records there was never another king like him. He reformed the religious practices of the Israelites, cleaned out the temple, and called for obedience to God's Law.

When you share a compliment, you are sharing hope because you have allowed God to use you. You are shining a light. And, in turn, you are helping others to glow. Compliment someone today, especially someone who is living a godly life like Josiah did. Encourage that person to be a light in the darkness.

Dear Father, thank You for showing me what is right and using me to help others glow with hope. In Jesus' name I pray, Amen.

Spring Hope

See! The winter is past; the rains are over and gone. Flowers appear on the earth; the season of singing has come, the cooing of doves is heard in our land.

—Song of Songs 2:11–12

Winter snow glistens and sparkles as it changes the scenery and whitens barren limbs. Children enjoy snowball fights, sled rides, and drinking hot cocoa to warm themselves. The cold lasts longer than the snow, and eventually we grow tired of winter games. As the earth slowly moves closer to the sun, the landscape is warmed. Spring has finally arrived. The trees are growing with new life. The birds are chirping, and the daffodils are beginning to bloom. We long to bring that newness into our hearts and our lives. After a season of wintery cold and stuffiness, we need to take stock and refresh our spiritual selves. The Bible says our bodies are temples and are places where Jesus dwells. We need to make sure that the place of Jesus is "holy and acceptable to God" (Romans 12:1 ESV).

Making it past the lingering days of winter seems difficult. Yet the very presence of winter is a reminder that spring will follow. Leave the cold behind, and give way to new life and new hopes. Also, let spring be a reminder that you may need to renew and refresh the place where Jesus dwells.

Dear Father, thank You for the new life that spring brings. May I use this time to renew my spiritual self. Amen.

A Caterpillar Journey

*Not that I have already obtained all this, or have already arrived at
my goal, but I press on to take hold of that for which Christ Jesus took
hold of me.*

—Philippians 3:12

Fuzzy, crawling caterpillars inch along with no understanding of the future and the freedom that wings will
give to them. Nothing daunts the little creatures that wiggle
over and under branches, leaves, and any objects they meet
on their way. A caterpillar is dedicated to moving a little at a
time, slowly filling up and storing its energy. Until one day it
stops, snuggles up to a tree, spins a cocoon for its home, and
rests contently inside. The caterpillar's labor is well worth the
work—it becomes a new, beautiful creature. Like a caterpillar,
the apostle Paul had a goal toward which he was pressing. He
wanted to become completely new by becoming like Christ. He
exerted all of his energy to reach his goal. With single-mind-
edness, he pressed forward. It was his primary hope in life.

We, too, inch along in life, moving toward the hope that is
within our hearts, not knowing what will happen when we finally
reach our destination, grow wings, and soar. Sometimes we
struggle over little bumps and wiggle through problems. When
our lives seem to be full of difficulty, it is good to remember that
we are God's creations, and we will one day reach our goal and
be transformed in ways we could never have imagined.

Dear God, though my journey toward my goal seems slow sometimes, help me to
remain single-mindedly focused. In Jesus' name I pray, Amen.

Soar like a Butterfly

"In this world you will have trouble. But take heart! I have overcome the world."

—John 16:33

An old English proverb says, "Just when the caterpillar thought the world was over, it became a butterfly." The caterpillar hid away to put on wings of beauty and begin life renewed. But within a cocoon is a butterfly that is unaware of the outside world. You may sometimes try to hide from pain and worldly troubles. Like spinning a cocoon, you may build walls around your heart. Use this time to spin new hopes and prepare to soar above the problems. Jesus guaranteed we would have problems in this world, so in our lives we should expect trouble. But He left us with a word of hope: He said He has overcome the world. Because the Spirit of God is in believers, we learn that overcoming is possible.

You cannot remain inside the cocoon forever. Eventually, you must come out and see the world. But use fresh eyes to see it from a new angle. In your dark resting place, seek to change by finding courage so you can sprout stronger wings. Realize too that hope does not always happen when you are watching. Hope's transformation often takes place deep within your heart and soul.

Dear Father, thank You for the lesson of the butterfly, and thank You for the overcoming power of Jesus that resides in me too. In His name I pray, Amen.

Chirping with Hope

"Because of the tender mercy of our God, by which the rising sun will come to us from heaven."

—Luke 1:78

The first tweets and chirps of spring signal the arrival of birds returning home. Their sounds fill the air with a joyful tune of praise as they celebrate the tender mercies of God. The winged creatures celebrate the newness of each day and respond by creating songs of greeting.

Sometimes the twittering seems to start too early, especially when you would rather stay snuggled in bed. But the tender mercies of God are for you as well. You are a part of the world that God has created. Life will go on whether you are a part of it or not, and a new day will begin even when you feel afraid.

Listen to the birds. They are beckoning for you to rise and start another day. So join them in their celebration and praise to God. Let the carefree chirping of the birds fill your heart with music to carry you through each hope-filled day. Respond to each day with a hopeful melody in your heart.

Dear God, my Father, thank You for the tender mercies with which You bless Your world every day. The birds are praising You for this wonderful gift. Like the birds, I celebrate and praise Your name. Your blessings fill my heart with hope. Amen.

Hope Chest

"For I know the plans I have for you," declares the LORD, "plans to prosper you and not to harm you, plans to give you hope and a future."
—Jeremiah 29:11

A hope chest made of wood was originally used to hold linens, candlesticks, and other items for the future. A young girl placed treasures into the chest. She may have embroidered items for her hope chest, and her family may have provided gifts to add to it. This treasure chest symbolized the dreams of parents and girls and was preparation for a bright future of love, marriage, family, and a happy home.

God gave a hope chest of sorts to the Israelites. God sent Jeremiah to deliver messages of hope that the Israelites could cling to like treasures. He told His people that after seventy years of captivity, He had not abandoned them. He was still their God, so He gave them plans for a bright future. He is your God as well, and He prepares for your future. He has made plans to give you a hope-filled life. God's plans for you are for your good. He loves you, and He will never harm you. Allow this promise and these truths to be your hope chest for the future. Then pray for wisdom and watch for God's path and openings as He reveals those plans. Be ready to embrace the future that God has prepared.

Dear Father, thank You for the plans You have for my future. I will rest on this promise and embrace every day with hope. In Jesus' name I pray, Amen.

Photos of Hope

These are the names of the sons of Israel (Jacob and his descendants).
—Genesis 46:8

Photos of our families often line our walls or tabletops. Your home likely contains special photos that connect you to priceless memories of loved ones who played a role in your life. The facial features in an old photo of a great grandparent may be reflected in a new photo of a young child. They may also share similar personality traits or passions. Family photos connect the past to the present. These photos are pictorial proof of our legacies. We are reassured that we are part of something larger, and all of the faces in the pictures are a reminder of the many hopes and dreams that are a part of us. According to the book of Genesis, Jacob, who was given the name Israel, had twelve sons. These sons were Jacob's legacy, and his legacy impacted the world. His sons became a nation, and from the nation of Israel, God gave the world the solution for the sin that plagues us. They became hope for the world.

Let the legacy of framed faces of people you love bring you hope as you recall encouraging words and stories of struggles, triumphs, and courage. These are the stories that make up your family, which is your personal legacy.

Dear God, thank You for the hope You have given me through my family. Amen.

Treasures of the Soul

Cast your cares on the LORD and he will sustain you; he will never let the righteous be shaken.

—Psalm 55:22

Deep in your soul and close to your heart is a place where dreams are stored and hopes are treasured. Your dearest thoughts are kept there, ones you may not have shared with others. Sometimes, though, you fill this special spot with burdens of which you should let go and allow God to carry. As king of Israel, David had many troubles during his dealings with his people and other countries. He had learned that the only way to maintain his hope and thrive was to cast his burdens on God. He humbly trusted that God would take care of him.

If you continue to carry your burdens on your own, then you have not committed them to God and do not trust Him with your life. Recognize that God has the power to handle anything you give to Him. Burdens can be too much to bear, so pour them out to God. He will always listen. It is never too late to build hopes, to renew a dream, and to revive your soul. Let go of your burdens, and fill your treasure trove with revived hopes and dreams.

Dear heavenly Father, today I humbly bow and commit to You my life and any burdens that are weighing me down. Thank You for being my burden bearer. In Jesus' name I pray, Amen.

Hope in the Cross

For the message of the cross is foolishness to those who are
perishing, but to us who are being saved it is the power of God.

—1 Corinthians 1:18

The beams of the cross are reminders of the hope we have in Christ. The upright beam points to heaven. In many ways, it is a bridge that stretches from here to eternity. The crossbeam represents the love of Jesus and reminds us that He spread His arms wide and died for us. The crucifixion of Christ is the foundation of all our hopes and joys. Those who do not believe in the work of Christ on the cross cannot comprehend that hope came through Jesus' crucifixion. It does not make sense to them. But for those who believe in the death, burial, and resurrection of Jesus, the cross represents the salvation that only comes by the power of God.

Let the outstretched beam of the cross remind you to spread the love that Jesus showed on the cross. Reach out with His message of love. Let the cross be the courage you need to share the unending hope of Christ. By the death of Christ we are made alive.

Dear God, by Your love and power You provided salvation for the world. It is through the cross of Christ that all who believe will be saved. Help me to share this message of hope with others. In Jesus' name I pray, Amen.

Finding Hope in Wisdom

If any of you lacks wisdom, you should ask God, who gives generously to all without finding fault, and it will be given to you.

—James 1:5

George Washington Carver, who was born into slavery, loved studying plants. He asked God to show him the great secrets of the universe. But God told him to study the little peanut. Through his studies he found many uses for that one plant, and those uses changed many lives. When we ask God for direction, He wants us to humbly follow the path He has made for us. Most of all, God wants us to seek Him. Because he asked God for answers, George Washington Carver went on to become one of the most prominent scientists and inventors of his time. He devised approximately three hundred useful products from a single plant.

God's knowledge is vaster than the universe and is available to you. Seek Him for wisdom and listen to His whisper as He points out a path for you to follow. He can multiply your efforts and what you offer Him by blessing you with knowledge and understanding. God will give generously to you when you seek Him and ask for wisdom.

Dear Father, thank You for the wisdom of heaven. Thank You that all I have do is ask and that wisdom will be imparted to me. Thank You for caring for me the way You do. Amen.

What Is in Your Heart?

"For where your treasure is, there your heart will be also."

—Matthew 6:21

What do you dwell on? What fills your thoughts? What are your desires? These thoughts reveal what lies in your heart. Jesus spoke about the treasure in the heart that really lasts. He contrasted the intangible treasures of heaven with wealth that can be stolen or destroyed by rust and moths. Christ advised us that owning more things does not necessarily bring you joy. Contentment is essential, and a heart that dwells on heavenly treasures will be content. The things on earth cannot be compared to the things of heaven. Placing your heart on earthly treasures enslaves your life to continuously seek material possessions that you cannot take with you to heaven. Seeking material possessions reveals an obsession that ultimately will destroy your hope.

Therefore, your priority should be to seek the treasures of heaven. What are these treasures? Anything that is of God is a heavenly treasure. Jesus also spoke of acts of generosity and charity to others as lasting treasures in heaven. This points to a focus on relationships and not on material possessions. Jesus wants you to realize that love and kindness are heavenly treasures that can give hope to others.

Dear Father, bless me to be a blessing to others by showing kindness from the heavenly treasure that is in my heart. Amen.

Treasuring God

For since the creation of the world God's invisible qualities—his eternal power and divine nature—have been clearly seen, being understood from what has been made.

—Romans 1:20

Pastor and author A. W. Tozer was correct when he said, "The man who has God for his treasure has all things in One." Look outside at the beauty of God's created world. If you have treasured a flower, sunset, or even someone's heart, you have treasured something God has made. The person who treasures these things, treasures God. God reveals who He is and what He is like through creation. He reveals that He is a God of power and love who is concerned about the smallest details. Creation has the power to draw you to God who made everything and everyone.

As you read the Bible and pray, you will learn more about God because He reveals Himself and speaks to you in His Word. Do you think of God at the beginning, middle, and end of each day? Have you asked God to draw you close to Him? Have you asked God to give you lasting hope? As you get to know God and all He has done for you, treasure Him and treasure your relationship with Him.

Dear God, my Creator, thank You for all You have made and for the blessing of Your Word. I will treasure You in my heart for as long as I live. Amen.

Healing and Hope

Do you not know that your bodies are temples of the Holy Spirit, who is in you, whom you have received from God? You are not your own.

—1 Corinthians 6:19

Paul tells us that our body is the place where the Spirit of God dwells. Through His Spirit, God lives within us, and we should do our best to take care of our bodies. Your body can be viewed as a vehicle that moves you from place to place. You should do your best to maintain it so that it serves you well all the days of your life. Your hope is that you will remain healthy, retain your youth, and be ambulatory for as long as possible. If any part of your body aches, take steps to fix the problem quickly. Take your body to a doctor for medical treatment when it is not running smoothly. You will leave with the hope of feeling better because the doctor may prescribe medicine, a change in diet, or rest.

Time changes the look of your body. After all, it does not take long before you realize you are no longer shiny and new. Even so, continue to treasure the life within you and the heart that keeps beating with hope. Remember, your body is a beautiful, unique vehicle in which God lives.

Lord, teach me to be healthy so that I can honor You with the body You have given me. Help me to take care of my body. Amen.

Protected Hopes

Joseph's master took him and put him in prison, the place where the king's prisoners were confined.

—Genesis 39:20

The soul of a person is where hope dwells. No matter what you face, even sickness or death, your soul will survive worldly problems and the evil schemes of people because it is eternal in nature. Therefore, the riches of love, hope, and inner peace that are in the soul can never be completely emptied. Think about how you have survived hardships such as broken relationships, divorce, deaths of loved ones, or abuse. Your soul, filled with its powerful wonders from God, has sustained you.

When you feel despair, look deeply past your heart and into your soul. You will find that hope is still there. Hope kept Joseph going when he was in an Egyptian prison. During his time, prisons had the vilest of conditions that included forced labor and cruelty. But Joseph looked beyond the cruelty, evil, and pain and clung to the hope within the depths of his soul. Oscar Wilde said, "Ordinary riches can be stolen from a man. Real riches cannot. In the treasury-house of your soul, there are infinitely precious things, that may not be taken from you." Rejoice that God protects the hope within your soul.

Dear Father, thank You that You are the keeper of my soul. No matter what happens in this life, the hope that dwells there will remain forever. Amen.

Precious Memories

But his mother treasured all these things in her heart.

—Luke 2:51

A movie or a book can make you cry or laugh. It is often because a scene stirs a precious memory or thought from deep within you. Something on screen strikes a chord that matches a hope within your heart and instantly brings back the memories you kept stored away. In that moment, your heart opens and tears or laughter flow out.

Mary, the mother of Jesus, pondered memories in her heart. They were memories that any person would treasure. In years past she had been visited by an angel who told her the Holy Spirit would come on her and she would conceive the Messiah. Her baby, the King of kings, had been born in a stable. When Jesus was twelve years old, his parents were looking for Him. He told them they should have known He would be in His Father's house, the temple. Mary treasured all of these things in her heart. Take time to dwell again upon the precious memories stored in your heart. Something cherished is worth letting your heart and mind dwell upon so that you can once again feel deeply. Use these treasured memories to inspire you to act in your life today. Let your past guide your future hopes.

Dear God, thank You for memories that I treasure. They have brought moments of laughter and joy at times when I have needed them most. Amen.

Hopeful Connection

I love those who love me, and those who seek me find me.

—Proverbs 8:17

Do you recall falling in love? You hoped to know the person better and learn all the details that made the individual special. You spent all your free time with your new love. You formed strong bonds to last through troubles and time. It was a moment when you felt connected to another person, when there was someone outside of yourself whom you could not picture your life without.

A. W. Tozer spoke of the desire to know God better. The moment God became real and special to him was when he was fifteen years old. He had heard a street preacher say that people needed to call on God if they did not know how to be saved. Tozer ran home to his attic, got on his knees, and began a lifelong pursuit of God. This moment inspired his pursuit to a deeper knowledge of God. He loved and grew in his connection to God for the rest of his life. Our pursuit of God should be lifelong. God is too deep, too wide, and too high for the knowing to ever end. The pursuit begins at the moment you understand that God truly loves you, and this begins your connection of hope.

Dear Father, I love You and long to know You deeper. Lead me in Your ways so that I may walk closer to You day by day. Amen.

Curious Hope

This is the confidence we have in approaching God: that if we ask anything according to his will, he hears us.

—1 John 5:14

Questions help you engage in conversation and explore the heart and thoughts of someone else. When someone makes a statement that you do not agree with, perhaps it is best to investigate by asking, "Can you explain that?" Or ask, "Does that belief help you face pain or death?" You can also question or evaluate yourself to explore your own thoughts and emotions.

There are questions you may avoid, but facing them makes you look deeper for answers. Questioning your hopes helps you evaluate them. When you ask yourself about your faith, it opens up your relationship with God and your hope of eternal life. So never be afraid to ask God questions about anything. He invites you to question and to turn to Him for answers. The book of John makes it clear that you can be confident that God will hear you. Make sure that your hope rests in His will and not your own. This means that His response to your questions trumps your expectations. Pushing to hear your answers will interfere with your relationship with God. God loves you and knows what is best, so ask confidently according to His will, and He will hear you and respond.

Dear Father, thank You for hearing me when I call out to You in prayer. May I always seek Your will for my life and live to please You. Amen.

Heirlooms of Hope

A good person leaves an inheritance for their children's children.
—Proverbs 13:22

*I*n 1963 President John F. Kennedy wrote a speech that he never got a chance to deliver because of his assassination. In the last lines of the speech, he wrote, "Let us stand together with renewed confidence in our cause—united in our heritage of the past and our hopes for the future—and determined that this land we love shall lead all mankind into new frontiers of peace and abundance." Those words became a part of the legacy he left behind. They were words that encouraged this nation to allow the past to unite us so that we could powerfully face the future.

That is what legacies are all about. You may not only pass down words, but you may have items that have given you hope. An old rocking chair, lace doily, or pearl necklace may have been handed down through generations. Each of these heirlooms holds stories of the struggles and successes of past owners. Each item provides a message to the new owner that whispers, "You have a legacy of love." The stories of your family's past are the seeds that gave birth to current moments of hope. Delight in heirlooms that give you confidence so that love and hope will continue.

Dear Father, thank You for the hope that has been handed down to me. May I continue the legacy for those who will follow. In Jesus' name I pray, Amen.

The Softer Side of Hope

Be kind and compassionate to one another, forgiving each other,
just as in Christ God forgave you.

—Ephesians 4:32

Wooly, new lambs; fluffy chicks; fresh flowers with soft petals; and furry bunnies add softness to springtime. There is even a softness about a spring rain in contrast to the hardness of a cold winter rain. Rejoice with a walk in spring, and enjoy the softness that surrounds you. Let it inspire new hope. Softness lightens our hearts. You also feel freer and happier when the softness of kind words touches your heart. Kindness should be second nature to believers. Paul encouraged us to imitate Christ, who showed kindness and forgave those who mistreated Him and nailed Him to a cross.

Jesus loved people so much, including those who hated Him, that He gave His life for all without distinction. Though it may be difficult, our love and kindness to others should be the same. Be thankful when someone gives you a compliment and smile. They are extending an act of kindness to you. Remember to share kindness with others as well. This will add softness and hope to someone's life.

Dear Lord, help me to be thankful for kind words and smiles. Let love soften my heart, and help me to pass on kindness in my words and actions. Let others see and feel the love of Christ that is inside of me. Amen.

Unstoppable Hope

"So is my word that goes out from my mouth: It will not return to me empty, but will accomplish what I desire and achieve the purpose for which I sent it."

—Isaiah 55:11

As suddenly as a flower buds and then opens to reveal new beauty, so the seasons change. Spring will always come year after year with its warmth and signs of new life. Hope is like the spring. Even when you think you are numb and dead inside, another season of hope will sprout and bloom within your heart. This is the kind of hope that God provides. Like His Word, God's hope is unstoppable. God's Word when sent forth has power to change a hardened heart and the most stubborn of minds. If you look back through history, you can see the great things that God has done. His past works give us confidence that the future He has promised will happen. Like the spring that comes every year, God will accomplish His desires.

So though you may grieve what has past, you can look forward to a new and refreshing hope with confidence. Allow a new song, a new bud, or another object of spring to strike a chord within you and bring a glimmer of hope. You may think that your problem or the sharp pain of grief will never end, but it will. Wait, and soon hope will find you.

Dear Father, thank You for spring and its promise of something new. Amen.

Oceans of Hope

Let the heavens rejoice, let the earth be glad; let the sea resound, and all that is in it.

—Psalm 96:11

Do you like walking along a beach barefoot so that your toes sink into the sand and the water splashes at your feet? Ocean tides ebb and flow, making small or large waves that splash and lick the sand. Looking out over the ocean as far as one can see is a reminder of the vastness of the world and limitlessness of hopes and dreams. You may have learned in school that there are five oceans and other bodies of water that cover more than seventy percent of the earth's surface. That vastness can hold a lot of dreams. The power of an ocean cannot be tamed but can be used as a source of energy in our lives and our homes. In spite of its power, the waters of great oceans exhibit a stillness that calms our souls.

Schedule a day to visit a beach and dream. Let the wide sky remind you to be open, and let the vastness remind you to keep dreaming big dreams. The expanse will serve as motivation to reach for your dreams, no matter how distant they may seem, because God is near.

Dear Father, thank You for the vastness of the ocean. Thank You for its inspiration to have big dreams and hopes. Amen.

Lightbulb Moments

Do not let any unwholesome talk come out of your mouths.

—Ephesians 4:29

An unexpected electric shock occurs when you touch a doorknob after you have rubbed your feet on carpeting. It is caused by electrons jumping from one object to another, and it is a tiny surprise that will put a little spark in your life.

Similarly, something tiny like a word can spark new thoughts that can be kindled into a blaze. Words have the power to affect others. This could be the reason that Paul advised that our talk and actions should not be frivolous. As followers of Christ and children of God, we are responsible to lead others to speak wholesomely. We are to share a standard of love and hope so that others will glorify God. Words also have power to create. God blesses us with lightbulb moments for our good and for the good of those around us. These lightbulb moments are words or thoughts that have the potential for something great. Ideas are all around you. Take a moment to reflect over what you see and experience. As you observe the world and capture passing thoughts, let these sparks fly in your direction. Lightbulb moments may be the start of a new hope. Embrace those hopeful sparks.

Dear Father, open my mind to new thoughts and new ideas so that I may be a blessing to others. Amen.

The God Factor

Come near to God and he will come near to you.

—James 4:8

There are moments you cannot predict because they are providential. An unexpected check arrives to fund your new idea; an encouraging friend calls at a moment you are feeling weak, or the sun simply peeks through the clouds to brighten a day that is filled with gloom. These are little blessings.

Have you noticed that some of the greatest moments of inspiration often follow times when you have stopped to thank God for all the little blessings He has sent? There is a God factor in realizing fulfilled dreams that should not be ignored. God made us to be in a relationship with Him, and there are two vital aspects of this relationship. First of all, it is a privilege that God would choose us to walk and talk with Him. Second, we need to open up and include God in the intimate details of our lives and our hearts. The actions that we extend toward God are reciprocated by actions from Him. Many times God's actions are exactly what we need as we strive toward our dreams. So do not forget God. Open your heart to tune in to Him and see the miracles He will perform in your life. Talk to God about your hopes, and expect an answer. Be ready for the surprise blessings He will send in response to a heart that is open toward Him.

Dear God, I want You to be a vital part of my life and my hopes. Amen.

Follow God's Leading

"My sheep listen to my voice; I know them, and they follow me."
—John 10:27

Have you ever stopped yourself from dreaming because it did not seem practical, as if it were too far out of your reach? Have you been afraid to hope because you thought something bad would happen? Did you give up on a dream because someone else kept putting down your idea? If so, you may need to reframe your thoughts. God speaks to us in several different ways: through His Word; through a still, small voice; through our circumstances; and through other people. Many times He may be using any one of these ways to communicate an action that you must do or a new path you should take. But we must learn to listen so we can know what God wants us to do.

Learn to hear when God speaks to you. He may be guiding you to reframe your hope. Then take steps to obey. Close your eyes, and remember what made your hope so special. Let such thoughts interrupt the disparaging thoughts and inspire you to think beyond your limits. Then look around with fresh eyes to find beauty in something ordinary, such as a leaf not simply falling but dancing happily in the wind. Free your thoughts from negativity, and follow God's leading to hope and dream even bigger than before.

Dear heavenly Father, thank You for speaking to me. I choose to follow You to my dream. Amen.

Money Is Not Hope

*Keep your lives free from the love of money and be content with
what you have, because God has said, "Never will I leave you;
never will I forsake you."*

—Hebrews 13:5

Too often people think that if they had more money they would follow their dreams. The truth is money should not be the heart or the means for fulfilling a dream. The pursuit of dreams should be dependent on hope. When you fill yourself with hope, finding the resources you need becomes a part of the dream, not something that blocks it. A survey of the richest people in the world revealed that many felt miserable and had no new hopes to pursue. They sacrificed too much in relationships for money and had given up their dreams.

The Bible identifies money as a master that will rule our lives if we allow it. Jesus said it is impossible to serve both God and money. The writer of the book of Hebrews advised that his readers should not love money. This does not mean we should not use money, but we need to keep it in its proper place. Do not depend on money to do what God can do. Trust that He will supply your needs and help you get the resources to fulfill your dreams.

Dear Father, thank You for providing what I need to fulfill my dreams. I trust in Your care for me. Amen.

Bouquets of Hope

Whoever does not love does not know God, because God is love.

—1 John 4:8

A child's fistful of weeds and a bouquet of long-stemmed roses have something in common. Both send a message of love and hope. The fragrance of roses may smell better than the more common scent of earthy weeds, but the love behind the weeds from a child is just as heartfelt as a gift someone bought at a florist. Both actions renew hope in your heart as someone has taken time to tell you that you are special. This love is how God wants us to relate to one another. Love is important to God because love is who God is. All of the characteristics of God grow out of His love, even His discipline. God expresses His love through discipline because He wants us to do well. If He did not care about you, then He would allow you to continue to make wrong choices.

The Bible reveals that a lack of love for others equals a lack of love for God. Therefore, show that you love God by loving others. Reach out and give someone a bouquet of flowers or some other gift. When given with love, a gift can touch someone's heart with hope.

Lord, thank You for special people in my life, people who care enough to shower me with smiles, little gifts, and words that show they care. Amen.

Friend Time

One who has unreliable friends soon comes to ruin, but there is a friend who sticks closer than a brother.

—Proverbs 18:24

Do you make friends easily? Or does it take you a long time? Either way, are you building lasting friendships? English author Thomas Hughes once said, "Blessed are they who have the gift of making friends, for it is one of God's best gifts. It involves many things, but above all, the power of going out of one's self, and appreciating whatever is noble and loving in another." In other words, making friends is not easy, especially today when independence is the rule. People would rather spend time on social media than with another person.

Making friends is like a treasure hunt. First, you have to find that person, maybe through a church fellowship, a football game, or another event. And once you find that person, dig in and discover the beautiful things about him or her. Appreciate the sparkle of hope when you discover a connection to another person. It is the fulfillment of finding someone with the virtues and qualities you admire. You will be rewarded with happiness and joy when you find a friend. After you find someone you admire, nurture the friendship by spending time together.

Dear Father, thank You for the gift of friends and for the hope they bring into my life. Amen.

Cherished Praise

Let someone else praise you, and not your own mouth.

—Proverbs 27:2

Compliments that mean the most depend on what matters to you. If you work hard and set goals, you probably appreciate compliments about your achievements and efforts. If you enjoy people and having fun, you probably enjoy compliments about the joy you bring to a gathering. If you enjoy sharing stories and jokes, a good reaction or laugh may be the compliment that satisfies you. Mark Twain said, "I can live for two months on a good compliment." The Bible does not have a lot to say about praising others. Even though our praise should primarily be toward God, expressing praise to others is acceptable. In the book of Proverbs, Solomon advised his son to let someone else praise him so that he would not think too highly of himself.

Expressing praise or giving someone a compliment creates an energy of hope. Make it a practice to share sincere compliments often. And when someone's unexpected words of praise touch you, write the comments down and post them somewhere so you can see them. They may become the wings of hope on which you soar. Cherish the praise given to you, especially from someone who is special.

Dear God, thank You for the praise I receive from others that keep my hope alive. Show me how to do the same for others. In Jesus' name I pray, Amen.

Smiles of Hope

A happy heart makes the face cheerful.

—Proverbs 15:13

Have you ever tried to collect smiles? You only need to smile at others and most will return the smile. Children are especially good at flashing back a grin or an ear-to-ear smile. Giving away smiles is like sprinkling joy into lives, a joy that returns to you. Smiles are free gifts of beauty. The muscles used to smile transform your face, and remind people that there is something in the world worth smiling about. It is a little reminder to hope. Smiling also has a positive effect on your mood. It communicates happiness and causes the energy and people around you to be uplifted. It is no secret that most people would choose to be happy rather than sad. So what makes us happy? What makes us smile?

Well, different people have different thoughts about what makes them happy. They will choose food, clothes, cars, and money as a means of happiness. But this is not God's idea of happiness. God's view is self-contained and comes from the heart where your hope dwells, and when you smile, you share that hope with others. When you pray and smile, you give God a gift, too, and He smiles back. Keep gifting people and God with smiles.

Dear Father, thank You for the happiness that is in my heart. Each day I will share it with others so they will experience happiness and hope. Amen.

Garden of Prayer

Jesus went with his disciples to a place called Gethsemane, and he said to them, "Sit here while I go over there and pray."

—Matthew 26:36

Knowing He would die, Jesus entered a garden to pray. He turned to His Father in heaven to present His case and to prepare for His suffering. His course had been set. He was the perfect Lamb of God who would pay for the sins of the world. But in His human form He struggled and prayed. Jesus could have chosen a number of other gardens, but for reasons of His own, He chose Gethsemane. He prayed there with great anguish and poured out His heart. The Father heard His prayer and gave Him strength to endure the cross. The tomb where Jesus rose was also in a garden that reflected new life and the wonder of the resurrection. Have you found a garden that is a wonderful refuge and place to pray? Have you found a place where flowers and plants lift your spirits and you can experience the presence of God? Amid the beauty of trees and flowers, there is hope.

Cherish your garden, and make it conducive for prayer. Enjoy the flowers as you walk and talk to God in your garden. Plants and the outside life can be reminders of the resurrection of Jesus Christ and of your hope in Him.

Dear Father, I choose to talk with You in my garden of prayer, asking for strength, love, fellowship, and hope. Amen.

APRIL

· • • ·· • • • ··· • • ·· • • • ··

*I am not solicitous to examine particularly
everything here, which indeed could not be
done in fifty years, because my desire is to make
all possible discoveries, and return to your
Highnesses, if it please our Lord, in April.*

—Christopher Columbus

Parks of Hope

I made gardens and parks and planted all kinds of fruit trees in them.
—Ecclesiastes 2:5

Solomon, the wisest man who ever lived and the wealthiest during his time, planted gardens and created parks. He filled them with foliage, fruit trees, and beauty. The first parks were primarily used for hunting deer; however, Solomon made gardens and planted plants for pleasure. Unless you live in the country, parks provide escape from busy city life. The asphalt and concrete buildings of the city can cause you to be tense and unable to relax. However, the openness and greenery of a park emits a soothing ambience that relieves stress. So daily walks in the park for reflection could be just what the doctor ordered.

Plan to spend time at a park often. As you sit or walk, you will find joy in being surrounded by all the living things of the natural world. They can become seeds of hope. Also, have fun making your own little park with a few seeds and plants. A little packet of marigolds springs forth quickly and continues to bloom all summer. Good soil and a little water will make them thrive. Then you will have a miniature park to enjoy where you can sit and reflect on Your hopes and dreams.

Dear God, thank You for parks where I can enjoy Your wonderful creation. Amen.

Waterfall Hopes

As the deer pants for streams of water, so my soul pants for you, my God.
—Psalm 42:1

Bubbling waterfalls overflowing and crashing down to another level fill the air with happy sounds of nature. As you walk near flowing water, listen and rejoice. Enjoy the wonder and power of nature. As you observe the flowing liquid, contemplate and dream. Niagara Falls is one of the most beautiful spectacles in North America. Millions of people visit every year to experience the wonder of these giant and magnificent falls. An explorer of North America, Louis Hennepin, wrote a description of Niagara Falls. He said, "The waters which fall from this vast height, do foam and boil after the most hideous manner imaginable, making an outrageous noise, more terrible than that of thunder; for when the wind blows from off the South, their dismal roaring may be heard above fifteen leagues off." Waterfalls are a reminder of the power of God. Just like the psalmist who thirsted after God, we should long for waters that will inspire us to let go and reach for our dreams.

Another amazing feature of the waterfall is that, because of its power, it will change rocks and land to repaint the canvas of the earth. Feel the hope of change when you feel wind and hear roaring sounds of nature, especially waterfalls.

Dear Father, thank You for waterfalls, which are reminders of the power that is at our disposal because of Your love. Amen.

Seeds of Hope

Whoever sows sparingly will also reap sparingly, and whoever sows generously will also reap generously.

—2 Corinthians 9:6

There is a joy that comes from digging into your own garden that you will not get from anything else. Starting with a patch of dirt or grass, slowly turning it over, breaking it up, and sifting out big rocks, you refresh the soil so that you can bury seeds that will grow and become something new. A trove of edible vegetables? A beautiful row of summer flowers? It can become whatever you imagine. There is a principle in planting that can be found in the Bible: if you plant a little, you will not yield a big crop. Of course, Paul was speaking about giving in this verse. Giving is like sowing seed. If you sow sparingly, you cannot hope for anything but a meager harvest, but if you sow generously, you will reap generously.

The process of digging and burying seeds allows new hopes to take root. The act of giving also produces hope in the lives of those who receive. So in your giving and your planting, sow as much as possible. The seeds of today are the beginnings of the hopes of tomorrow.

Dear God, may the seeds that are planted in my heart yield great hopes for tomorrow, not only for myself but for those to whom I give. Amen.

Garden of the Mind

Set your minds on things above, not on earthly things.

—Colossians 3:2

What do you fill your mind with each day? Is it knowledge, gossip, or trivia? What you plant will produce results, so be careful what you sow in your head. The apostle Paul told the believers in Colossae to set their minds on heaven. Thoughts of heaven include spiritual blessings, hope, and the will of God. It is the same attitude that was found in Christ when He was on the earth. His mind and heart were focused on the Father's will. Because you are human, some of your thoughts should be reflective of your human nature. But you should also focus on thoughts that are reflective of your spirit.

James Allen said, "Man's mind may be likened to a garden, which may be intelligently cultivated or allowed to run wild; but whether cultivated or neglected, it must, and will, bring forth. If no useful seeds are put into it, then an abundance of useless weed seeds will fall therein, and will continue to produce their kind." You can weed out insults, discouragement, and nonsense that choke your hopes to make room for better thoughts in the garden of your mind. You will discover that filling your mind with biblical truths, helpful information, and encouragement will nurture your hopes.

Dear Father, I choose to have heavenly thoughts by only planting seeds in my mind that honor You. Amen.

Hope Among the Thorns

*As the mountains surround Jerusalem, so the LORD surrounds his
people both now and forevermore.*

—Psalm 125:2

Thorns are prickly things that can stab and wound. Tiny slivers get under your skin and irritate. Yet with the prickles you will find fragrant and lovely flowers in myriad colors. There are many plants that characteristically have thorns, such as roses, of course, the prickly pear cactus, and some fruit trees and vines. These thorns are like little soldiers who protect and defend its fruit and blooms. In God's sight you are a flower, and He is the thorn who guards and protects you both day and night. Just as He surrounded and protected Jerusalem, He will surround and protect you too.

Let the roses be reminders of God's protection. Roses take root in clay and sand, where many other plants cannot thrive. Thorns grow from the stems before the flower buds and blooms to protect the plant from predators. Roses continue to return year after year as reminders of God's protection so that your hope can bloom too. Be thankful for the prickles in life that protect your hopes. They are God's gift of protection.

Dear Lord, thank You for the gift of roses. Their precious blooms remind me of
the hopes of my heart. Their thorns remind me of Your protection. Amen.

Charming People

Rejoice always, pray continually, give thanks in all circumstances;
for this is God's will for you in Christ Jesus.

—1 Thessalonians 5:16–18

Some people are naturally charming. They spread the sunshine of laughter and sprinkle joy wherever they go. They strive to make others happy and think about the needs of others before their own. Paul encouraged the Thessalonians believers to be like this. He wanted them to rejoice. He wanted their joy to always be evident, in good and difficult times, because he recognized that their joy came from God. Paul also encouraged the believers to pray. This is not surprising because Paul had devoted his life to prayer and understood its powerful benefits. Finally, he told them to give thanks because he knew that God was always working on their behalf. These three actions made the people into examples, impacted others positively, and were the will of God.

So be an inspiring person. Look people in the eye with a smile and joy that reaches from your heart. Remember names and events, support their hopes, and ask questions so you can know and encourage people. Speak with kindness and desire to sprinkle joy in the day. Enjoy those who bring out the best in you.

Dear Father, thank You for the good examples who are in my life. They do Your will by encouraging me to remain hopeful and by sharing their joy. May I be a person who inspires others. In Jesus' name I pray, Amen.

Flourishing Hope

At least there is hope for a tree: If it is cut down, it will sprout again, and its new shoots will not fail.

—Job 14:7

To feel the earth, dig in the soil and place a seed in the little hole you have dug. This brings a feeling of satisfaction. You are a friend to the earth and nurture growth in its plants. Not all plants grow easily. Because of bugs, droughts, or storms, they may become damaged or destroyed. But Job wanted readers to know there is hope when conditions for a plant or tree are not favorable. To his dismay Job did not believe this hope could be applied to him. He had been subjected to dire circumstances, and he believed that his only hope was his death. He believed there was hope that the tree would grow again but there was no hope for him.

We know this is not true because of the resurrection power of God. With Him we will flourish in glory, just as He causes plants to flourish in your garden. When you plant a whole garden, you can see great growth. Rely on God to bring the sunshine and rain so that your plants can flourish. And trust He will supply what is needed for your hopes to flourish as well. He wants you to succeed.

Dear God, I trust You to cause my hope to flourish. Amen.

Yanking Weeds That Destroy Hope

If we confess our sins, he is faithful and just and will forgive us our sins and purify us from all unrighteousness.

—1 John 1:9

Weeds pop up even if you mulch or spread barriers of newspaper or plastic over the ground. They are persistent and if left untended can choke out what you have planted. The weeds in our gardens are like the sins that pop up in our lives. Sin is not something easily covered, although you may continually struggle to yank it out. Some sins, like gossip, are difficult to remove. But a good gardener works diligently to remove all the weeds, even if they return again and again. You can be assured, though, that no matter how much sin reveals itself in your life, God will forgive you and will help you to remove these sins. The only requirement is that you confess your sins. In the Greek language, the word *confess* means "to say the same thing as another." When you confess to God, you are saying the same thing that He believes about your sin. Sins are not just mistakes. They are offenses against God.

As you struggle to remove weeds of sin that attack your hopes, remember that God will forgive you and help you to remain free from sin. As you cultivate and tend your hopes, He will help them grow.

Dear God, thank You for forgiving me and cleansing me of sin. Amen.

True Growth

"Though it is the smallest of all seeds, yet when it grows, it is the largest of garden plants and becomes a tree, so that the birds come and perch in its branches."

—Matthew 13:32

Jesus spoke about the mustard tree that grows from the tiniest of seeds. It grows tall and opens its branches for birds to rest upon them. The growth that Jesus spoke about is unnatural because a mustard seed usually sprouts to become a bush, not a tree with such height and breadth that birds could build their nests. Jesus used this as an analogy to emphasize the extensive growth of the kingdom of God. It is represented as a tiny mustard seed that will grow to something beyond its potential. He wanted His listeners to know that the kingdom of God, though seemingly tiny like the mustard seed, would have extensive growth.

God wants your hopes to grow and be fruitful like a beautiful mustard tree in a lush garden. He wants your hopes to grow into something useful for others and to provide comfort and nourishment. God delights in watching you grow and seeing you bring comfort, joy, and hope to others. Like the growth that Jesus spoke about for the kingdom of God, this is supernatural and is true growth that will last.

Dear Father, I want that true and supernatural growth for my hope. Thank You that You have this same desire for me. Amen.

Fragrant Faith, Hope, and Love

And now these three remain: faith, hope and love. But the greatest of these is love.

—1 Corinthians 13:13

Fragrant flowers touch us deeply as we breathe in their sweet scents that fill the air. We can imagine that the scent is the flower's expressing joy and sharing that joy with the world. The scents we share from our hearts are affected by our feelings, words, and circumstances. Anger has a nasty odor, but love, along with hope and faith, has a sweet scent. Paul spoke about all these virtues but focused especially on love because he wanted the Corinthian believers to be united. He described faith as "confidence in what we hope for and assurance about what we do not see" (Hebrews 11:1). For him our faith is the trust we have in God. He encouraged us to "rejoice in hope" (Romans 12:12 ESV). But he said love was greater than hope and faith because love will increase when we see God and it is descriptive of who God is.

A heart full of hope, faith, kindness, love, and joy produces sweet fragrances. Forgiveness is what it takes to pull the weeds from your heart and make room for new seeds to grow, ones that bring positive emotions that fuel your hope.

Dear Father, thank You for faith, hope, and love, and thank You for the fragrance of joy that is in my heart. Amen.

Fruitful Living

"Build houses and settle down; plant gardens and eat what they produce."

—Jeremiah 29:5

Be fruitful in your life, and nurture growth as you make your home a haven. Let your home be a place that offers spiritual nourishment to visitors and family. God commanded the Israelites to rebuild their homes. When they returned from seventy years of exile in Babylon, they found that their city, including their houses, lay in ruins. God, who is a God of decency and order, wanted their homes to be refreshed, repaired, and rebuilt. He wanted them to get on with their lives and be fruitful, even though times were difficult.

Added little touches make your home a welcome place for all who enter. Keeping a home clean and lovely makes it extra welcoming. Clutter is distracting and creates a collection of things that are not needed or used. Dust and dirt invite bugs, not people. In the busyness of life, it is nice to have a place to relax and be comfortable, no matter how large or small. When your home is neat and orderly, you will be ready to spread sunshine and hope to all who visit.

Dear Father, bless my home so that I can be fruitful in my everyday life and interactions with others. Bless my home to be a house of hope and love where You will be glorified. In Jesus' name I pray, Amen.

Countless Hopes

"See if I will not throw open the floodgates of heaven and pour out so much blessing that there will not be room enough to store it."

—Malachi 3:10

Counting blessings is a cheerful activity that lessens the pain of problems. When you start to count the beauty of each flower in your life, each kind word, and each friend, hopefully the blessings become too many to list. Each one can be linked to a past hope or may spark new hope to plant in the garden of your heart. There is an old gospel hymn whose words encourage listeners to count and name their blessings. This implies the possibility of receiving numerous blessings. God desires to open up the floodgates of heaven and pour more blessings than you can count and store. His only prerequisite is the same one that He gave to the Israelites, that you be obedient to His commands. Obedience to God is an indication that you trust Him. When you trust God, He will never let you down. So get ready for the blessings to roll in.

As you add up your blessings and the reasons for your hopes, they combine to become the little helpers that give you the encouragement to pursue your dreams.

Dear God, I choose to be obedient to Your commands. Thank You for the many blessings with which You have blessed me. Amen.

H-O-P-E

There is surely a future hope for you, and your hope will not be cut off.

—Proverbs 23:18

There is a website that invites people to create and submit an acrostic using the word *hope*. What words, phrases, or sentences would you use to communicate the message of hope? Words for the letter *h* could be *help* or *hopefulness*; for the letter *o*, *optimism* or *open* could be used; for the letter *p*, *positive* or *pushing* emphasizes a hopeful future; and for the letter *e*, *eager* or *excitedly* reveals the thrilling nature of hope. Use these words or others to get you started on your message of hope; then share it in various ways with others. God wants to use you to inspire hope.

Begin by sharing your message of hope with family and friends, and then share with those who are not so friendly. God loves everyone and wants to give hope to each person. To reach out and love the unlovable is difficult, especially people who have hurt you out of their own pain. It means letting go of selfish anger and hatred. Your faith helps you to believe your love can make a difference even when you do not see the change. Let hope inspire you to continue reaching outward with the message of hope.

Dear Lord, thank You for the message of hope that You have placed in my heart. Give me the courage to share it with others. In Jesus' name I pray, Amen.

Passionate Hope

*He humbled himself by becoming obedient to death—even death on
a cross!*

—Philippians 2:8

Passion means intense emotion. Passion energizes you beyond your normal strength. The image of real passion is the suffering of Jesus that started with the events of the week of His crucifixion, including a prayer in a garden, the betrayal of a friend, an unjust trial, and being scourged and abused at the hand of His captors. Jesus showed us a love so intense that it would not give up in the face of the most difficult struggle and the torture that He would endure. His passion concluded with His endurance of death on a cross, where nails were driven through His wrists and His feet, and a spear was plunged into His side. It was a cruel death that He endured for the sins of the world.

A few days before He died, He entered the garden and prayed for more strength. His prayers were the seeds of strength. His passionate love kept Him focused on the reasons He willingly suffered. The blood He shed and the love He showed became the seeds of hope for people in the centuries that have followed. Let His love nurture your passionate hope.

Dear God, thank You for Your great sacrifice of Your Son. I will always be grateful for His passion and what He endured not only for me but for the sins of the whole world. Amen.

Millions of Seeds

Jonathan became one in spirit with David, and he loved him as himself.
—1 Samuel 18:1

You probably cannot pinpoint one reason why a particular friend is so important. It is the accumulation of so many tiny actions, words, and kindnesses that make the friendship special. Jonathan, the son of King Saul and the soon-to-be king, and David made a covenant with each other that bound them together as lasting friends. David sacrificed for Jonathan, and Jonathan sacrificed for David. On one occasion, without jealousy or envy, Jonathan gave David his robe and military garb in recognition that David would someday be king instead of him. They were loyal to each other. Jonathan stood with David against his own father when Saul sought to kill David. They expressed heartache and pain with each other. Jonathan and David cried when David escaped harm.

Do you have a friend you can call on whenever you have a need or whenever you just want to hear a cheerful voice? Memories of laughter and tears shed remind you of joys and sorrows shared. Each laugh, tear, and smile exchanged becomes a seed to keep the garden of friendship growing. As you pray for your friends each day, be thankful for the hope of friendship. Pray for their health, and be thankful for their availability.

Dear God, bless my friends who brighten my days and encourage me to remain strong when facing challenges to my hope. Amen.

Hopeful Words

The tongue has the power of life and death.

—Proverbs 18:21

What is your favorite saying or phrase? Does it bring you comfort or laughter? Does it spread hope or show love? Or does it cause you to be discouraged, thinking thoughts like, *I can't do it.*

People proliferate love or hate and encouragement or discouragement through their words. James, the brother of Jesus, said words can cause a lot of damage that cannot be undone. James compared this damage to a fire that is out of control. It begins as a small flame that grows to engulf a forest; then it jumps from one hill to the next. Measure your words before you speak by asking yourself if the words will cause pain. Words that hurt include lying, gossiping, putting someone down, cheating, and bragging, among others.

Try adding a few encouraging words into your daily vocabulary, such as *awesome, amazing, way to go, thanks, I appreciate you*, and *I love you*. It only takes a word or two to lift someone's spirits, appreciate someone, or give a compliment. It is easy to scatter good thoughts everywhere you go. Be ready for kind words to return to you. They will lift your hopes too.

Lord, thank You for words that encourage and bless. May my words be encouraging and help new friends and inspire new hopes. Amen.

Blessed Forgiveness

Blessed is the one whose transgressions are forgiven, whose sins are covered.

—Psalm 32:1

*I*t is easy to pass on dejection to others by being grumpy or unkind. It is also easy to push to get your way and sulk if you do not get your way. Essentially, it is easy to hurt other people. However, it is a blessing to be forgiven for these offenses and to forgive others.

Jesus taught His disciples about forgiveness. On one occasion Peter questioned Jesus about how many times a person should be forgiven. Peter then asked if forgiving seven times was enough. Jesus responded, "I tell you, not seven times, but seventy-seven times" (Matthew 18:22). Jesus wanted Peter, and us, to know that we should never keep count of the number of times we forgive someone, and we should always forgive those who sincerely ask for forgiveness. Each evening as your mind wanders over the day, ask yourself if your actions and words may have hurt someone. Be quick to ask for forgiveness or send a note to apologize. Also, forgive anyone who slights you, with the hope that you will be forgiven for your offenses. Be thankful when you are forgiven.

Dear Father, thank You for the forgiveness that is available to me because of Jesus. Help me to forgive others and quickly ask for forgiveness when I have caused hurt. Amen.

Unusual Sprouts

John's clothes were made of camel's hair, and he had a leather belt around his waist. His food was locusts and wild honey.

—Matthew 3:4

A little bird drops a seed into the ocean, and it floats to some distant shore after splashing among the waves. It sinks into the soil and sprouts. A new plant grows and shoots up to give off more seeds and fills an area with new growth. The wind picks up a seed and blows it among the rocks where it wedges inside a little crack and sprouts in a most unlikely place. Seeds grow under unusual circumstances. They are delivered by unusual means and grow in unexpected places. This is God's work of replenishing the earth. God also uses unusual people. Consider John the Baptist, whom God used to prepare the way for Jesus Christ. John was unusual in his dress and in the food that he ate, and John preached an unusual message. It brought a message that planted seeds of hope in the hearts of people. It was the hope of a Savior.

Seeds of hope are like the little seeds that are tossed by the wind and waves and carried by birds. Pray that God will bless the seeds of hope you sow and help them sprout even when it seems unlikely.

Lord, help me to scatter seeds of love and joy in faraway hearts, especially those hearts that seem like unlikely places for love to grow. Amen.

The Plans of God

*As a plan for the fullness of time, to unite all things in him, things
in heaven and things on earth.*

—Ephesians 1:10 ESV

A handful of small, brown seeds look dull and lifeless, yet they hold the promise of tomorrow's garden. Inside each seed is the potential to grow and change. A seed must be buried and sit in the darkness of the soil while water nourishes it and causes it to split open and sprout.

Tomorrow's blooms take time. The seeds of our hopes also take time. God is the soil in which we plant our seeds. Are you ready to plant your hopes with God? God's plan is for the world, but many people do not understand His plans. His plan is to unite all people in Jesus Christ, and He uses people to execute His plans. You must be willing to allow God to guide your hopes and dreams. He will cause them to grow and use you for His purposes. Be willing to open up to God, asking Him to allow your true longings and dreams to grow. As you grow toward the light and warmth of the Son of God, watch your hopes sprout with new life, and watch God use you in His plans.

Dear Father, as I place my hope in You, use me in Your plans to bring others together under Christ. Amen.

Real Expectations

Praise be to the God and Father of our Lord Jesus Christ!

—1 Peter 1:3

As you praise God, you name His abilities and amazing promises. Remembering what God has done and what He can do will give you great expectations of what the future will bring. The Bible reveals who God is and all the wonders He has done. In particular, the book of Psalms includes praises to God and celebrations of the mercies of God. It helps you to focus on God and moves you to praise Him. David, the primary author of many of the psalms, includes many themes for praising God because of his personal experiences with God. David praised God, the One who crowned him king of Judah. He praised God for protecting and providing for him. David praised God just because He is God and deserves praise. David trusted God and expected by faith that God would be with him to help, guide, and protect him in the future.

As you praise God, you remind yourself that God is in charge and, like David, you simply must trust His will and His ways. Every step does not rest on you, but it rests on God. You can trust the outcome to God who is powerful, loving, and almighty. May this relieve any pressures concerning expectations you may have because you know that God cares about you and your hopes.

Dear God, I praise You for all You have done in my life to this point and praise You for what You will do in the future. Amen.

Hope at Home

When Herod realized that he had been outwitted by the Magi, he was furious.

—Matthew 2:16

Herod the Great was someone with whom most did not trifle. On a particularly bad day, he had all the little boys in Bethlehem who were two years old and younger killed. He was a man plagued by paranoia and even had members of his family put to death. Herod, who married ten times, had three of his own sons killed. Herod's family probably waited in dread for his arrival home every day. In fear they may have wondered what kind of mood Herod was in. Herod allowed his emotions and fear to determine his actions toward others. We, on the other hand, should let our love, peace, and hope guide our actions.

When we arrive home tired and worn, it is sometimes difficult to be nice. We may hope to be alone or want to express our complaints to others, so consequently, we show a little impatience toward our families. But if we show love and care in these weary moments, we will make our home a happy place that fosters hope.

Dear Lord, may I show the kind of love at home that fosters hope. Amen.

Hope of Wisdom

If any of you lacks wisdom, you should ask God, who gives generously to all without finding fault, and it will be given to you.

—James 1:5

Wisdom is not just about knowledge. The dictionary defines *wisdom* as discernment and insight, which are necessary when an important decision needs to be made. James said God would provide wisdom if you ask Him for it. He gives wisdom to all believers who will request it. God gives you the kind of wisdom that goes beyond the thinking of people and beyond common sense. God's wisdom will lead you to godly solutions for living. God's wisdom nurtures hope for today and for tomorrow. This means that God's wisdom will help you to advance toward your dreams.

Consider keeping a journal about the progress you are making toward realizing a dream. This will help you to sort your thoughts and make wise choices. As you write about each step you have taken, you can review your experience and reflect on lessons learned. You will be able to process your responses as you write about them and create a record of your progress. It is amazing how journaling can increase your chances for success as you gain understanding and wisdom. Challenge yourself to write in your journal on a regular basis, especially about your hopes.

Dear God, I choose to ask for and use Your wisdom to make decisions about life and hope. Thank You for the promise of wisdom. Amen.

Friendship Surprises

When Elizabeth heard Mary's greeting, the baby leaped in her womb.
—Luke 1:41

Like seeds that blow in the wind and take root to surprise us with something unexpected, our friendships can bring surprises as well. You never know what will blossom in the relationship or what type of fruit will grow as you nurture a friendship. Though Mary and Elizabeth were relatives, they were also friends who loved each other. Both had been blessed—and surprised—with unusual pregnancies. Elizabeth had conceived in her old age, and Mary had conceived by the Holy Spirit. When an angel visited Mary and told her about her baby, the angel mentioned Elizabeth. So Mary decided to visit Elizabeth because she knew that Elizabeth would understand what was happening to her. Elizabeth was the friend that Mary could talk to about what was happening in her life.

God knows it is not good to struggle or rejoice alone, so He blesses you with friends. Be ready for laughs, tears, and surprises with each friend. Sharing your life with another will gain the hope of a good friend who will bring more joy to your days. Rejoice in the unique differences of each individual. Thank God for each friend you have made, and treat each one as a gift from God.

Dear God, thank You for the gift of friendship and the little surprises that mean so much. Amen.

Seeds of Love

Therefore, as we have opportunity, let us do good to all people.
—Galatians 6:10

Passing out compliments, encouraging others, and lending a helping hand are ways you sow love and hope. With these simple gifts you plant seeds that you can nurture with more loving actions and thoughtful conversations. Many of the letters in the Bible that were written by Paul contain an exhortation or encouragement to be kind to one another. This is important for believers who are to model a God of love before the world.

Every day as you respond to people, you continue to sow seeds, so let's sew the good seeds of love. Your loving actions will bring out the best in others. And as you open up to talk and share, the friendship grows. Paul also said to continue to do good and to carry one another's burdens. These actions will help you reap many blessings. Every time you use an opportunity to do good, the seeds of friendship show signs of growth. Enjoy the fruit your seeds produce as friendships blossom. You will soon grow a garden of friends.

Dear God, keep me focused on what I can do to help others, especially my friends. Help me to sow seeds of love wherever I go. Help me to never miss an opportunity to show love to those around me. Amen.

Legacy of Hope

"'He is the one who will build a house for my Name.'"

—2 Samuel 7:13

The seeds of a tree are able to grow many trees; then those trees will continue to produce more seeds until a forest emerges. Similarly, the seed of one dream can birth many other dreams and possibilities. Your dream can be a seed of hope for coming generations to build upon and increase.

King David was living in a beautiful palace, and finally there was peace in the land around him. So he called the prophet Nathan and revealed his dream to build a temple for God. But God spoke to Nathan, giving him a message for David. God said David would not be the one to build His temple; David's calling was for another purpose, and he had been successful in what God had asked him to do. God said his son Solomon would build His temple. Therefore, David began to collect materials, and he described his vision to his son so that Solomon could begin to build God's temple. Share your dream with future generations, especially if your dreams are unfulfilled, so that they may capture your visions and be the ones to germinate the seed you had hoped to plant.

Dear Lord, thank You for those who come behind me to fulfill the dreams that I leave. Amen.

Dreamweaver of Hope

Joseph had a dream, and when he told it to his brothers, they hated him all the more.

—Genesis 37:5

Before you were born, God knew all about you and formed you in your mother's womb. When He created you, He had a specific plan for your life. During the passage of time, God will equip you to fulfill His plan and purpose for you. The amazing story of Joseph is a great example of how a dream can be weaved from hope to reality.

Joseph had been given dreams of God's plan for his life; so with confidence and strength, he endured being sold into slavery by his brothers, being thrown into prison, and being accused of a crime he did not commit. Joseph's years of steadfast reliance on God resulted in his dreams being fulfilled. It allowed God to weave a plan together that brought about not only the reunion of Joseph's family, but Joseph also was given a high position in Egypt so that he was able to save a nation from starvation. God as the Dreamweaver will help you to discover your dreams and purpose, give you hope, turn disappointments into opportunities, and make choices that impact your destiny. Trust Him to weave the impossible.

Dear God, thank You for all that You do to make my dreams possible. Amen.

Future Hopes

Do not boast about tomorrow, for you do not know what a day may bring.

—Proverbs 27:1

Weather forecasters can only theorize about future weather conditions based on patterns and signs that occurred in the past and that are occurring in the present. Only God really knows the future. God has not given us the ability to see the future, so we should not arrogantly talk about tomorrow as if it will be a sure thing. No person is assured of one moment in the future. You cannot even be certain that you will have tomorrow what you have today. But do not allow this to cast a shadow on your hopes for the future. Not knowing the future does not forbid preparing for tomorrow. You must not put off any great work for fear that it will not be fulfilled.

If you knew you had only a few days left on earth, is your dream so important that you would pursue it? If you believe deeply in what you want to do, then invest time to do it now with the hope that God will give you time to complete the work. Have faith that your dream will produce good results and is worthy of your effort.

Dear God, I am not guaranteed tomorrow, so help me to work hard every day with the knowledge that my future is in Your hands. Amen.

United in Hope

Finally, all of you, have unity of mind, sympathy, brotherly love, a tender heart, and a humble mind.

—1 Peter 3:8 ESV

Someone saw a boy struggling in the waves and undertow. That person reached out to help, and other people joined to help him. They formed a string of joined hands. The first person in the line waded into the swirling water and stood against the waves to grasp the boy's hand. They pulled and tugged together and saved his life.

It is a biblical principle that people who stand united in love and trust can accomplish many great things. Divisiveness and dissention, however, cause turmoil and make dreams begin to fade. The apostle Peter said we should be one. As believers in God, it is essential that we be united. But we are also individuals. It is obvious that we are not the same in many aspects. However, the tie that binds us, according to Peter, is that we are of the same mind. This means we should believe the same things about God and His love. This will join our hearts and hopes together.

Joined hands make a difference that give strength and hope. Reach out with an open hand to join someone who hopes like you and wants to work with you. Rejoice as your strength and hope increase and produce results.

Dear God, help me to reach out to others who have the same hope as me so that together we can make our dreams come true. Amen.

Hope Remains

"He will wipe every tear from their eyes. There will be no more death or mourning or crying or pain, for the old order of things has passed away."

—Revelation 21:4

In the wake of major storm damage, like hurricanes and tornadoes, people search through the debris for their meaningful possessions. Irrepressible hope is found in discovering beauty that remains. In the aftermath of Hurricane Katrina, people who experienced the devastation or those who reached out to help shared many stories of hope. One story is told of a hymnal that was found among the ruins of a church. It was a symbol of hope, and the volunteers believed it was a message from God that everything would be okay. Their hope was born out of the debris and remained to strengthen them.

You are programmed to seek hope and fight with all you have to survive the storms that come into your life. Fireproof safes and placing photos in online storage provide hope that, if disaster comes, you will still have a little something left, a reminder of past pleasure and loved ones. Reflect on what you have already survived. What gave you hope to go on? Then thank God for the beauty and the love that remains in your life to give you hope for the future.

Dear God, in spite of storms that come my way, I will seek the hope that remains so that I may be strengthened to rebuild and move forward toward Your plan for me. Amen.

Peril and Hope

Whoever dwells in the shelter of the Most High will rest in the shadow of the Almighty.

—Psalm 91:1

David Vetter lived his entire life in a bubble. He was born without an immune system, so his body could not fight off diseases. David was a brave little boy who hoped that one day the doctors would find a cure. But until then he had to spend all his time in a bubble where he ate, slept, and played. The bubble was David's shelter from harm until he was twelve years old. At that time the doctors took a risk on a procedure that gave his family hope for a cure, but instead it caused David's death.

We cannot live in a bubble and be protected from all danger any more than David could. The world is full of pain and grief, but it is also full of beauty and love. Seek love and beauty to let your hope grow to overcome the darkness of troubles. And when you face troubles, you have a place where you can find comfort. David called it the shadow of the Almighty. Under His protection, we have unending hope, knowing that our difficult circumstances in life are temporary. In Christ we can have eternal peace and joy.

Dear God, thank You that there is hope in spite of peril. Amen.

MAY

· • • · · • • · ·

Green is the fresh emblem of well-founded hopes. In blue the spirit can wander, but in green it can rest.

—Mary Webb

The Miracle of Life

For you created my inmost being; you knit me together in my
mother's womb.

—Psalm 139:13

A baby jumps inside the womb to the mother-to-be's delight. She notices each turn, twist, and hiccup within her. The first stirrings of movement amaze a woman as she wonders about the baby's looks and personality. Only God can create life. It is He who formed each person in the womb. It takes power, skill, and a delicate touch to make such a tiny baby in such a small space. For us it is a mystery, but for God it is His crowning achievement. In verse 14 of Psalm 139, David could only praise God for this amazing work, saying, "I am fearfully and wonderfully made." Anyone who looks upon another human being should have the same awe. Life and birth are miracles because of the development process in the womb.

Therefore, we should be joyful during the birth of a child. There is joy in hearing of a baby's arrival or in holding a newborn bundle. To experience new life is the very essence of hope. The same is true when something new enters our lives. We are excited with new hope of what miracles may come. Rejoice at the delight of a new hope, and give thanks to God for the gift.

Dear God, like David, I praise You because I am fearfully and wonderfully made. Amen.

Belief Beyond Troubles

"Do not let your hearts be troubled. You believe in God; believe also in me."

—John 14:1

*I*n the play *Peter Pan*, a mischievous boy named Peter, who lives in a place called Neverland, decides he will never grow up. He lives among other boys, pirates, mermaids, Native Americans, and fairies. On one occasion one of the fairies, Tinker Bell, had problems with her light. It began to fade, so Peter Pan turned to the audience and stated that to help her they must believe in fairies. This fairy tale is a reminder of the importance of faith.

Jesus reminds us that we do not have to let trouble take root in our hearts and shut out hope or faith. Instead, we must cling to faith and believe that God has the ability to overcome any struggle. It takes courage and strength to challenge a troubled heart. But Jesus said to put your hope and faith in Him. Because of our faith in Jesus, we are sure that one day He will return to earth and will take His followers to heaven. But while you are here, know that Jesus wants the best for you. He may not prevent trouble, but He sees past your current problems and knows the good that is to come. Therefore, hope in the One who loves you dearly, and believe He will help you.

Dear God, I believe in Your Son, Jesus. Thank You that He is my hope during times of trouble. Amen.

Hope Redesigned

For you know that the testing of your faith produces steadfastness.
—James 1:3 ESV

When making or altering a dress, sometimes you need to rip out a seam to make it fit better. The material is good and still strong, but you have to make a few adjustments. So you use a little seam ripper to rip apart the old seam and yank out the threads, but it does not harm the fabric. This fashion adjustment will make the dress fit and look so much better. Similarly, adjustments may need to be made in your heart or your life because of troubles that are ripping apart your life. James challenged believers to be joyful when adversity tests our faith because the end result will be better. Difficult times help you to develop patience and can teach you to stand stronger and hold on to your dream. Difficult times will produce a stronger faith, which should be an important characteristic in you as you strive for your dream.

So if you feel like troubles have tugged, pulled, and ripped apart a dream, maybe it is a fashion adjustment. The fabric of your dream is still intact, but it may need a slight refitting. Review your dream, and see where you might sew the pieces together differently for a better fit. A little redesign could make all the difference.

Dear God, thank You for those times when I need an adjustment. I know the results will make me better able to reach for my dream. Amen.

Rest in Jesus

"Come to me, all you who are weary and burdened, and I will give you rest."

—Matthew 11:28

Have you ever tried everything you could think of to work out a problem and nothing fixed it? You may feel exhausted and do not know how you can continue, but that does not mean you have exhausted all the possibilities. Jesus said if you are weary, He will give you rest. Sometimes you may become weighed down by responsibilities, work, or whatever you are doing to accomplish your goals. Jesus compared your burden to being harnessed to a yoke. A yoke is a wooden frame used for carrying a load or fastening animals together so they can do double the work. Jesus said if your burden is heavy, then you should put down your yoke and put His yoke on because His yoke is easy.

When you feel hopeless and cannot find a solution, take a break and look to Jesus. It might be time to refresh your mind and spirit with rest. Indulge in a favorite activity, or visit a favorite spot. Relax, pray, and let your troubles go. Then remember that there is always another possibility, another idea to try. Jesus will lead you every step of the way. Once you are relaxed, have recharged your mind, and have renewed your spirit, take a new look, but this time look with Jesus.

Dear God, thank You that I can go to Jesus for rest when I am weary and weighed down. Amen.

There Is Always Tomorrow

Therefore we do not lose heart. Though outwardly we are wasting away, yet inwardly we are being renewed day by day.

—2 Corinthians 4:16

Just as the winter snows melt and give way to warmer, sunnier weather with bluer skies, so a new day arrives and a new story unfolds. Today holds new possibilities. Katie Scarlett O'Hara, one of the characters from the book *Gone with the Wind*, is a spoiled and insecure young woman. She spends much of her young life in pursuit of a man who is promised to her friend. Her pursuit destroys many lives and challenges her relationships. Toward the end of the book when Scarlett finally realizes her pursuit was a childish romance, it is too late. However, though her home is destroyed and her life is in shambles, she rises up and determines to think of a solution the next day.

A new day will have its own challenges, but it also has new moments for spinning your dream and weaving together a new story. The book of 1 Corinthians reveals that with each day, you are inwardly being renewed. Therefore, like Scarlett, you should consider how to plan for the new day. Look to make connections that will help you strengthen your plans. Pay attention to the opportunities to build onto your dream. Cheerfully choose to make the most of this new day.

Dear Lord, thank You for this new day. Amen.

Confidence

For the LORD will be your confidence.

—Proverbs 3:26 ESV

A new outfit and hairdo can boost your confidence. You feel good because you know you look good. This simple way to boost your confidence can be just what you need to continue to pursue your dreams. When difficult times come and you doubt your abilities, or doubt that your dreams are achievable, ask God to give you a new look.

God longs to have you trust in Him and know how much He believes in you. Ellen G. White said, "We need to have far less confidence in what man can do and far more confidence in what God can do for every believing soul. He longs to have you reach after Him by faith. He longs to have you expect great things from Him." God wants to bless you with opportunities and bring people into your life to help you. He wants you to be safe and secure from all fear and discouragement. God will support you and help you to maintain your hope. He does not want you to lose heart and cast it away. Ask Him to boost your confidence with His love, and expect great things from Him.

Dear God, thank You that You are my confidence. Thank You for Your love and support of my dreams. Amen.

Why?

Why is light given to a man whose way is hidden?

—Job 3:23 ESV

Too often hearts are broken and dreams are shattered. Job suffered great losses and asked God why. There were many questions asked and many implied in the book of Job, some by Job, others by his friends and his wife. They asked questions such as these: Why do the righteous suffer? How can God allow the righteous to suffer? Who is man to judge God? But the question that most people ask is why. That is a natural question to ask when you are suffering or in pain. When Job asked why, God responded by asking Job questions. He asked, "Where were you when I laid the earth's foundation?" (Job 38:4). This question humbled Job because he realized his own feeble stature, and he learned that in spite of heartbreak, God had the power to make everything brand new.

God never actually told Job why, but Job listened to God and remembered that God is almighty and wise. Job looked beyond the why of heartbreak and instead trusted in and found comfort in God, and God gave Job new hope and restored his prosperity. In heaven there will be no pain and wickedness, but until then, here on earth, suffering will exist. Be grateful that God will continue to comfort you, strengthen you, and give you renewed hope.

Dear God, when I experience heartbreak, please remind me of Your love and care. In Jesus' name I pray, Amen.

Touch of Hope

But Jesus said, "Someone touched me, for I perceive that power has gone out from me."

—Luke 8:46 ESV

Helen Keller, who was both blind and deaf, remained at a distance from the world. Her circumstances seemed hopeless until Anne Sullivan touched her hand and taught her how to communicate. Then Helen heard and experienced the world through Anne's fingers. Anne's fingers gave Helen's heart a touch of hope. Helen said, "Once I knew the depth where no hope was, and darkness lay on the face of all things. Then love came and set my soul free. Once I knew only darkness and stillness. Now I know hope and joy." A touch can speak volumes. A soothing touch speaks of tenderness and love. While in a crowd of people, Jesus felt a touch that drew power from Him. It was an intentional touch from a woman who had been suffering from a disease. It was a touch of hope and faith that healed her and made her whole.

Touch is necessary for life. If Helen Keller did not have the sense of touch, she would have remained in a dark and hopeless world. The sense of touch is used for learning, protection, and showing affection. Most importantly, a positive touch from someone else will encourage you and give hope. So today take time to reach out with a loving word and a gentle touch to fuel someone's hope.

Dear Lord, thank You for touch. Lead me to reach out and touch someone who needs hope. Amen.

Hope in Stillness

I will meditate on your precepts and fix my eyes on your ways.
—Psalm 119:15 ESV

When a cloud invades your day and you start to complain, remember the sun is still there and God is still in control. Take a moment to be still, meditate on God, and look for the silver lining. You will feel the warm rays of the hidden sun. King David said He would hide God's Word in his heart so that he would not sin against God. God's Word is like gold and is worth hiding away, and the heart is a good place to store it. David meditated and fixed his eyes on the ways of God. God promised that when we meditate on His Word, we will be blessed and find peace (Psalm 1:1–3). The benefits of meditation, being still and calm, are many, and the most important is spiritual health and wellness.

So do not be bothered by the clouds. There is peace and calm in stillness, while complaining agitates your mind and heart. Grumbles and gripes stir up hurt, pain, and discouragement. Plus, complainers point out the criticisms and miss seeing what is good. When you cease complaining, you turn off a dripping tap that pings noisily and irritates. As you let quiet fill your heart and look for what is good, you will find hope again.

Dear God, I will meditate on Your Word so that I can be a blessing to You, myself, and others. Amen.

Unexpected Hope

Jesus called in a loud voice, "Lazarus, come out!"

—John 11:43

A new friendship, the budding of a flower, a stranger's smile, or a sweet greeting can interrupt a dull day and make it burst with joy. Like the surprise ending of a good joke or a romantic story that you did not guess, unexpected surprises in life can inspire you and even cause you to giggle throughout the rest of your day. This is when hope catches you unaware. Jesus was always doing the unexpected. He walked on water, stilled a storm, made the blind to see and the lame to walk, and, yes, He raised Lazarus from the dead. No one expected Jesus to do such an extraordinary feat. Lazarus's sisters, Mary and Martha, sent for Jesus when Lazarus became ill. Their expectation was that Jesus would heal their brother. But when Jesus waited too long, Lazarus died, and all hope was lost. But hope returned when Jesus called Lazarus from the grave. It was an unexpected blessing for all who held him dear.

You give unexpected hope whenever you smile, call a friend, or give a little gift of homemade goodies to someone who does not expect it. Try it. It may be just what someone needs.

Dear Lord, send a surprise blessing to bring a smile or giggle in my day. Send the unexpected hope to lift my spirit so that I can share unexpected hope with someone else. Amen.

Diligently Prepare

Study to shew thyself approved unto God, a workman that needeth not to be ashamed, rightly dividing the word of truth.

—2 Timothy 2:15 KJV

Abraham Lincoln received only eighteen months of formal schooling as a child, but his passion for reading and studying prepared him to become president. He wielded an ax to help build his family home and worked as a clerk in a store where he earned a reputation for honesty. Later he took advantage of opportunities to become a lawyer and politician. In the book of Timothy, Paul provided two reasons that a person should diligently prepare. First, prepare so that you meet God's approval. Your life is not about pleasing yourself or others. All your time should be spent in earnest pursuit of seeking and doing God's will. Second, prepare so that you will not be ashamed in the work that God has called you to do. Lincoln would not have represented the country well if he had not known what he was doing. Likewise, you will not represent God well if you do not prepare for what is ahead.

You may devote time to a hobby or study topics that you are passionate about. Then the passions may become hopes of something bigger. Continue to learn and prepare to reach your goals. As you look for opportunities, be ready for a happy match of your hopes to your knowledge.

Dear God, strengthen me and prepare me to reach my goals so that I will represent You well. Amen.

Inventing Hope

For though the righteous fall seven times, they rise again.
—Proverbs 24:16

Have you ever experimented with trying to solve a problem? You may have tried various ways to remove a stain or adapted recipes to incorporate an ingredient found on sale. Solutions to common problems inspire inventions. Some famous inventors include Thomas Edison, Alexander Graham Bell, George Washington Carver, Eli Whitney, and Benjamin Franklin, among others. Their inventions began with an idea, which more than likely addressed a need. It was Plato who said, "The true creator is necessity, who is the mother of our invention." Thomas Edison investigated problems to find solutions. He brought hope to people as he solved problems. In solving problems he also created opportunities and jobs, becoming a source of hope for many people.

When a problem frustrates you, consider turning it into an opportunity to help people. To solve the problem, begin by thinking outside the box. Ask yourself questions about what you want to accomplish with the solution. Apply your skills and study to what has already been tried, with the hope of finding a new solution. It may take repeated efforts to find an answer, but keep trying. Following up on your idea may open up new ways to bless your family, friends, and others.

Dear God, my Father, when I find problems, whether they are my own or whether they are problems others are facing, give me the fortitude to persistently seek a solution. In Jesus' name I pray, Amen.

Bring Health to Your Body

Do not be wise in your own eyes; fear the LORD and shun evil. This
will bring health to your body and nourishment to your bones.

—Proverbs 3:7–8

Taking a few seconds to notice a problem and prevent an accident can keep away guilty thoughts such as, "If only I had done something." Benjamin Franklin cautioned, "An ounce of prevention is worth a pound of cure." This is one of the points that King Solomon made in the book of Proverbs when he cautioned his readers against arrogance. We should not be wise in our own eyes. When you choose this route, it means you do not trust God and look to yourself for direction. Rather, Solomon advised that you should fear God and stay away from evil. Adherence to these recommendations will prevent deterioration of your health—physically, mentally, and emotionally—and loss of your hope.

When a day ends in peace and calm, it meets the hope of a day without crisis or accident. You may not recall the little reactions of changing lanes to avoid a collision, keeping an eye on the stove while cooking, or other steps that prevented accidents or harm and bring health to your body. Routine safety prevention becomes normal procedure and makes a difference. Be grateful for uneventful evenings, and hope for more of them to come.

Dear God, thank You for keeping me safe and for the wisdom of prevention so that I can keep my whole body healthy. Amen.

Prepared for Change

"Be strong and courageous. Do not be afraid; do not be discouraged,
for the LORD your God will be with you wherever you go."

—Joshua 1:9

Keeping assorted greeting cards, envelopes, and stamps in a drawer will help you to be prepared to offer hope to others who face challenges or celebrate milestones. Congratulations, get well, sympathy, and blank note cards are reminders that change is coming and that change can be good, bad, or unknown. People do not know the future, but there is One who does.

Preparation, which includes trusting God, would be wise. Joshua was faithful to God in obedience and trust. Because of what God had commanded him to do, he faced intense changes not only for himself but for the Israelites. In preparation God told Joshua that he should not be afraid because He would be with him. Joshua knew that God would do what He promised. He is the great God who is faithful. Therefore, Joshua purposed to trust God in the face of changes.

You may not know the future, but you can be ready to greet it and hope that your heart is prepared to face unforeseen joys and sorrows. Strengthen your heart for change through prayer. Prayer helps your heart to be ready for the unknown. Trust in the One who knows what will happen.

Dear God, thank You for Your promise to be with me as I face unknown changes. I trust Your promises. Amen.

Heavenly Hopes

And he carried me away in the Spirit to a mountain great and high, and showed me the Holy City, Jerusalem, coming down out of heaven from God.

—Revelation 21:10

Have you thought about spiritual things lately? Are you prepared for the next life? Jesus is preparing a place in heaven with many rooms for all believers. God, who will be enthroned in heaven, is only a whisper away to those who pray. In the Bible only one person, the apostle John, had a glimpse of heaven and described its beauty and the joy he experienced. In verses 10–21 of Revelation 21, he provided a preview of what heaven is like. He called it the Holy City, Jerusalem, and said it shone like a jewel and crystal. He saw a great high wall around the city of heaven with twelve gates made of pearls and twelve angels. The wall was made of jasper, and its foundation was decorated with many different precious stones, including sapphire, emerald, and amethyst. But John was not done yet; he said the streets of the city were of gold, as pure as transparent glass.

What a joy to think heaven is ready and waiting, a place lovelier than any vision or dream. John saw it, and you can too. It is a hope that will be fulfilled if you believe in Jesus.

Dear God, thank You for preparing a beautiful place like heaven. I look forward to being there with You. Amen.

Positive Dream Catchers

But hope that is seen is no hope at all. Who hopes for what they already have? But if we hope for what we do not yet have, we wait for it patiently.

—Romans 8:24–25

Have you seen the colorful, spider-like weavings called dream catchers? In the tradition of Native Americans, dream catchers are hung in the place where a person sleeps. They are used to capture bad dreams and allow good dreams to come through. What if you turned a dream catcher into something more positive, made it into something that would display turning your hopes and dreams into beautiful realities?

What are you hoping for on this earth? Do you dream of a new home, a successful career, freedom from debt, or a family? What are you hoping for beyond this earth: no more heartache, no more diseases, rest from suffering, or rewards of heaven? In both of these cases, you should not be impatient. Just grab ahold of your hope in a dream catcher, and wait patiently for it.

Begin by describing your dreams for earth in vivid color to others so they can help you catch the vision and passion of all that you hope will come true. Share the splendor of the dream, and let God fill your heart with hope. But hold your dreams for beyond earth in your heart, and wait patiently for them to be filled in eternity.

Dear God, I will grab ahold of my hopes and wait for the day You will fulfill them all. Amen.

Armed for Hopes

Prepare for war! Rouse the warriors! Let all the fighting men draw near and attack.

—Joel 3:9

Have you wanted a new appliance and started a list of the pros and cons of the purchase? You may have thought of ways to cut corners to save for the purchase and may have kept an eye out for the best sales. As you considered it, you may have discovered that your finances and timing were not ready, and you needed to hold off on acquiring the desired item until the timing was right.

During the Revolutionary War, George Washington had to hold off until the time was right. In 1777 he had faced two defeats at the hands of British soldiers. He and his men then encamped at Valley Forge for the winter. During that time, George Washington and his men's supplies were replenished, and they were trained in new war strategies. These strategies were not only taught to the soldiers at Valley Forge but to all enlisted American soldiers at that time. George Washington and his soldiers, prepared and strong, went on to attack the British at the Battle of Monmouth and proved that the troops could stand against the British army.

Just as an army must build its strength to defeat its enemies, you may need to wait and build up your resources before you can achieve your goals.

Dear God, bless me to wait until You have armed me to reach for my dreams. Amen.

Prayer-Prepared Hope

[God] went ahead of you on your journey, in fire by night and in a cloud by day, to search out places for you to camp and to show you the way you should go.

—Deuteronomy 1:33

Before taking a family trip or taking children to an event, you probably make plans. You check the map or program the GPS to the right address, and you pack snacks and supplies. For longer trips you pack a suitcase with clothes, toiletries, and items to make the journey pleasant. Do not forget to invite God on your trip as well. Moses reminded the Israelites of their march through that great and terrible wilderness toward the promised land. He reminded them that the presence of God was with them in the fire by night and the cloud by day. God journeyed with them to protect and provide for them. When the cloud lifted up above the tent, they journeyed, and when it rested, they pitched their tents. God was in the fire at night to help them find their way through the darkness.

God was with the Israelites throughout their journey in the desert. He provided food, water, and His presence. He planned a long trip where they would learn to trust Him. Praying before a trip should be included in your preparation. It brings God on the journey with the hope of His protection and care.

Dear Father, bless my journey with Your presence for protection and care along the way. Amen.

Time Is of the Essence

Teach us to number our days, that we may gain a heart of wisdom.

—Psalm 90:12

If you have ever sewn a T-shirt or simple top, you may have spent more time selecting the fabric, choosing the pattern, cutting the material, and matching the design than actually sewing. Once at the machine, you need to thread it, check the needle size, and adjust the stitch length. During these preparations you envisioned the finished piece and may have dreamed of wearing it or thought of the person who would receive it as a gift. Did you feel that your time was spent wisely as you sought to accomplish your goal? Preparation is important, but we must make sure that what we are planning and doing is necessary. The psalmist encouraged us to number our days. In other words, he said you should work as if today is your last day on earth. He advised that there is wisdom in doing this. This wisdom is what inspires you to seek the most important duties and choose the most important actions to take.

God is eternal, but we are temporary. Therefore, you should value time and plan and work on your hopes and dreams with the understanding that the time in which you work is all you have. The hours and days before you belong to eternity.

Dear God, my Father, teach me to number my days so that I may value time and do what is essential. Amen.

Pay Attention

To present her to himself as a radiant church, without stain or
wrinkle or any other blemish, but holy and blameless.

—Ephesians 5:27

Have you ever noticed when something was amiss with yourself, but no one ever mentioned it? Maybe you left a curler in your hair or wore a shirt inside out, and you only discovered the error at the end of the day. You may have wondered if anyone noticed the mistake. Sometimes it is easy to be distracted or to miss the unexpected. But an important part of showing love toward others is to notice the details.

In the book of Ephesians, Paul encouraged husbands to love their wives as Christ loves the church. Christ notices every detail about His bride. Jesus serves and honors the church, and He notices any aspects that need to be strengthened. He also delights in who we are and our good works accomplished through Him. In any relationship there will be failures and defects, but there will also be successes and joys. The key is that each person should notice. Paying attention to detail makes others feel loved.

Friends may hope you will notice a frown, a stray tear, a downcast look, or something amiss. Or they may hope you will see a special twinkle when they have good news they want to share. When you meet with friends or are with loved ones, pay close attention, and you will bring more joy to the relationship.

Dear Lord, help me to be more attentive to details in the lives of those I love.
Amen.

Work On

Go to the ant, you sluggard; consider its ways and be wise!

——Proverbs 6:6

Little ants march along, undaunted by obstacles. They spend time stocking their underground cupboards with picnic crumbs, tiny seeds, and bits of fallen fruits. They build their anthill much taller than their short bodies and climb up and down the mound. Ants never let anything distract them. These focused workers prepare for winter during hot summer days. As the book of Proverbs advises, we should consider the ant and its ways. The ant is not slothful. Slothfulness or laziness should not be a characteristic that defines a believer in Christ or one who has big dreams. You should diligently and conscientiously put your best efforts in all you do. Being lazy has the potential to keep you from accomplishing your dream and becoming what God has called you to be.

Do not allow your hopes and dreams to be ruined because of slothfulness. Be like the ant. You can prepare for your dreams by storing supplies, building skills, and developing a network. You will be building your hopes like the ants build their home, one grain of sand at a time. Before long you will have built something bigger than you thought possible.

Dear God, when I become lazy, give me the fortitude to complete my work and build the future of my dreams. Amen.

Conversation Building

"How can this be?" Nicodemus asked.

—John 3:9

Connecting to people's hearts and communicating with them builds friendships. Do you consider the other person's needs and feelings before you speak? Do you remember past conversations that shared hopes and fears? A Pharisee named Nicodemus went to Jesus one night. He wanted to talk to Jesus about rumors he had heard. The conversation that Nicodemus had with Jesus would become the most important conversation for the world. He asked Jesus, "How can someone be born when they are old?" (John 3:4). Jesus responded with an explanation about the Holy Spirit and being born again. Jesus shared God's love and said what must be done to enter eternity. He gave Nicodemus the gospel in a nutshell. Nicodemus connected with Jesus through questions, and Jesus responded. It was a conversation of hope.

Conversations can be a powerful source of hope. You can bridge the past with the present to strengthen the bonds of your friendships. When you want to share your hopes, it is also a time to ask about their hopes too. Share how your dreams will make a difference and touch lives, and listen as they give suggestions and share their opinions. Communicate with your friends, and embrace each other's hopes.

Dear Father, thank You for the conversation between Nicodemus and Jesus that brought hope to the world. I will use my voice to communicate and connect with others about hope. Amen.

First Aid of Hope

Be prepared in season and out of season.

—2 Timothy 4:2

Many people, especially parents, make sure there are bandages, ointment, tweezers, and other items in a first aid kit in case of accidents. It is normal to prepare for unexpected accidents or changes, especially unwelcome ones. Nurse Clara Barton understood the necessity of being prepared for the unexpected. During the Civil War, she worked to aid injured soldiers who were brought into the hospital from the battlefields. But soon she saw a need to go to the battle lines to carry supplies and help the soldiers. Many times she arrived just when medical supplies and bandages had run out. Using her own funds, she risked her life to aid others. The soldiers called her "Angel of the Battlefield." Clara Barton later founded the American Red Cross. She devoted her life to being prepared to aid others.

It is always good to prepare your heart for unexpected changes. When life goes wrong, it can be devastating. Be prepared by staying in touch with friends and family so you can keep your support group strong. They will be there to lean on when you need them. Give thanks for all that you have and all those around you who help protect your hopes and keep you prepared.

Lord, help me be prepared for unknown challenges. Be with me as I face the future and prepare my heart to stand firm. Amen.

Creative Thinking

Do not be overcome by evil, but overcome evil with good.

—Romans 12:21

John D. Rockefeller, one of the richest men in the world, once said, "I always tried to turn every disaster into an opportunity." His work philosophy paid off, and through hard work and determination, he founded Standard Oil Company and became a leading businessman and philanthropist in the United States. Thinking creatively, he took on a number of business ventures as a teenager but soon ventured out on his own. Eventually, he tapped into one of society's needs and established an oil refinery, which grew very quickly and became the largest company in America.

Creative thinkers look deep to find opportunities in disasters. They do not default to evil, but they strive for the good that lies underneath. Think through how you survived past crises and became stronger. You probably discovered you are tougher than you thought and found new abilities within yourself. This means you are a survivor and that is a reason to celebrate. Let problems draw out the best in you, never the bad. Consider the journey of your life and how much you have been through and what you have accomplished. Keep that in focus, and renew your hopes.

Dear God, disasters come and go. I pray to never try to overcome them using evil but to think creatively so that good will be the result and so that my hope will be renewed and bless others. Amen.

Thoughts of Hope

If anything is excellent or praiseworthy—think about such things.
—Philippians 4:8

Each morning you wake with new energy so that you can begin your day strong. Spend that energy on what you want to do instead of dwelling on regrets or fighting old battles. Focus on what moves your hopes forward and helps build your dream.

Think on what is true, good, and beneficial about your dream. The apostle Paul wrote to his Philippian friends that "whatever is true, whatever is noble, whatever is right, whatever is pure, whatever is lovely, whatever is admirable—if anything is excellent or praiseworthy—think about such things" (Philippians 4:8). Paul wanted them to produce what was good, so he encouraged them to think about good things. Then he wrote, "Whatever you have learned or received or heard from me, or seen in me—put it into practice. And the God of peace will be with you" (v. 9). He identified himself as one who lived a life that was worthy to be copied. Each morning when you arise, recharge your hopes with the energy of your dreams. Focus on the desires that God has placed in your heart. Allow your thoughts to center on how your goals will benefit the world. Your thoughts will be lived out through your actions and, like Paul, you will impact the lives of those around you.

Dear God, may I think only thoughts that will bless You and give hope to others. In Jesus' name I pray, Amen.

Courage to Change

Therefore, if anyone is in Christ, he is a new creation. The old has passed away; behold, the new has come.

—2 Corinthians 5:17 ESV

M any people know or have heard the serenity prayer. Though the wording has been adjusted for various reasons, most pray the following: "God, grant me the serenity to accept the things I cannot change, the courage to change the things I can, and the wisdom to know the difference." This prayer has been adopted by Alcoholics Anonymous and several other twelve-step programs. It is a prayer that focuses on a desperate change from the negative to the positive and is an appeal for wisdom. The Bible reveals that spiritual change will come if you are in Christ. But situational and other changes require prayer.

You grow a little wiser every day when you take time to evaluate and learn from your experiences. There will always be some things you cannot change. But there will be things you can change. Wisdom helps you know the difference. Take time to pray about things you can change; then map out a direction for that change and the self-improvements you hope to make. You will find there is plenty of work ahead, work that will yield good results. As you change within, you will change your attitude. You will have peace, knowing you are always striving to improve.

Dear God, my Father, give me the wisdom and courage I need to make necessary changes to improve. Amen.

Winding Road

The steps of a man are established by the LORD, when he delights in his way.

—Psalm 37:23 ESV

As you ride along on a rambling country road, you will discover a different surprise at every turn as the scenery changes along the way. You may see a different field, a wild animal, a bubbling brook, or a rolling hill. Your journey in life is like traveling on a winding road. Each day is a bend in the road that is filled with laughter, pain, lessons, celebrations, and special moments. Occasionally, there may be obstacles on the road that will need to be overcome. But you can rest assured that when you delight in God, He will establish your steps. Furthermore, God has promised that when you face an obstacle, you "shall not be cast headlong, for the LORD upholds [your] hand" (Psalm 37:24 ESV).

The turns in your life do not have to be the end of the road. They are little twists that allow you to see a new phase of your life unfold. Find the reasons to be grateful for new opportunities or challenges that help you reach your dreams, and remember the One who travels with you. You may want to keep a journal as you journey along the way to reaching your hopes. Looking back at your journal entries will remind you that God has established each day on your winding road of life.

Dear God, thank You for traveling with me on my life's journey. I am full of hope, knowing that You are traveling with me. Amen.

Closing Gaps

The woman said, "The serpent deceived me, and I ate."

—Genesis 3:13

Have you heard the anecdote about a woman who was riding in a wagon with her husband and remarked about how the space between them had widened through the years? He looked at her and replied that he had not moved. Obviously then, she was the one who put the distance between them. In the book of Genesis, we learn that God made Adam and Eve for relationship with Him. But one day they moved away from God through disobedience. They choose to believe the serpent and ate forbidden fruit. At first Adam and Eve lived in a beautiful garden and walked and talked closely with God. But they focused elsewhere, away from God and their relationship with Him, creating a gap between them. God said only forgiveness could close the gap.

When you hope to regain lost closeness in a relationship, maybe it is time to check your position and attitude. Notice whether you have moved in new directions and left friends behind. If you hope to restore closeness, you may need to bridge a gap that you have made. It might be that jealousy, anger, or bitterness caused you to distance yourself. Forgiveness will bridge the gap. See if you need to make the first move to restore closeness.

Dear God, thank You for closing the gap that was created by Adam and Eve. Help me to move forward to close gaps in my lost relationships. Amen.

Lasting Change

"Truly, truly, I say to you, whoever hears my word and believes him who sent me has eternal life."

—John 5:24 ESV

Jonah LeRoy "Doane" Robinson worked as a farmer and then a lawyer before following an inner dream to become a historian. He dreamed of carvings in the Black Hills of South Dakota that would draw people to come and see the beauty of the state. He enlisted artist Gutzon Borglum and sought state and federal funding. Borglum carved four presidents in the rock, which became known as Mount Rushmore. Millions of people visit the national park each year to see the lasting beauty of the area and the majestic carvings.

Doane Robinson's legacy is lasting, but there are few things that last in this life. There are no guarantees that life will remain just as it is today. People change, and whether that change is lasting is up to you. Just as only you can make the decision about where you will spend eternity, only you can decide whether the change within you will last.

Lasting change begins as a hope. Are you ready to pursue your dream? Who can you enlist to help you make the changes that will last?

Dear God, thank You for eternity that will last throughout the ages. Bless me to make changes that will last so that I can pursue my dreams. Amen.

The Unchangeable God

Every good and perfect gift is from above, coming down from the Father of the heavenly lights, who does not change like shifting shadows.

—James 1:17

Mount Everest looms high in the distance for those who live in its shadow. It is there every day, peaking high into the sky. Erosion changes it so slowly that people do not notice. Yet it changes. The words of Psalm 46 emphasize who God is and what He can do. Though a mountain like Mount Everest may crumble and fall, God will never change. That means He will always love you and stand with you, protecting and guiding you as you reach for your dreams. With this reality in mind, the psalmist declared there is no reason to fear. God is your refuge, even though life gets demanding. Though earthquakes may tumble mountains, they cannot shake God. Trusting the God who never changes offers the greatest stability and hope in your life.

The next time you get discouraged, think about Psalm 46 and James 1:17. No matter what is going on around you, God in all His power, might, and greatness will never change. Though the mountains change, God never will. Therefore, it would be wise to continue trusting an unchanging God to help you reach your hopes.

Dear Father, it is such a comfort to know that You do not change. Thank You for the confidence this gives me to reach for hopes without fear. Amen.

Ever Changing

But grow in the grace and knowledge of our Lord and Savior Jesus Christ.

—2 Peter 3:18

If you could change anything in the world, what would it be? Most people say that they would take away crime and war. Others would eliminate poverty and homelessness. Still others would close all the orphanages and make sure that every child had a home. These are noble responses that may never occur as quickly as we would like. But anything is possible because change does take place. For example, think about technology. It changes all the time, and it changes fast. It seems that just as you figure out how to use a new type of phone, computer, or social media app, the model or interface is changed. Change is continually happening. Even nature transforms coastlines, riverbeds, and other landscapes.

On a personal level, you change too, including physical, mental, and character changes. These changes, if they are founded in virtues and God's grace, help you grow and mature. Think of what changes you want to bring about in yourself and your dreams. Start growing today with one little action. Ask God to help you make the changes needed to see your dreams come to fruition.

Dear God, bless me to change so that I can grow to be strong and mature and so that my dreams will help others who want to change too. In Jesus' name I pray, Amen.

JUNE

· • · · · • · · · • • · · ·

And what is so rare as a day in June?
Then, if ever, come perfect days.

——James Russell Lowell

Thinking Outside the Box

We have different gifts, according to the grace given to each of us.

—Romans 12:6

When you venture out to do something new or different, you enlarge your world and add adventure. When you think of a new activity to try, it restarts the process. The thought leads to action, and the action impacts your world and brings change. This new venture comes from thinking outside the box, which is a metaphor for thinking differently or creatively. This type of thinking causes one to venture out beyond the ordinary to accomplish greater works or service. Our God is a creative thinker. His creation testifies to that, and He made us to think creatively too. He has graciously given us different gifts to be used to fulfill our calling and reach our goals in life. Utilize the gifts, skills, and talents that God has given you by thinking outside the box.

As you think creatively, consider what you hope to accomplish and the possible changes your decision will spark. As you consider a desired outcome, also consider if you need to change your thinking to make it happen. You really can influence and change the world around you just by thinking outside the box.

Dear Father, thank You for the unique gifts You have given me that help me to think outside the box and change the world. Amen.

Pressing Forward

Forgetting what is behind and straining toward what is ahead, I press on toward the goal to win the prize for which God has called me heavenward in Christ Jesus.

—Philippians 3:13–14

To accomplish your hopes and goals, you must head in the right direction and move forward. You may move backward for a moment to seek forgiveness or restore a relationship, but then turn around and press forward again. Paul had an amazing goal. In verse 10 of Philippians 3, he said he wanted to know Jesus. This was a noble goal that many during his time thought they had already accomplished. But Paul realized he had not arrived at his destination. Therefore, he said with determination that he would "press on" (v. 12). There was no looking back. He had put his hand to the plow so that he could reach his goal and win the prize, which was heaven (Luke 9:62).

When you are pressing forward to your goal, you may come to a fork in the road, which can mean choosing a new direction. Both options seem to head forward in the same direction. But first look ahead to see which choice moves you closer to your goal. Keeping your eye on your hopes helps you to press forward to reach your goal.

Dear God, I am pressing forward to accomplish what You have placed in my heart. Keep me focused so I can reach my goal. Amen.

Exercising Your Heart

"'I will remove from you your heart of stone and give you a heart of flesh.'"

—Ezekiel 36:26

Have you checked on the condition of your heart lately? A doctor will run tests to make sure it is healthy and strong. For the average person, the heart usually beats from sixty to one hundred times per minute. What is more, the heart pumps an average of six quarts of blood throughout the body. But there is more to your heart than the numbers that tell you how fast it is beating or how much blood pumps through it. Your heart is kept in shape by the things you do to take care of it. The same is true for our emotional heart too. Forgiveness removes the hardness of your heart that comes from envy, anger, and hurt. God told the Israelites that He would remove their heart of stone and give them a heart of flesh so that they could love and obey Him.

When your heart is healthy, it allows you to hope in people and in dreams. If you overflow with kind words and joy, then your heart is soft, generous, and loving. Your heart benefits from exercises like praise, acts of kindness, and sharing hope. Keep your heart in great shape every day.

Dear God, thank You for my heart of flesh that allows me to love, give, and hope. Help me to keep it healthy and strong. Amen.

Live Fully

You make known to me the path of life; you will fill me with joy in
your presence, with eternal pleasures at your right hand.

—Psalm 16:11

When you hold on to pain and anger, you will stifle the joy that is around you. Letting go brings freedom to move forward and pursue new dreams. Choose to live fully and trust in your hopes. Henry David Thoreau, a man of many talents, is widely known as an author and writer. His diverse talents and interests could have been a stumbling block, but he chose one path of life and lived it to the fullest. Of course, he choose to be a writer. To be that writer that he dreamed of, Thoreau wrote excessively, maintaining dairies and journals. He also spent time reading and reflecting on nature.

Imagine the life you want. Envision the details, the people involved, and eventual success. If you believe in your hopes, you will move forward with confidence. Franklin D. Roosevelt said, "We have always held to the hope, the belief, the conviction, that there is a better life, a better world, beyond the horizon." As you live each day to the fullest, you should make the most of every moment and opportunity. Treasure the journey as you live the life you envisioned.

Dear God, my Father, my desire is to live the dream fully that You have placed within my heart. Empower me to move forward with intentionality to make my dreams come true. Amen.

Deep Roots

"Therefore everyone who hears these words of mine and puts them into practice is like a wise man who built his house on the rock."

——Matthew 7:24

A bamboo tree grows slowly the first five years. It spends the time growing deep roots that spread out in all directions. Then once it is firmly in place, it grows five feet a year. A firm foundation is important for the life and stability of any tree. If the roots are shallow, it will not withstand severe weather like storms or drought. Trees without deep roots will have withered leaves and produce little to no fruit and would eventually dry up and die. But a tree with deep roots has a firm foundation. It will not topple over in a storm, and during a drought, its roots reach deep enough into the earth to find water. Having deep roots is the same as building on rock. Jesus said if you build your house, which is your spiritual life, on a rock, which is Jesus, the storms of life will not topple you over. You will have a firm foundation on which to build your hope.

Take action to build deep roots in Jesus Christ. When you do, you will spark new growth. Once your root system has this firm foundation, your hopes will shoot forth and produce fruit.

Dear God, strengthen me to build deep roots so that my hopes will grow and produce fruit. Amen.

Hope for Tomorrow

Weeping may endure for a night, but joy cometh in the morning.
—Psalm 30:5 KJV

Today may be filled with pain that seems unbearable as tears flow freely. You may even want to scream because of the intensity of your hurt. Loss and grief are difficult and may leave invisible scars that continue to plague you for a long time. It is difficult when you lose part of your heart because a loved one has passed on or you face devastating news that shakes you to the core. The psalmist understood such emotional trauma. He knew that devastation was imminent because he had received a prophetic word from God. But once the event had passed, his weeping would be replaced with joy. He had hope for tomorrow because tomorrow promised to be free from pain.

Your pain may overwhelm your faith for a time. But people who love you will surround you and bring comfort. Take courage—your tears will not last forever. The God of all comfort is with you to comfort you. Your loved ones still need your presence with them. They need you to be healthy and whole. So look forward to tomorrow and wait with hope. Your loved ones will see your beautiful smile again. Tell God how you feel, and put your hopes in tomorrow, when your pain will be replaced with joy.

Dear Father, thank You for the joy and hope of tomorrow. Amen.

Hope of Overcomers

Blessed is the one who perseveres under trial because, having stood the test, that person will receive the crown of life that the Lord has promised to those who love him.

—James 1:12

It took a blind and deaf woman named Helen Keller to show the world that it is worth the struggle to overcome darkness and loneliness. She overcame obstacles and learned to see and communicate effectively. The world is filled with those who have overcome struggles. Watching the news on television reminds us that suffering continues everywhere, but so does hope. One such story was of a man, Louis Jordan, who was lost at sea for sixty-six days. He left the coast of South Carolina two months earlier but did not return. His mother filed a missing person's report, but the search was suspended after ten days. Though his sailboat had capsized, Jordan did not give up. Eventually, he was spotted and rescued by a container ship. He said he lived off of fish he had caught, rationed his water, and prayed. He did not give up hope.

Jesus wanted us to know that though the world is filled with trouble, it is possible to overcome hardships because He did. Overcomers share the experience of moving beyond hardship to grasp what is good and worthy. You, too, are an overcomer when you have come through difficult experiences or have risen higher than your problems and pain.

Dear Lord, when troubles come, I have hope that I can overcome because of Jesus. Amen. In Your name I pray, Amen.

Words That Polish

"Do not judge, or you too will be judged."

—Matthew 7:1

When you ask a mentor to help you or get a professional critique, you hope for constructive criticism. You hope the reviewer will be kind, but truthful, and will guide you to improve but not judge you. During biblical times, Pharisees were religious leaders who thought they were more righteous than others. They felt that the way to show their righteousness was to be judgmental. Jesus condemned this practice as wrongdoing. He taught that we should love one another. This means not judging when people do something of which we do not approve. Our responsibility is to offer sound correction or criticism in love. When critiquing another's work, remember to speak with gentleness and love. This will put the focus on building someone up rather than tearing him or her down.

Harsh or judgmental criticism hurts as it rips apart your creation, the product of your mind, heart, and hands. However, a constructive critique shows you how to edit your design and polish it to make it shine. Although constructive criticism may be difficult to hear, receive it as necessary; then step back and note the comments with new eyes. Accept beneficial remarks and ideas as you refine your hopes.

Dear God, thank You for friends and family who help me through constructive criticism. May I offer the same service in love to others. Amen.

Cherished Bliss

"Oh, that you would bless me and enlarge my territory!"
—1 Chronicles 4:10

Bliss is deeper and longer lasting than laughter or the simple pleasure of a favorite activity. Bliss is extreme happiness. The real secret of blissfulness, even in difficult times, is faith in eternal life with God. Nothing on earth could be cherished more. In the book of 1 Chronicles, Jabez believed in God and prayed that God would bless him. He wanted God to bless him not in a small way but excessively. He also requested of God, "Enlarge my territory! Let your hand be with me, and keep me from harm so that I will be free from pain" (4:10). There is not anything else written about Jabez in the Bible. The Bible only mentions that when he prayed this prayer, God "granted his request" (ibid.).

There is nothing wrong with asking God to bless you. The word *blessed* actually means bliss or happiness, and God wants you to be happy. When you suffer and feel great pain, you need a little blissfulness, a little blessing from God, and a little more faith. Just reflect on God, and ask for His blessings and blissfulness. Some blessings may not come in the form of what you want but what you need. Cherish God's blessings, and accept His grace and comfort.

Dear Father, thank You for your willingness to bless me and for the blissfulness that Your blessings bring to me. Amen.

The Art of Gratitude

Give thanks in all circumstances; for this is God's will for you in Christ Jesus.

—1 Thessalonians 5:18

Parents begin teaching their kids manners at an early age. They are taught to respect adults and to be polite. Politeness includes thanking others when it is appropriate. There is power in being thankful and appreciating what you have. You can turn your problems into joys when you view them as opportunities to change your circumstances. Paul taught that in connection with everything we go through in life, we are to face it with gratitude. Thankfulness is the first step to opening up your mind and heart to replace hurt with hope. Thankfulness means there is a recognition that God is in control, and no matter the outcome, your troubles will soon be gone and all will be well.

Gratitude is the art of using your faith to seek and discover the blessings within problems and in routine, ordinary tasks in life. Thankfulness evolves from a heart of hope and joy as you dwell on God's mercy and His work on your behalf. Take time each day to think of a way that God has blessed you. Spend time in prayer, acknowledging God's goodness and thanking Him for His many blessings.

Dear God, with joy I give thanks to You for all You do in my life. Amen.

Troubles

But understand this, that in the last days there will come times of difficulty.

—2 Timothy 3:1 ESV

Trouble is all around us and comes to every home and heart. The apostle Paul confirmed that trouble will come, especially during the days following Christ's resurrection. No one is exempt from pain, but you can choose how to react. In verse 7 of Psalm 112, the psalmist said, "They will have no fear of bad news; their hearts are steadfast, trusting in the LORD." Fear is dangerous to your hope and means your trust in God has failed. Fear comes in all shapes and sizes: the fear of death, of getting an incurable disease, of losing a loved one, and of the future. Fear is a horrible monster. As a believer in Christ, you are to trust in the Lord. But if fear overwhelms you, just turn to God and ask for that fear to be removed.

God promises to walk with you through your pain, sorrow, and trouble. He has overcome the world and will help you be strong and courageous. He will give you a sense of peace when something goes wrong and discourages your hope for the future. As you cling to hope, look to God with every struggle. Trust Him to help you overcome all doubts and problems as you hope for better times.

Dear God, when trouble comes and I am afraid, please remove the fear and help me to keep my eyes on You. Amen.

Give God Glory

"Rabbi, who sinned, this man or his parents, that he was born blind?"

—John 9:1

Jesus' disciples wanted to know who was at fault for a man's blindness whom they had met along the way. Jesus did not blame anyone but said his blindness would reveal the power of God. Jesus wanted to use the man's blindness to teach about faith so that God would be glorified. A physically blind person will not see a beautiful landscape, and a spiritually blind person will not see the blessings of life. A person who is deaf will not hear the sweet sound of birds chirping, and a person who is spiritually deaf will not experience hearing God's voice. Although no one is to be blamed for one's physical deafness and blindness, all of these instances can be overcome by the power and goodness of God.

Jesus healed the blind man whom He and the disciples encountered so that the people who followed Him would give glory to God. Perhaps you miss out on the wonders of life because you are spiritually blind or deaf. You may not be able to receive everything you want or hope for, but God is ready to heal you today. Just reach out and asked for healing. Then give God glory for the hope of many pleasures He will bring your way in the days to come.

Dear God, thank You for Your miraculous works of healing. Amen.

Tested

Because you know that the testing of your faith produces perseverance.
—James 1:3

As a student you may have cringed at taking a test or worried about studying the right materials. Tests measure what you remember. Tests also reveal what you do not know and where you could improve. The apostle James said testing, particularly the testing of your faith, has great rewards. James understood that tests would develop your spiritual qualities so that God could use you. When you are tested, you will soon learn to stand strong and face troubles without grumbling and unbelief. Those who prevail in a spiritual test acquire perseverance, which then leads to obtaining wisdom.

Tests in life come daily. You will face problems and will struggle with limitations. They reveal strengths and weaknesses as you dig deep to find solutions. Let tests be assessments that help you grow. In the process of improving or enhancing your strengths, you develop useful skills and face the future with more hope and confidence. When you have been tested and have mastered it, look around for those who would benefit from your guidance. Helping others through their struggles will grow hope in them and yourself.

Dear God, thank You for the tests in life that help me to grow in my faith. Help me to face each test with confidence that You are with me. In Jesus' name I pray, Amen.

Help the Hurting

And do not forget to do good and to share with others, for with such sacrifices God is pleased.

—Hebrews 13:16

Actress Audrey Hepburn, who was the star of the legendary movie *Breakfast at Tiffany's*, was also a humanitarian. Although she won many acting awards and made pacesetting fashion statements, she devoted the last years of her life to children who had little hope. As an ambassador for the United Nations International Children's Emergency Fund (UNICEF), Audrey Hepburn traveled the world to bring awareness to children's needs. She was often videotaped holding and feeding starving children. Her legacy continues through the Audrey Hepburn Children's fund, which was set up by her family following her death.

Every smile, word of kindness, and action of assistance brings hope to hurting hearts. Silent cries for help may be seen in the posture and eyes of people around you. Look into the eyes of people, and pause to discover how you can give someone hope. There is never too much kindness or too many smiles in the world. In a few extra minutes a day, you can offer hope that someone longs to receive.

Dear Lord, use my hands to help someone else in need today. Use me to bring hope to others as part of the work I do in fulfilling my dream. In Jesus' name I pray, Amen.

Love Relieves Pain

If I give all I possess to the poor and give over my body to hardship that I may boast, but do not have love, I gain nothing.

—1 Corinthians 13:3

The apostle Paul had a problem he had to address. He had received a letter from members of the church of Corinth about difficult issues. These issues divided the church and caused some to sin. Paul confronted them about their sin and encouraged them to live a loving life if they wanted to make a difference for God. Some of them were arrogant and proud as they helped others, thinking that giving was all that was needed. But Paul taught that without love, their giving did not profit anything.

When you are hurt, you may turn to a loved one, a friend, or a co-worker who listens with compassion. Or you may knock on the door of a friend and be invited in for a cup of tea, or you may call a friend and plan to meet up for a snack and a chat. Compassionate friends offer the hope of being accepted and affirmed. You should extend the same kind of love to others. The pain of loneliness and rejection is healed when someone offers love. When people care enough to drop other activities and spend time with you, they show their care. Caring brings comfort that restores your spirits.

Dear God, thank You for the love that is shared between others and me in a time of need. Amen.

Compassion

When Jesus heard what had happened, he withdrew by boat privately to a solitary place.

—Matthew 14:13

Most people believe that the only suffering Jesus experienced was His passion during the week of His crucifixion and His death on the cross. But according to Scripture, Jesus suffered and grieved several times in His life. On one occasion Jesus was grieved at the loss of His cousin, John the Baptist. Herod had thrown John in prison. Then Herod's wife tricked Herod into beheading John. She was angry at John for condemning them for living together because she was the wife of Herod's half-brother. When Jesus heard about this, He withdrew to a solitary place. Disasters, loss, and crises help us understand the pain and misery other people experience. Once you have suffered, you can provide comfort to someone else. Through the death of John, Jesus understood what it meant to suffer the loss of a loved one. He understands your grief.

Support groups arise because compassionate people want to offer hope to those who may face similar situations. When you experience a new type of suffering, it is comforting to turn to someone who understands and has faced something similar. Supporters reach out with empathy and share your sorrow to help you renew your hope.

Dear God, thank You that others understand my losses because of their experiences. Thank You for the compassion we share. Amen.

Hurting Conscience

If we confess our sins, he is faithful and just and will forgive us our sins and purify us from all unrighteousness.

—1 John 1:9

Have you ever felt guilty about a sarcastic comment you made or because you left some work unfinished for someone else to do? Your conscience speaks because you know you caused pain in a moment of anger, laziness, or indifference. You dashed the hopes of someone who trusted you. Although this is an extreme case, consider how Judas Iscariot must have felt after he betrayed our Lord Jesus Christ. Judas was a trusted disciple, but he allowed greed to get the best of him. So for thirty pieces of silver, he betrayed Jesus with a kiss. The guilt and remorse were too much for Judas, who ended his life in suicide.

The book of 1 John reveals that no one is without sin, and we must confess our sin to God who will forgive and cleanse us (1:8–9). Choosing to live without regrets means to consider actions and words carefully. One moment of reflection before speaking or acting helps keep your conscience clear. When you choose wisely, you will fulfill your hopes of living in peace. But when you fall short or sin, just confess it to God. He will forgive you and clear your conscience.

Dear God, when I fall short by sinning, give me strength to confess to You so that I will not carry the heavy weight of guilt. Amen.

Acidic Anger

Whoever is patient has great understanding, but one who is quick-tempered displays folly.

—Proverbs 14:29

There are several people in history who have been described as angry, most notably, Henry VIII. Former king of England, Henry VIII received this reputation because he infamously ordered the execution of two of his wives. Anger is an extreme emotional reaction. It often means that a standard or boundary to which you hold strongly has been violated. Anger is a healthy human emotion, but it can get out of control and be destructive to you. Anger hurts you because it adds to your stress, raises your heart rate and blood pressure, and causes you to tense your muscles. Anger can be said to be an acid that corrupts relationships and causes bitterness.

In chemistry adding a base solution can balance an acid. So, too, in life adding something sweet can bring a balance to anger. Proverbs 15:1 affirms this idea: "A gentle answer turns away wrath." Laughter and positive thoughts help you let go of anger and diffuse negative emotions. Forgiveness removes the anger. When you are hurt and filled with anger, seek healing from God that will ease the pain and bring peace. You will enjoy balance and feel happier.

Dear God, help me to remain calm when I am hurt. Instead of displaying anger, let me show love and inspire hope. Amen.

One Simple Act

For he has rescued us from the dominion of darkness and brought us into the kingdom of the Son he loves.

—Colossians 1:13

Sometimes the smallest things can have the greatest impact. For example, an e-mail to an old acquaintance read, "Forty years ago, you offered thanks to our Lord as comfortably as placing a napkin in his lap. You and our Lord were close." The sender explained that the simple prayer brought the writer back to the Lord, and he started praying with his wife. One simple act can change someone's world. Adversely, one simple act, if not done, can have devastating effects. For instance, the mother of Henry VIII and his third wife, Jane Seymour, both died of the same disease—childbed fever. This disease is a bacterial infection caused when doctors do not wash their hands thoroughly. If the doctors had performed this one simple act, King Henry VIII's wife Jane, whom he loved more than any of the other women he had married, would have lived through giving birth.

Many are happy that God did not renege on the one simple act that saved the world—the resurrection of Christ. You may never know how your prayer or words can change a life or impact others. You matter to God and can trust that He will use your actions, even the simplest ones, to touch lives and spread hope.

Dear God, thank You that Your one simple act saved humanity, including me. Amen.

Lovable You!

Let love and faithfulness never leave you; bind them around your neck, write them on the tablet of your heart.

—Proverbs 3:3

Two commandments sum up the life of a Christian. The first commandment is that we should love God, and the second one is that we should love our neighbors (Matthew 22:37–39). The most important characteristic of a believer is not obedience or service but love. We are to give of ourselves—passionately and deeply. This means showing mercy, giving to meet needs, praying for others, and offering sound advice when others are confused. We are also to express sympathy with those who are in trouble and forgive faults and offenses toward us. These actions are just a small fraction of the love we are to express. God has wired people for love. Love makes your life flow with laughter, excitement, and peace.

When you give of yourself, you trigger a reaction to which people will respond. Nurture friends with kindness, loving actions, and sharing interests. With each drop of love you pour out, your circle of friends will grow and respond with love toward you. You already have talents, lovable qualities, and a heart that cares. As you allow love to flow freely, you will discover other people with the same hope. You will be filling your river of life with new friends, and love will overflow.

Dear God, I choose to love others as You have commanded. Amen.

Inner Glow

*Let your adorning be the hidden person of the heart with the
imperishable beauty of a gentle and quiet spirit, which in God's
sight is very precious.*

—1 Peter 3:4 ESV

Too often when we look in mirrors, we see the lines that are
drawn on our faces and wonder how we can erase those
wrinkles. We search for the perfect skin care product and diet
that we hope will make us look younger. But the world's view
of beauty merely focuses on temporary, outward looks. Real
beauty shines forth from inside. Inner beauty of character
remains and grows more beautiful as you continue to love
others and develop virtues. In the book of 1 Peter, women are
encouraged to work on their inner beauty rather being concerned with their outer appearance. This does not mean that
you should not care for your hair, skin, and clothes, or that
you should not wear makeup. It means that your spirit needs
nurture and care so that you will be pleasing to God.

God looks deep into your heart beyond outward blemishes to discover your inner sparkle. Those who love you see
the hope that is within you through the beauty of your smile,
and they will hope to have that same inner glow.

Dear Lord, I pray that what You see within me is pleasing to You, and I pray
that others will be inspired to hope not only by my actions but by what is in
my heart. Amen.

Enough?

Yet to all who did receive him, to those who believed in his name, he gave the right to become children of God.

—John 1:12

People long to be accepted and have their efforts approved. You may have thought, *Am I good enough?* You may work diligently to be good or appreciated and feel dejected when someone rejects you or overlooks your effort. In that same light, have you ever wondered if you are good enough for heaven? Do you listen to people who say the good they do is enough to get them into heaven? Or do you listen to God, who beckons you to believe in Him? Many Christians wonder about their salvation. They question whether they are going to heaven. If you struggle with this uncertainty, then ask yourself these questions: Do you believe in Jesus Christ? Have you trusted in Him as your Lord and Savior? Are you basing your salvation on what God has done for you rather than what you do? If you responded yes to these questions, then your salvation is sure, and you are a child of God.

There is only one way to heaven. Wearing a cross is not enough. It takes faith in Christ and believing He died for you. God's love is enough. Be thankful that faith in Jesus is enough for eternal hope to be realized.

Dear God, thank You that you provided a way to heaven through Your Son, Jesus Christ. Amen.

Amazing Kindness

Therefore, as God's chosen people, holy and dearly loved, clothe yourselves with compassion, kindness, humility, gentleness and patience.
—Colossians 3:12

In the story *The Wonderful Wizard of Oz*, Dorothy and her dog, Toto, had been whisked away to the Land of Oz in her house by a tornado. In this mysterious land of munchkins and witches, Dorothy met and befriended a scarecrow, a tin man, and a lion. Each of them, including Dorothy, had overwhelming needs. The scarecrow needed a heart; the tin man needed a brain; the lion needed courage; and Dorothy need to find her way home. The answer lay in the Wizard of Oz in Emerald City. But once they arrived, instead of finding a wizard, they discovered only a man with no magic powers to help them. It was Dorothy's character that helped to fulfill their needs. Through her kindness to the scarecrow, the tin man, and the lion, each character displayed the characteristic they formerly lacked. It was her amazing kindness that strengthened them to do amazing feats.

Simply being a friend works wonders. Therefore, you should put on kindness every day so that you can make an amazing difference to people around you. Your example really does inspire hope. As you hope for answered prayers, continue to be kind and loving.

Dear God, today I put on kindness so that the people I meet will be strengthened in their hope. Amen.

Undeserving

For by grace you have been saved through faith. And this is not your own doing; it is the gift of God.

—Ephesians 2:8 ESV

Take a walk, and look at the beauty around you. Your life is filled with plants and trees, beautiful sunsets, and flowing streams of water. They are gifts from God you never earned and blessings from above that fill your life with awe. By grace God also has given you salvation. Grace means unmerited favor, something that you can do nothing to earn. It also means you do not deserve it. Every person was born into a world of sin, separated from Him because of sin. But God in His great love extended this undeserving gift to you so that you could spend eternity with Him.

You did nothing to deserve the beautiful world God created. There is also no way to deserve God's grace. You did nothing to save your own soul and set yourself on the path to your hopes and eternal life. Therefore, you should appreciate the beauty around you and be thankful for God's gift of grace. Let these truths fuel your hope and your sense of wonder.

Dear God, thank You for the blessings that I do not deserve such as the stars, the sunset, and Your grace. Help me to appreciate the beauty of my surroundings each day. Amen.

The Ripple Effect

Jesus replied, "Very truly I tell you, everyone who sins is a slave to sin."
—John 8:34

A pebble tossed in the water creates a series of circles. Each circle surrounding the splash where the pebble fell becomes larger and pushes out to create another ripple. This is referred to as a ripple effect. The dictionary defines a ripple effect as a situation in which one event causes a series of other events to happen. Many times after the first event has occurred, subsequent events are unintentional. In the case of sin, Jesus called this slavery. After committing the first sin, other sins follow without much effort and with very little resistance to control them. The way to overcome being a slave to sin or creating a ripple effect of sin is to trust Jesus to set you free.

Little lies lead to covering up something and to bigger lies that create a ripple effect. When you think, *it won't hurt anyone*, you are hoping you will get away with something you know is wrong. You care more about getting your way than being honest and truthful with someone in your life. Hope is never strengthened through these actions. If you stumble in this way, allow Jesus to be the truth you need to move forward. And always be careful to make choices that avoid sin.

Dear God, I choose to trust Jesus so that I will not become a slave to sin. Thank You for the strength to overcome when I do fall short. Amen.

Enough Time

"Mary has chosen what is better, and it will not be taken away from her."
——Luke 10:42

I do not have time for that, we say to ourselves. Busyness fills our schedules and can keep us from following our dreams. The items on your calendar reflect your choices. With each choice you make, you control the hours before they arrive. The question is does God like our busyness and the choices on our schedules? The story of Mary and Martha in the book of Luke helps us to reflect on our schedules. These sisters who were friends of Jesus had welcomed Him into their home. Martha busied herself with the chores of the house, including preparing a meal, while Mary relaxed at the feet of Jesus. Many times we are like Martha with many tasks and activities vying for our time at our jobs, churches, and with our families. The to-do list can be unending and fill our schedules so that time for God seems impossible to find.

If you want time for something, you need to evaluate how you are spending your weeks and hours. Decide if you need to let something go. It may not be the time for a new hope. You can choose to dedicate days or hours to your dream when the right time comes. But for now make God your priority, and then allocate time for everything else in your life, including your hopes.

Dear God, today I choose to sit at Your feet. Amen.

Investing in Others

But encourage one another daily, as long as it is called "Today."
—Hebrews 3:13

In the play *My Fair Lady*, Eliza Doolittle, a dirty flower girl who cannot speak proper English, finds herself at the mercy of phonetics professor Henry Higgins. Mr. Higgins makes a bet with his friend that he can change her into a proper lady within six months. Eliza's opening song reveals the dream of a home somewhere with lots of chocolates to eat. She hoped for a better situation in life. When Mr. Higgins fulfilled that dream, she found that what she really wanted was respect, appreciation, and love. She realized that the material things and her proper manners did not bring happiness.

You may have a wish list of things you think will make you happy. You hope a desired item will make your life easier and happier. Like Eliza discovered, it is not things but good relationships that bring fulfillment. The idea is that we are responsible for one another, to help one another through struggles and to grow spiritually. There is no such thing as being a private child of God. With this attitude you will not experience a fulfilled life, and your hope will not last. You need others as much as they need you. Choose to invest in people. Sharing love and hopes brings harmony and peace, as well as joy.

Dear Father, thank You for investing in me with hope and love. I choose to invest in others as well. Amen.

Wanted: The Right Person

Do not be yoked together with unbelievers. For what do
righteousness and wickedness have in common? Or what fellowship
can light have with darkness?

—2 Corinthians 6:14

Every romance book ends with two people finding each other and believing they have met the one person who will complete his or her life. You may sigh and think, *I want a happily-ever-after ending.* You may be married or not, but you can choose to be happy with the people in your life. You already have the One who really can meet all your needs. God promises to provide for your needs, and that includes the right people. The apostle Paul encouraged his readers not be in romantic relationships with people who do not hold similar beliefs. This does not mean you should not have friendships with people with whom you have nothing in common. We are responsible to be an example of God's goodness and grace to those who do not believe. However, our close relationships should be with those who can strengthen our commitment in Christ and in our journey toward hope.

Be thankful for each person in your life, and find reasons to celebrate your relationships. Spend time with friends and with God.

Dear Lord, bless me with the right people in my life, and help me grow in my relationship with You. Bless me to be a light to those friends who do not know You. Amen.

Do Not Limit God

"Go from your country, your people and your father's household to the land I will show you."

—Genesis 12:1

It takes faith, courage, and imagination to try something new. If you limit yourself by thinking you do not have the resources or talent, then you limit your hopes and imprison your dreams. Abraham's name was Abram until God changed it. One day God told Abram to leave his home and everything with which he was familiar, including his family. Only his wife, Sarai, and his nephew Lot traveled with Abram. God did not tell Abram where he was going. He simply said to leave. It took a lot of faith and trust in God to pack up and leave his home, but that is what Abram did. God also told Abram that He would bless him and make him into a great nation. God placed a promise and hope within Abram's heart. Abram did not place limits on God. There was no doubt that God would be with Abram to guide him and help him fulfill his dream.

Faith in God opens possibilities when you believe He can show you connections, provide for your needs, and help you reach your goals. If God has called you to do something, trust that He will provide everything you need. Ask God to reveal and send the opportunities. Open your mind to new possibilities without placing limits on God.

Dear God, through faith I choose not to limit Your help and care. Amen.

God Hears

Evening, morning and noon I cry out in distress, and he hears my voice.

—Psalm 55:17

Chronic pain is a harsh reality for many people, possibly for you too. We live in an imperfect world, and nothing we do prevents all suffering and pain. You can take action to ease your pain or the pain of someone else, and you can hope and pray for a cure. You also can look to the One who can help. King David was suffering great distress because a friend had betrayed him. This broke his heart, and though he was not suffering physically, he suffered great emotional trauma. In spite of this, he took comfort in the knowledge that God heard his cry for help.

Your suffering causes you to empathize with others and creates an awareness of how others feel when they are in pain. When you live bravely and cope well with your pain, you can be an example to others that pain does not have to control them. The greater hope is that God hears when you cry out to Him. Thank God that there will be no pain or tears in heaven, but when you suffer while here on earth, you can be confident that God hears your cry.

Dear Lord, thank You that You hear me when I call to You in distress. Help me to bear my sorrow one moment at a time. Amen.

JULY

. . . .

This, then, is the state of the union: free and restless, growing and full of hope. So it was in the beginning. So it shall always be, while God is willing, and we are strong enough to keep the faith.

—Lyndon B. Johnson

Who Is It All About?

"Indeed, the very hairs of your head are all numbered. Don't be afraid; you are worth more than many sparrows."

—Luke 12:7

Ask yourself how much time do you spend thinking or worrying about other people, especially about what someone else has said or thought about you. It may be helpful to know that most of the time others are not thinking about you at all. Most people have personal worries and life concerns to think about rather than about you.

But with God it is all about you. He would have sent His Son to die for you even if you were the only person on earth. The human head averages one hundred thousand hairs, and each day it loses fifty to one hundred of those hairs. God cares enough to count the hairs on your head. Not one of them will fall to the ground without His knowledge. He also listens to your every thought, sees each tear, and cares about what is hidden in your heart. Therefore, do not be afraid or dismayed about what others may or may not think of you. God values you more than the sparrows, and they are lovingly cared for by His hand. God wants to fill you with hope because He cherishes you.

Dear God, my Father, thank You for lovingly caring for me. You know about me, even the number of hairs on my head. This brings me great comfort and gives me peace. Amen.

Waves of Time

"What no eye has seen, nor ear heard, nor the heart of man imagined, what God has prepared for those who love him."

—1 Corinthians 2:9 ESV

You cannot guess what the next wave will be like as you stand at the shallow edge of the ocean. You can hope for a great wave so that you can surf or hope for a small one just to splash at your feet. You must wait to see what comes and prepare for the next wave train. You cannot control the waves, but you can watch them roll in, confident that you will be ready for any degree of force that the wave brings. These waves are like different events throughout a lifetime that are rolling toward you.

Although you do not know your future, you can always pray for God to prepare you for whatever the day may bring. At the beginning of the day, pray and hope for the best. Rejoice at the splashes of blessings, and try to stay afloat during the tidal waves of life. Trust God will give you His best. And be sure that He will equip to survive the thrashing waves that will occasionally come your way. Remain hopeful as you encounter wave after wave, remembering the waves you have conquered in your past.

Dear Lord, I pray for waves that delight me and blessings that make me stronger. Keep me from toppling over at troubles as I hope in You. Amen.

Anchor of Hope

Cast your cares on the LORD and he will sustain you; he will never let the righteous be shaken.

—Psalm 55:22

A small anchor holds a ship in place against raging waves and winds. An anchor weighing less than fifty pounds is enough to keep a two-ton ship secure and grounded in place, linked to the land below the surface.

Like an anchor, it only takes a little hope to hold on to your dreams. The anchor is attached to the boat with a heavy chain, and the sailor slowly lets it down. The unseen anchor remains underwater to stabilize the ship against storms and the current. Hope in God is like an anchor. It is an anchor to your soul. Do as Alfred Tennyson said: "Cast all your cares on God; that anchor holds." Cast your worries and concerns about life on Him. They can become too heavy at times for you to carry. This is God's desire for you. He does not want you weighed down. He wants you free to dream and do what He has called you to do. Commit your life and work to Him. Trust Him to sustain you, and be satisfied with His blessings. Let His invisible gift of hope hold you through storms of doubt and waves of troubles that toss and pound against you.

Dear God, today I cast my cares on You so that I will be protected from the storms that are in my life. Amen.

Secure Knots

We have this hope as an anchor for the soul, firm and secure.

—Hebrews 6:19

Sailors tie strong knots with twists and loops to prevent slipping. To secure a boat to a dock, the knot must be dependable. Campers, climbers, and fishermen also use knots for safety and security. In tying a boat to a dock, a cleat hitch is simple to tie and holds fast. A poorly tied knot may slip and cause the loss of the anchor or boat.

You are like a ship on the sea of life. Sometimes life, like the sea, will toss you up and down. When times seem turbulent, you need an anchor to hold you steady. That anchor must be tied to a rope with a firm knot, which is your hope. Your hope will slip away if it is not well fastened. Doubts cause a knot that is tied to the anchor to be loose and slip. A rope that is not cared for will also weaken a knot. Always take care of your rope through prayer, Bible reading, and developing strong relationships with other believers. These priorities will help your knot remain secure. Confidence in your hope, like confidence in a good knot, is essential during turbulence.

Dear God, help me to hold fast to You with hope so that I will not slip and be lost. Amen.

Fortified in God

The LORD is a stronghold for the oppressed, a stronghold in times of trouble.

—Psalm 9:9 ESV

Early armies used forts and towers as strongholds against enemy approach. Modern techniques use underground bunkers, radar, missile detection systems, and satellites to provide protection. During the days of the American West, forts were not built to protect soldiers and pioneer families from hostile Indians, as they are depicted in movies. The forts were made to promote peace among the tribes and between Native Americans and immigrants. However, when settlers encroached on the land looking for gold and silver, the Indians retaliated to protect their land. Then the fort served as a stronghold to protect the settlers from harm.

In times of trouble, your prayers become towers of strength that cannot be toppled. Your friends become your stronghold too. Your friends become a supportive safety net that holds you, comforts you, and prays for you, as your hopes begin to fall apart. Fortify your life with friends. Strengthen your stronghold, which is the Lord. You can go to Him and depend on His power and promises to protect you.

Dear God, my Father, thank You for being my stronghold during times when I need protection. Help me to grow stronger with each attack on my hope. In Jesus' name I pray, Amen.

Safe Harbor

The LORD is my shepherd, I lack nothing.

—Psalm 23:1

It is wonderful to arrive home at the end of a weary day and know you can rest, confident of your safe harbor. You can sit and be grateful that you survived the trials of your day. David must have felt the same way when he penned Psalm 23. David worked as a shepherd of sheep. Although he was not a sailor who worked at sea, he faced similar challenges as the seaman, like storms and winds, and faced some challenges that were not the same, like lost sheep and ferocious wolves. David understood sheep and realized it was his responsibility to protect them at all cost, fighting against lions and bears to keep the sheep safe. As a matter of fact, he even saw himself as a sheep who was kept safe by God, his Shepherd. God made sure David had everything he needed. When David needed rest, God provided rest. When David faced distress, God led him to safety.

During the day you may struggle and fight against the winds of change and storms of discouragement, but you must avoid drifting off course with distractions and worry. Remember that God is your Shepherd to keep you safe. As you wrestle with problems, keep your heart focused on Him. He will guide you to your destination.

Dear God, thank You for Your care as my Shepherd. Thank You for keeping me safe. Amen.

Remain Steadfast

Let us not become weary in doing good, for at the proper time we
will reap a harvest if we do not give up.

—Galatians 6:9

A mushroom anchor looks like an upside-down mush-room. It is used to secure lightweight boats like canoes and rowboats. It holds well in soft bottoms of mud, sand, or silt where there is little turbulence.

In little problems of life, you may only need a mushroom anchor, not a huge anchor with wide arms. Take a lesson from tightrope walkers, who must be steadfast as they walk across a wire that is extended between two points. By placing one foot in front of another, they advance to their destination. Sometimes objects such as a pole, an umbrella, or a fan are used to help maintain balance. Tightrope walkers must also remain focused and keep from being distracted so they will not fall. Deal with little issues as if you were walking a tight-rope. Remain steadfast, and hold on to your hope without letting distractions or less significant problems disrupt your peace. A quick, calm response will help resolve small mat-ters without arguing or causing havoc. Paul advised that you be steadfast in maintaining goodness because of its many rewards. So let steadfastness and goodness form the mush-room anchor for your lesser difficulties.

Dear God, bless me to remain steadfast when dealing with little problems. May I also maintain goodness so that I can be a blessing to others. Amen.

Mooring Lines to Friends

"Remain in me, as I also remain in you."

—John 15:4

Mooring lines keep boats connected to the dock. Multiple lines may be used in each boat in case one line snaps. The mooring lines connect the ship to the world as they come into port. Sailors have to toss the line to shore so that someone on shore can pull it and tie it in place. Jesus wants us to be moored or connected to Him. As He spoke to the disciples a few days before He was crucified, He revealed that one way they could be connected to Him was to be connected to each other. Jesus knew that His time with them on earth would soon be over. He had taught them all they needed. They now needed to depend on each other.

Being moored to friends and other people is important to your success. It helps if you form relationships with people who are mature in their faith. When you spend time with other believers, you stay connected with God. Mooring connects your dream to reality and to people who can help you. Cooperation with friends and others builds trust and establishes unity. These relationships help you remain linked to God and help you strive to accomplish your dreams.

Dear God, I pray to be connected to friends who can help me stay connected to You and support me as I live the life You intend for me. Amen.

Plow Anchors

But test everything; hold fast what is good.

—1 Thessalonians 5:21 ESV

The sturdy plow anchor resembles the front of a plow. It swivels and uses a scooping motion to hold hard in mud, weeds, and rocky bottoms. It holds fast, yet it pivots as wind turns the boat above the surface. This gives passengers a gentler time while anchored. God understands that life gets rocky, making it difficult to hold on to your faith, and situations change as quickly as the wind. In these moments reading the Bible may be a struggle, and prayer time becomes a drudgery. Sometimes you may even wonder if God is still there. But hold on to your faith. Even when you do not feel God's presence, He is always there. Strong faith can be developed in spite of the way you feel. Strong faith results in a positive outlook with positive outcomes.

With strong faith you can hold fast against hardness in people, weeds of ill will, or rocky obstacles. The plow anchor does not dig in with its sharp point, but it gently scoops like a shovel gliding through rocky soil. Strong faith considers the needs of others while holding to the truths of God. Coping with problems gently like the plow anchor will help you hold steady to your hopes.

Dear God, help me to develop strong faith that keeps me anchored to my hope and gives me a compassionate heart so I can be a blessing to others. Amen.

Anchor of Truth

"Then you will know the truth, and the truth will set you free."

—John 8:32

The fluke anchor penetrates into sand, mud, and gravel with two hooks. It buries itself into the bottom to form a powerful hold. Sailors trust the fluke, which is designed like a whale's tail, and know it is reliable through harsh storms.

If your hope is built on the anchor of truth, you can depend on it to bring stability through struggles. Jesus called Himself Truth that sets you free. He was not equating Himself to an academic standard. His truth was not about general knowledge but about knowing the Father and allowing His own life to be the standard for your life. Jesus frees you from living a lesser life of uncertainty. His truth is the righteousness by which you can be strong when facing storms. It starts with knowing you are honest and dependable so others can trust your ideas and dreams. If you are in the midst of a struggle, you might benefit by letting truth be your anchor of defense. And always be mindful that your truth is not the world's standard of truth, but it is the truth of Jesus.

Dear God, I choose Jesus as my anchor of truth so that I can overcome the storms and struggles of life. His truth is the standard by which I anchor my hopes and dreams. Amen.

Kedging

Now to him who is able to do immeasurably more than all we ask or imagine.

—Ephesians 3:20

During the War of 1812, Americans used kedging to save a ship from capture. The dictionary defines *kedging* as moving a ship by using a line attached to an anchor, which is dropped at the distance and in the direction desired. As enemies chased the *USS Constitution* for more than two days in light winds, Captain Isaac Hull used several tactics to elude their enemies' pursuit, including a kedge anchor. He sent a small boat out a few thousand feet and dropped two anchors. The crew then wound up the rope to let the anchors haul the ship forward. They repeated the process for two days and nights and stayed out of range of the enemy ships. The kedging saved the ship from attack. Unless there is knowledge about this strategy, one may think it is impossible for small boats to pull large ocean vessels. Yet kedging works. Many times our thinking about our hopes and dreams are limited. God is able to do much more than you can imagine.

As you cast your hopes in the direction you want to move, make sure that you cast them in God's direction. Like a small boat pulling a ship, God can cause your hopes to grow exponentially more than you could ever imagine.

Dear God, show me how to release my hopes to You so that You can make them grow. Amen.

Anchored Hope

We have this hope as an anchor for the soul, firm and secure.

—Hebrews 6:19

An anchor with a grasping claw digs deep to cling to gravel, rock, and coral. The powerful anchor holds on with all its might and prevails against the stormiest seas. When you encounter the most demanding trials or rockiness of abuse, let hope be your claw anchor. One of the most difficult tests written in the Bible was when God asked Abraham to sacrifice his son Isaac. Abraham obediently prepared Isaac for slaughter, but God stopped him and provided a ram instead. Abraham passed the test, and God promised to bless Him. When God made that promise, He swore an oath. The author of Hebrews explained, "Since there was no one greater for [God] to swear by, he swore by himself" (Hebrews 6:13). The promise was Abraham's hope; the oath sealed the promise like a claw anchor because it is impossible for God to lie.

What God has promised, He will do. With hope like that you can dig in deep against the difficulties that tug at you. Push deep, and hold on to your dreams and your faith. Use all your strength and willpower as you hang on tight. With such strong faith in your hopes, you will overcome your struggles.

Dear God, thank You for Your promises that give me hope. I trust that You will do what You have promised. Amen.

The Maker of the Stars

Lift up your eyes and look to the heavens: Who created all these?

—Isaiah 40:26

As long as sailors have ventured in ships upon the ocean, they have used the stars to light their way and guide them at night. They measure the angle between the horizon and a star to map their position. The stars sit in the heavens in reliable positions, and the sky moves in a predictable way. Sailors look up to chart their course. God made the stars that guide them, but the stars should not be worshiped. God was angry at the Israelites because they worshiped the stars and other idols just as the Canaanites who were around them did (Zephaniah 1:5). These pagans named the stars, but God gave them their real names. God knows each one and controls every heavenly body, including the stars. Isaiah said, "Because of his great power and mighty strength, not one of them is missing" (Isaiah 40:26).

Today people follow stars for different reasons. They consult the stars, reading their horoscopes for guidance and to discover something about their future. The Bible calls this "divination" and warns against it. God wants you to look only to Him for guidance. You can look above the turmoil around you to your hope and chart a course, and let the One who made the stars and heavens guide you.

Dear God, guide me by Your power in the direction You want me to go. Amen.

Launching

And Noah and his sons and his wife and his sons' wives entered the ark to escape the waters of the flood.

—Genesis 7:7

A ship in port makes a pretty scene against the backdrop of the sky and water. However, a boat is useful only when it sets sail out to sea. Ships are built to glide on the water, cross the seas, and take people or cargo to destinations. Ships are built for a purpose. God called Noah to build an ark for a purpose. The story of Noah's ark has been shared in many churches. Adults and children alike know the reason for the ark. God wanted to send a flood to cleanse the earth because of the wickedness of the people's hearts. Hence, God asked Noah to build an ark so that he and his family along with a number of animals and birds of every kind could be saved.

Noah's ark served its purpose. It was launched, spent forty days and forty nights at sea, and then landed on top of a mountain. Hopes and dreams also need to set sail and not just remain in your imagination as a lovely painting. You were created for a purpose and are meant to move forward and succeed. Be ready for the joy of putting your hope into action and setting sail to the destination of your dreams.

Dear God, help me to launch the dreams in my heart so I can fulfill my purpose. Amen.

Anchored in Friendship

I am a friend to all who fear you, to all who follow your precepts.

—Psalm 119:63

There is nothing like a close companion who encourages your hopes. You can trust that person and turn to them for support. If you feel like you are drowning, your companion will throw a lifeline to pull you back up and encourage you to keep hoping. But what if that friend were also a friend of God, and what if there were millions of friends like that? Indeed, there are millions of people across this land and around the world who love God. A relationship with God makes our friendships with one another have a closeness that is very special. There is a spiritual connection with one another and with God so that you should never feel alone or without support.

Share your hopes with a friend, and together seek to become friends of God. You can laugh together at what goes wrong and rejoice together at what goes right. You will find your friend investing in you and your dream. You can discuss the struggles and problems to get ideas from a different perspective. You can also be a companion who invests in your friend's dreams to encourage his or her hopes. But more than that, you will have the wisdom and love of God and the support of others like you because of your common focus as believers.

Dear God, thank You for the support of friends who love You the way that I do. Amen.

CPR for Hope

Because of the LORD's great love we are not consumed, for his compassions never fail. They are new every morning; great is your faithfulness.

—Lamentations 3:22–23

When hopelessness tries to creep in, it is time for revival. You need a little CPR to revive your hope. In overcoming, you gain confidence that you can continue and not let difficulties win. The Bible refers to these mishaps as "afflictions." The word *affliction* suggests great pain and suffering. This hopeless state can be brought on by illness, hurt, catastrophe, loss, and failure, among other events. Do not allow these difficulties to make you feel hopeless or overwhelmed. Do not give hopelessness the attention that it demands. God's love is what matters at this point. In the book of Lamentations, you receive the CPR that you need. It reveals that God's great love never fails. Every morning when you wake up, His love and compassion are still strong, even in the midst of hopelessness.

When you take a deep breath and slow down to look at a problem, you may think of another approach. With each little conquest and with the love of God to spur you on, hope recovers, and you breathe a little easier again. Smile and rejoice when you give new life to your hopes and revive your dreams.

Dear God, thank You for Your compassion that is my focus and my revival for overcoming the struggles of the day. Amen.

Revived by Forgiveness

See to it that no one falls short of the grace of God and that no bitter root grows up to cause trouble and defile many.

—Hebrews 12:15

Someone may sabotage your efforts or bring pain into your life that halts your work toward your dreams, deflates your ego, and crushes your hopes. A cruel word may hurt or discourage you. People may cause problems unknowingly or on purpose. The simple antidote is forgiveness. Many who watched the movie *Magnolia*, starring Tom Cruise, longed to give him a heaping teaspoon of forgiveness. The scenes reveal the emotional lives of many characters who are caught up in disappointment and hurt. The Tom Cruise character cannot escape from the disappointment in his father, who left him with his sick mother when he was a kid. With many resentful feelings toward his father, the movie showed how a grudge hurts the one who is holding it.

We are encouraged in Scripture to let no bitter root in our hearts grow or develop. But let forgiveness unlock your heart to allow pain and anger to flow out and make room to be refilled with hope, love, joy, and peace. Free your heart and hope by forgiving someone, instead of letting the hurt become a prison. Let forgiveness put the hope back into your dreams.

Dear God, bless me to choose forgiveness over pain and love over holding a grudge. Amen.

A Gentle Breeze of Hope

David and Samuel and the prophets, who through faith conquered kingdoms, administered justice, and gained what was promised.
—Hebrews 11:32–33

A gentle breeze feels cool and can have a calming effect, but the swirling winds of tornadoes, fire whirls, and waterspouts leave great damage in their wake. After the storm passes, the cleanup, rebuilding, and restoring of hope begins. What restores hope following such loss? David, Samuel, and others like them used faith. According to verse I in Hebrews 11, faith is the next step up from hope. This verse helps you to understand that "faith is confidence in what we hope for and assurance about what we do not see."

Use your faith to believe God will help you and to believe in your ability to restore what seems hopelessly destroyed. In rebuilding you may transform your hope into something new. Just as the land remains after a windstorm, build upon the foundation of your dream that remains. It is a new start that gives you an opportunity to tweak things and redesign it to fit new needs. Let hope be the gentle breeze that whispers, *You can do it; you can build something new and better.*

Dear God, sometimes I need a gentle breeze of hope. Strengthen my faith to believe that restoration is possible when hope is gone. Amen.

Childlike Hope

"Anyone who will not receive the kingdom of God like a little child will never enter it."

—Luke 18:17

Children love cardboard boxes. They can transform them into forts, spaceships, caves, and other products of their imagination. Even when flattened, the box transforms to a canvas for artwork or a wall to section off an area. Jesus understood the nature and importance of children. While Jesus was teaching, His disciples were bothered by children who sought His attention. He gently rebuked His disciples and said, "'Let the little children come to me, and do not hinder them, for the kingdom of God belongs to such as these'" (Luke 18:16). Furthermore, Jesus said the hope and faith of children are what adults need to have. There is nothing pretentious about the faith of children. Their faith is grounded in humility because of their dependence on others.

Children and their ability to find joy in the simplest of things are gifts of hope. They explore brokenness to discover how things work and find a new purpose for seemingly useless items. Children bring hope as we watch their zest for life and their ability to imagine and dream. Watch a child at play. Let it renew your hope and fuel your imagination.

Dear Father, help me to rediscover childlike hope and faith so that I can enter Your kingdom with joy. Amen.

Step-by-Step Toward Hope

Your word is a lamp for my feet, a light on my path.

—Psalm 119:105

Workers nail each board of a house one at a time. Each stroke of the hammer seems so insignificant, but each one is important. Little jobs may seem trivial and even a nuisance when working toward big accomplishments, but they are the proving ground of realizing hopes. They are the steps you need to take to get to where you are going. Each step propels you forward to the next step. Even when you step in the wrong direction, God can still use it for His purposes. Just retrace your steps when you get off the path, and though situations may have changed, make the adjustment and return to your course. Learn from your missteps. Trust that the path you are on is the one that God has placed you on. Allow His Word to direct you step-by-step toward your hope.

Completing each little task of a big job brings you one step closer to completing something grand. You build confidence in finishing the little jobs, which will make it easier to tackle big ones. Let your little successes inspire bigger dreams, step-by-step.

Dear Lord God, guide me along the way as I walk this journey step-by-step toward my hope. And if I stumble, gently place me back on the path. Amen.

God's Guidance

"Before I formed you in the womb I knew you, before you were born I set you apart."

—Jeremiah 1:5

When your spirit remains unwavering and loyal to your hope, you can depend on your ability to continue. Consistent work leads to success. As you faithfully plug away and daily apply your talents to your hopes, you may find yourself wondering, *Am I almost there yet?* Never forget from where you have come and how you have arrived at where you are. God's hand has been with you to guide you, even before you were born. Just like He called Jeremiah while he was being formed in his mother's womb, God formed you. And also like Jeremiah, God called you for a specific purpose. The hope in your heart leads you to that destination. It is your life's journey that only you can walk. It is God guidance that will get you there.

The road to a goal may seem like an unending journey, yet each day of unwavering faith brings you a little closer to the goal. When you pause to look around you, you may be surprised at how far you have come. Look back to where you have traveled, and thank God for His guidance. Let the distance traveled bolster your steadfast spirit to continue.

Dear God, thank You for Your guidance since my birth. I look forward to the rest of my journey with You. Amen.

Reach for the Impossible

"Is anything too hard for the LORD?"

—Genesis 18:14

The song "The Impossible Dream" from the musical *Man of La Mancha* challenges people to follow a dream no matter how hopeless it appears. Stories of people who overcame great challenges and forged ahead inspire us to continue our quest. One such story is that of Abraham and Sarah. Although they both had reached very old ages, Sarah conceived and bore a son. Sarah, who dreamed of giving Abraham an heir, laughed at the promise from God that she would conceive. She overcame the unbelief that her body could no longer carry a child when she was challenged by the question, "Is anything too hard for the LORD?" (Genesis 18:14).

Within stories of success, there are usually failures and struggles along a journey where little possibilities led to achieving what seemed impossible. Do what you already know you can do well to reach your goals. Celebrate the success, and let it give you the momentum to try something more difficult. You will soon find yourself doing what you once thought was impossible but still hoped you could do. Soon you will discover that nothing is impossible for God. Trust in the journey God has for you, no matter how unattainable your hopes may seem.

Dear God, because nothing is too difficult for You, I will seek You every day to do the impossible. Amen.

Overcoming Obstacles

I consider that our present sufferings are not worth comparing with the glory that will be revealed in us.

—Romans 8:18

In an obstacle course, a player may leap over an object, jump through a hoop, and crawl under another object. The person proceeds by meeting one challenge after another. Paul understood the nature of obstacles, having experienced so much suffering for the cause of Christ. His sufferings, however, were but obstacles that could be overcome, because he looked forward to the future glory. That future glory is eternal life in heaven. This gave him strength to continue his journey. We may encounter our own hurdles to jump, walls to climb, or even a mud pit to wade through. But overcoming these obstacles builds strength.

As you face real challenges with hope, you develop courage when your focus is on eternity. Sometimes you must reach higher than you imagined, and at other times, you need to get down low on your knees in prayer. What obstacles are you facing today? Do not go around them, face them head on. They can be overcome when you set your eyes on heaven. And when you face them with heaven in view, they will strengthen you.

Dear God, thank You for obstacles that allow me to see the glory that is before me. May each obstacle strengthen me and help my journey toward my final destination in heaven. Amen.

Your Season for Hope

"Look at the fig tree, and all the trees. As soon as they come out in leaf, you see for yourselves and know that the summer is already near."

—Luke 21:29–30 ESV

Summer is the warmest season of the year, but it falls within different months within different parts of the world. In the Northern Hemisphere, summer extends from June to September. But in the Southern Hemisphere, summer begins in December and ends in March. Summer is the season for daisies. They grow when the weather is warm and favorable. In fact, summer is the season for the greatest plant growth. When you see green leaves and flowering plants, then you know that summer is approaching.

Your hope may require a particular season for strong growth. If things do not seem to line up, it may be the time to ask if the timing and season is right for you to move forward with your plans. It may be that your hope needs to sit and simmer in the recesses of your mind and heart for a while until you enter the right season of your life. As you reflect on your life, you will discover what hope to nurture in this season.

Dear God, when the season is right, strengthen and lead me to reach for the plans You have for me. Amen.

Eyes on Your Vision

Where there is no vision, the people perish.

—Proverbs 29:18 KJV

At boot camp a soldier may cringe at the sight of a swamp to cross with a swinging vine or rope. Looking down brings fear, and the soldier's hands may sweat and slide. It is much easier to swing high and far if the warrior looks at the rope and land ahead, rather than staring at the muddy waters below. Goals are set to be conquered or achieved. Where you focus your attention as you are striving for your goal can mean success or failure. That is where having a vision comes in. A vision is the picture in your heart of what you are hoping to achieve. It helps you to overcome obstacles and to keep going when the road is rough. In order to develop a vision, you must know exactly what you hope to achieve. Write down your thoughts, and make goals to achieve each step. Accomplishing your goals is possible with a vision. Without one you may not fulfill your dreams.

Your vision instills hope and courage. Obstacles are simply hurdles to cross along the path. As you focus on your vision, your fears will lessen. As you aim for the target, let your vision strengthen your willpower.

Dear Father, bless me with a vision that helps me reach my goals and fulfill my hopes and dreams. Amen.

Inspired Living

All Scripture is God-breathed.

—2 Timothy 3:16

Breathing is essential. Your body needs air flowing into it to continue life. The word *inspire* comes from the Latin words *spirare*, which means "to breathe," and *in*, which means "into." Inspiration is about breathing life into an idea. This is what God did to His Word. God breathed life into the Bible. There are some who believe that the Word of God does not come from God. They believe it is merely a book of stories and wisdom, and nothing more. But the Bible has changed many lives because of the power that God has placed within its covers. Its words have the power to teach when instruction is needed, to rebuke when someone veers off God's path, to correct when someone is wrong, and to train in righteousness when someone lives in sin. God breathed this power and life into His Word to help us live. In a similar way, your soul needs the continual flow of ideas and hopes to really live.

Ideas are everywhere. You will find them in conversations, in books, while looking at the world, through prayer, and by asking questions. Through His Word, God is the ultimate source of inspiration and the One who wants to breathe new life into your soul. As you read the Bible, keep your mind open to ideas, and continue to hope. God will inspire you.

Dear Father, thank You for Your Word that inspires me and helps me to live. Amen.

Dream Big

I do believe; help me overcome my unbelief!

—Mark 9:24

$\mathcal{J}$magine the life you want. Be brave, and let your mind dream. Dreams energize your mind and bring new hopes or revitalize unfulfilled hopes. You naturally aspire to something bigger or more important in life. You are wired to dream big and to hope without limits. Your dreams come from within you and from God. Never allow doubt to steal your dreams. Jesus' disciples allowed unbelief to steal their power from performing a miracle on one occasion. They could not heal a boy who was possessed by a demon. Then his father took his son to Jesus for healing. Jesus said, "Everything is possible for one who believes" (Mark 9:23). In many ways Jesus was telling the father that he needed to dream big so that his son could be healed. If the father doubted, his dream of seeing his son whole would have been crushed. That is why the father asked Jesus to help him to overcome his doubt. The father wanted the dream of his son's healing to be realized.

Be encouraged by what you learn from failures and past efforts, because mistakes develop wisdom to help you make better choices. Out of the lessons learned come new hopes and dreams. Let your imagination renew your mind and help you to dream bigger. Never doubt that you can reach your dream.

Dear Father, when I doubt my dreams, please strengthen my faith and help me to believe again. Amen.

Renewed Energy

But those who hope in the LORD will renew their strength.

—Isaiah 40:31

Have you felt a bit weary or overwhelmed lately? Life gets busy, and sometimes dreams get lost in the daily routine. The prophet Isaiah encouraged the people whose dreams had faded right before their eyes. The people of Judah had spent seventy years in captivity, and Isaiah helped them to see that their Creator, God, had not abandoned them. They thought that God had forgotten, but Isaiah said that God knows everything that He has created by name, so how could He forget His people? Isaiah encouraged them to focus on God and open up their eyes to what they already knew about Him. God is strong and powerful, and He shares His power with those who need it.

When you take a break and spend time on yourself and with God, you allow yourself to rest and be refreshed. Calm your spirit and revitalize your tired body with an hour at a spa, or bask in the sun to let the failures and commotion dissolve from your mind. Pray and reflect on God and your favorite Scripture verses to renew your soul. If you hope in Him, He will renew your energy and prepare you to pursue your hopes again.

Dear Father, You are a powerful and strong God. Thank You for renewing my energy when I become weak. Amen.

Hope from Within

"Do not be afraid of those who kill the body but cannot kill the soul."

—Matthew 10:28

A candle burns from the inside out once the wick is lit. The absorbent wick pulls the wax to itself, and the flame burns the wax once it turns into a gaseous state. The wick only burns when it needs to move down to reach more wax. Just like candle wax, your physical body will waste away, but your soul will never die. Your soul is the part of you that is not physical and the part that will last throughout eternity. Some theologians believe the soul to be the most important part of your human makeup. In other words, they believe that without your soul, you are nothing and would cease to exist. That may be the reason that Jesus taught that you should not be afraid of those who could destroy your body but could not destroy the soul. As long as your soul is safe, you are safe.

Your hopes are deep within you too. Like the wick inside of a candle, your hopes light up as they are fueled. Encouragement, faith, and trust fuel hope. Your hopes may need to be re-lit at times when you let winds of discouragement blow them out, but they are still there within your soul, waiting for you.

Dear God, keep my hope burning brightly from within my soul. Amen.

Weavings of Hope

So that there should be no division in the body, but that its parts should have equal concern for each other.

—1 Corinthians 12:25

The artist weaves many threads together to form a tapestry. The threads intertwine to create a beautiful design. Throughout history tapestry art has graced the dwellings of people all over the world. A tapestry is woven on a loom and composed of two sets of interlaced threads. Like a tapestry, your life is woven together with relationships. When a relationship fails, it is like ripping out threads in your life's design, so it will need mending. Henry Melvill said, "Ye live not for yourselves; ye cannot live for yourselves; a thousand fibers connect us with your fellow men, and along those fibers, as along sympathetic threads, run your actions as causes, and return to you as effects."

Paul encouraged us to have equal concern for each other, and when someone falls, we should help restore that person. A hole in the tapestry of your relationships leaves everyone open and vulnerable. Thankfully, your friends will come together to help each other mend. The pricks of sorrow are reminders that new threads are being woven along with new hopes.

Dear Father, help me to remember at all times the obligation I have to support my family and my friends so that nothing pulls us apart or destroys our individual hopes. Amen.

Touch Points

Keep me safe, my God, for in you I take refuge.

—Psalm 16:1

I'm home" are words that echo through a house when a loved one returns home from a trip or after work. It is a warm greeting of joy that waits for a response. Too often loneliness replaces homecomings. A home is a safe refuge where we are surrounded by love and family. In the Bible, David sometimes referred to God as His refuge. David had learned from difficult experiences that he could always go to God for safety and care.

After the loss of a loved one or a broken relationship, there is an empty feeling, much like a hollowness, that echoes in your soul. Reaching out to connect with someone else may fill the emptiness for a time. But reaching out to God as your refuge will revive your hope. With the use of the Internet, people are less connected in person but still long for face-to-face interaction as a way to connect with others. If you are experiencing this emptiness, you may benefit more from volunteering or joining a group where you will find people in need of hugs or warm words. As you create new relationships and invite others into your life, you will find new hope. And when you go to God, He will take you in. He is your refuge and will keep you safe.

Dear Father, You are my refuge and my strength. Thank You for awakening my hope. Amen.

AUGUST

· ·

Tears of joy, like summer raindrops,
are pierced by sunbeams.

——Hosea Ballou

One Moment

You will fill me with joy in your presence.

—Psalm 16:11

Death is a veil, and for now we cannot see beyond it. Death separates us from loved ones but leaves behind a treasury of moments. One moment is all it takes to wipe a tear, to share a hug, or to say, "I love you." In one moment, a mind or a heart can be changed to reflect a new opinion or a new attitude. Consider the moment that changed America on September 11, 2001. On that day many people routinely went to work but returned home in shock because of the devastating events of that morning. On that day terrorists flew two planes into the World Trade Center buildings in New York, killing more than two thousand people. Mothers, fathers, other relatives, and friends lost loved ones. Many desired one more moment to express their feelings with their loved ones.

Fulfill every moment, and capture them in a journal or photo album so that when death steals someone away, you will have memories of those moments. As the moments live in your heart, so do the hopes the person shared and the encouragement they gave you. Cherish the moments, and let the joy they rekindle fuel your hopes.

Dear God, thank You for precious moments that fill my heart with joy and hope. Amen.

New Horizons

He marks out the horizon on the face of the waters for a boundary between light and darkness.

—Job 26:10

When you look out as far as possible, you see the horizon where earth and sky meet. It may seem close, but you can travel for miles and miles and never reach the horizon. When you stand in a forest, the horizon may be obscured or invisible, but it is still there. The horizon has several special usages. First, God the Creator uses the horizon as a boundary over the waters between light and darkness. Aircraft pilots also use the horizon to keep the plane flying at a level of consistency. To control the aircraft, the pilot makes sure that the plane's nose lines up with the horizon. Even artists use the horizon to determine perspective in landscape drawings or paintings.

Each day has a new horizon, but you cannot see what will happen beyond it. It can limit your vision. However, we must have faith that the One who created all things and loves us knows what is beyond the horizon and is looking out for us. Whenever you see the horizon, let it remind you that God cares and there is more to life than what you can see.

Dear God, by Your great hand the world was created, including the horizon. Thank You that it is a reminder that You are looking out for me. Amen.

Escaping Sorrow

Be not quick in your spirit to become angry, for anger lodges in the heart of fools.

—Ecclesiastes 7:9 ESV

Anger is often a first response to hurt, and it boils over when you let it take control. Patience and forgiveness turn down the heat to control the anger and help you cool off. A Chinese proverb puts it this way: "If you are patient in a moment of anger, you will escape one hundred days of sorrow." Patience is the key to overcoming anger. Anger is a strong and often uncontrolled emotion that leaves regret and heartbreak in its wake. According to the book of Ecclesiastes, anger is the mark of a fool or an arrogant person, indicating that a person is wise when anger is controlled and abated.

Returning kind words when you are faced with anger can stop many battles from escalating into wars. Even if the other person continues with abuse and hurt, you can protect your heart and hopes. You escape sorrow with forgiveness, staying in a safe place, and reminding yourself that you are lovable and wise. Choose to dwell on your dreams and joys, not on angry words or actions, to keep your heart filled with hope.

Dear God, give me strength to choose patience over anger and love over hate so that my hope and the hope of others will flourish. In Jesus' name I pray, Amen.

New Life

Whoever sows sparingly will also reap sparingly, and whoever sows generously will also reap generously.

—2 Corinthians 9:6

Dry, little seeds that are planted and watered will sprout, grow, and bloom. The seed holds life within it even though it appears to be lifeless. There is a legend about a man named Johnny Appleseed, who was a pioneer apple farmer in the 1800s. Johnny Appleseed brought new life to the countryside in many cities and towns across America. According to the legend, his dream was to make sure there were plenty of apple trees so no one would go hungry. Therefore, the story is told that he wandered from place to place, planting apple seeds. Throughout a period of more than fifty years, Johnny planted apple seeds far and wide. He was a generous man who sowed generously, and as the Bible promised, he reaped an abundance. Johnny Appleseed brought new life and hope to many people.

Seeds are reminders of the hope of new life. One cannot easily tell what a seed will become just by looking at it. So, too, we cannot see what our hope will become. Trust in God's plan, and sow seeds of hope. Then watch as new life springs forth.

Dear God, I choose to sow seeds of hope abundantly wherever I may be. Like Johnny Appleseed, bless me to produce new life. Amen.

Cleansed

The blood of Jesus, his Son, purifies us from all sin.

—1 John 1:7

No home works well without a good ventilation system to circulate the air and remove contaminants. The system should filter out unwanted particles and keep the air flowing. Its main function is to replace the stale air with fresh air. From a Christian perspective, it could be said that sin is the stale portion of a person's spirit. There is only one way to be cleansed of sin, and that is through the blood of Jesus. In the Old Testament, the Israelites had a system, which had been put in place by God, of using the blood of animals to cleanse a person from sin. The sins of the people were transferred to the animal in a sacrificial ceremony. When Jesus died on the cross, He became the perfect sacrifice for all humanity. Now we can have a relationship with God and spend eternity with Him.

Just as your soul must be cleansed from sin, your heart also needs to be cleansed. Do not let the contamination of bitterness and rage clog your heart. As soon as you feel a twinge of anger, let it go with forgiveness and respond with kindness.

Dear God, thank You for the blood of Jesus that cleanses me from sin. May I use the principle of cleansing to be free from anger and other contaminates in my heart. Amen.

Lonely No More

The LORD God said, "It is not good for the man to be alone. I will make a helper suitable for him."

—Genesis 2:18

God saw the ache of loneliness within Adam when no creature could be the companion he needed. God created Eve, and Adam rejoiced. This completed God's creative work. He had made man, whom He named Adam, and woman whom God made from the rib of man. God had deemed, "It is not good for the man to be alone" (Genesis 2:18). God could have made woman from the ground like He made man, but He choose to make her from flesh and bone. This signifies the oneness of man and woman. It was a union of their hearts and their lives.

Loneliness is difficult. Breaking up from what was once a close relationship hurts. You are made for relationships. God sees your pain when you feel lonely. The good news is that God is always with you and ready to listen. There is more good news: God created many people, so you can fill your life with new friends. Step outside your home and your comfort zone to meet someone new. Join groups at church or join a group that shares an interest, like gardening or painting. Rejoice as you make new friends.

Dear God, thank You for the solution You have provided for loneliness. Help me to find ways to meet this need not only in myself but in others. Amen.

Mending the Home

But as for me and my household, we will serve the LORD.

—Joshua 24:15

Homes are places where children grow up and family traditions are made. Memories of home are planted in the deep recesses of the mind so that in years to come, there will always be longings of home. Sometimes divorce, busyness, and extramarital affairs harm the home, making many of them places of anger and hurt. But houses can be rebuilt after a storm has damaged them. So, too, you can rebuild the atmosphere of your home.

How do you mend the brokenness of a home? In the Old Testament, Joshua decided that he and everyone else in his home would serve God. With this decision he not only strengthened his home but made God its foundation. So begin by laying a firm foundation, which is the Lord. Then restart by loving the people in your home and loving those who visit. Choose peace and forgiveness over anger and fear. Sprinkle joy into the lives of your family members by preparing favorite meals, giving bright smiles, and sharing amusing anecdotes. As you sit together for meals, linger to share hopes and dreams. These little actions will transform your house into a home.

Dear Father, lead me to make my home a place where Your love is shared and forgiveness is practiced. Amen.

Tears Today; Joy Tomorrow

Those who sow with tears will reap with songs of joy.

—Psalm 126:5

Tears have many important functions. They clean and lubricate the eyes, and a stream of tears will flow when the eyes become irritated. Tears are also formed from laughter, or even a yawn draws tears. Most of the time, though, tears mean sadness or joy. Therefore, tears express intense internal emotion. One of those emotions is sorrow. Sorrow overflows with weeping or crying. Each salty tear that is shed commemorates a loss or hurt. With each tear there may be a memory of a past pleasure that is now lost. The psalmist wrote about the sorrows of the Israelite people, who returned from captivity to a parched land because it had lain seventy years without cultivation. He helped them to understand that although they were weeping now because of harsh labor, they would experience future joy when everything was restored.

Tears can be reminders that something or someone brought you joy and delight. Tears can also show that you are stressed or sad. You express your loss in tears that words cannot do. It is good to have a shoulder to cry on, someone to comfort you and share your pain with, and help wipe away the tears. Although you may weep today, look forward to tomorrow when your hope and joy returns.

Dear Lord, thank You for tears today and for hope tomorrow. Amen.

It Is Your Choice

There is a way that appears to be right, but in the end it leads to death.

—Proverbs 14:12

The grains in an hourglass slowly drop to the bottom. The pinch at the center of the glass allows only a few grains to flow through at a time. Some sand timers measure only a minute, allowing just sixty seconds before the last grain falls.

A minute is short, so the minutes of your life should be spent on hope and not wasted in anger. Someone's words or actions may have upset you. The choice is yours. You can choose to relax and let go of the tension that anger brings. Or you can allow the anger to keep you tied up in knots. The best response is to choose to forgive the person. Although anger seems right because of the hurt, it is not beneficial to those involved. God's Word offers insight on how to deal with these situations. It also helps you to see the end of some dark paths so you can avoid them. Do not fill the minutes with anger. Spread kindness, and you will find that kindness will be returned.

Dear Father, each minute is a precious gift that You have given to every living being. Help me to be one who chooses to spend each minute sharing joy and kindness. Amen.

Torn Apart

"What God has joined together, let no one separate."

—Matthew 19:6

There is such a final sound and hardness about divorce. It is a lost hope and a turning point in the lives of those who go through it. For too many it has become a fact of life. Statistics have remained consistent in recent years, citing that fifty percent of marriages end in divorce. Even Christians have fallen victim to this trend. Although marriage is a permanent agreement between a man and a woman, the Bible does provide conditions for divorce for certain situations.

When you or someone close to you faces a divorce, allow time to grieve the loss of the relationship. Avoid letting your heart become hard from anger or bitterness. At this turning point in your life, choose to hope for a better future. Jesus linked divorce to hard hearts. Like sin was not a part of God's design for us, neither was divorce, but God permitted them both. And the forgiveness that God provided for sin also covers divorce. Just as plaque builds up in arteries and causes a blockage, so the negative emotions of divorce can build up and cause emotional blockage. Forgiveness from one another and from God softens your heart and lets you turn toward new hopes and love.

Lord, help each person going through a divorce recover and find new hope. Help their hearts be softened and filled with love again. Amen.

Haven of Beauty

He has made everything beautiful in its time.

—Ecclesiastes 3:11

The television network HGTV has renovation shows where homeowners remodel their homes because, in their current conditions, the homes do not meet the families' needs. The work can include anything from painting walls to tearing out rooms to removing everything down to the foundation. But the final result grips the heart of the viewers as beauty is revealed in every room.

Similarly, the Bible reveals God's desire for beauty for our lives. In the book of Ecclesiastes, Solomon said God made everything beautiful. This means that the world we live in is naturally beautiful. But sometimes the relationships in our homes can become like a dilapidated house.

The atmosphere of a home may even appear beautiful, and visitors may get a false impression of a happy family. In reality, however, the family has lost its beauty. Therefore, God must renovate our homes, sometimes even starting over from our very foundations. We must put our own efforts into making a real home. Fill your home not only with beauty, good food, and comfortable seating but with joy and happiness. Rejoice as you transform your home into a haven where people feel safe to talk and share their hopes.

Dear God, just as You made our world beautiful, help me to make my home a haven of beauty. Amen.

Solving Puzzles of Love

Whoever reads this writing and tells me what it means will be clothed in purple.

—Daniel 5:7

A picture must be cut into pieces of irregular shapes to make a jigsaw puzzle. Then everyone has fun putting the pieces together, usually starting with the corners and outside edges. Puzzles, riddles, and problems are enjoyable, but some can be difficult to solve. King Belshazzar in the book of Daniel had his hands full trying to solve a riddle of sorts. A hand had mysteriously appeared and wrote words on a wall in a language that was not familiar to anyone. The king called for Daniel, whom God had given the gift of interpreting visions and dreams, and God gave Daniel the interpretation to the writing on the wall. For this Daniel received the king's favor.

Love is like a puzzle of tightly fitted pieces. But when a loving relationship starts to fall apart, there is still hope of restoring it and fitting the pieces back together again. It takes time and may take extra people, like a counselor and praying friends. Look for the smooth edges as places to start, and rebuild the frame to protect the more fragile and broken insides. Like God helped Daniel solve the puzzle on the wall, God will help you figure out the pieces of your relationships.

Dear Father, when the loving relationships in my life come apart, help me to work to heal and restore our hearts so we can be whole again. Amen.

Galaxies of Stars

Over the heads of the living creatures there was the likeness of an expanse, shining like awe-inspiring crystal, spread out above their heads.

—Ezekiel 1:22 ESV

Clusters of stars form the Milky Way and other galaxies in space. The twinkling spheres in the inky blackness of space bring light and move in great harmony. They remain so constant that throughout time, travelers have used them, particularly constellations, as guides. Navigators and early explorers used constellations to determine their locations. The sky changes at night as the earth rotates, and it does not look the same from different parts of the earth. Early travelers could figure out where they were just by looking at the sky, even when they had no landmarks and were traveling without maps.

Many people today gaze at the stars because of their beauty and because God made them. They are part of His great expanse. The countless stars shine in the night sky, each glowing in its own path and with its particular brightness. The stars beckon you to live in harmony, shine with your own inner glow, and follow your path. Encourage others to shine and fill the earth with brightness.

Dear God, my Father, You have made the heavens, including the galaxies with their constellations. Thank You for the hope they inspire and for the light they give, guiding travelers on their way. Amen.

Living Together

Live in harmony with one another. Do not be haughty, but associate with the lowly. Never be wise in your own sight.

—Romans 12:16 ESV

Pride causes much disharmony as it causes a person to look down on someone and envy those who seem better off. Pride is a negative personality trait that God wants people to overcome, or it will cause devastating problems. The Bible says, "Pride goes before destruction" (Proverbs 16:18). Nothing good will come from being prideful. It destroys those who are proud and hurts those who are not. Prideful people have a tendency to be unthankful because they think they are special and deserve only what is good. They find difficulty in getting along with others due to their lack of humility.

As God's people, we should try to be bouquets of beauty. Flowers in a bouquet mix together to produce a sweet scent. Whether a shrinking violet, bright red rose, morning glory, or other type of bloom, you are lovely. Embrace the people around you rather than pushing people away. Check your pride and practice humility when you start to overlook someone. Look more closely to discover the fragrance in the individual. Reach out and nurture that person's hopes to help them to blossom.

Dear God, teach me humility so that I will not be prideful. Help me to get along with others so we can live and work together in harmony. Amen.

Getting in Harmony

Praise him with trumpet sound; praise him with lute and harp.

—Psalm 150:3 ESV

When one instrument in an orchestra is out of tune, the notes stand out, but not in a good way. However, it is easily fixed with a little adjustment. Harmony is often just a simple modification away. The musicians, under the leadership of a conductor, tweak their equipment until the sound is in accord. One of the most leading conductors of the twentieth century was British conductor Leopold Stokowski. He is credited with making Philadelphia's orchestra the finest in America. He also appeared in the Disney film *Fantasia.* Stokowski had a reputation for being a master of sound, which means he understood music and harmony in a way that placed him above the rest. The psalmist also understood music and harmony and used it in a way that celebrated and praised God. God's faithfulness to those He loves calls for celebration. He is worthy to be praised in the most harmonic of ways.

You may not be in an orchestra or even have a knowledge of music, but harmony and consistency in the pursuit of your dreams is mandatory for their fulfillment. If you are experiencing conflicts in achieving your dreams, you may want to find what is out of tune with the rest of your goals and make adjustments to get back in harmony.

Dear God, bless me to pursue my dreams with consistency and harmony. This is my hope and my prayer. Amen.

Process to Harmony

"First be reconciled to your brother, and then come and offer your gift."
—Matthew 5:24 ESV

Some major conflicts have given birth to hope, such as the racial disharmony that led to Martin Luther King, Jr.'s speech titled "I Have a Dream." His speech gave hope to many people and lifted their spirits. The prejudice against women has spawned unrest and disharmony, too, as women have protested and won many rights. Traditionally, women were the keepers of the house who were responsible for rearing the children and other household duties while the men worked outside of the home. But when men went off to war, women took the jobs their husbands left vacant to make ends meet and to keep the economy running. Through the years, women have not been treated fairly in the workplace and continue to fight for respect and equal treatment.

The emotional toll of strife is a little alarm reminding you to make peace. As you recognize conflicts in your dreams or relationships, let them motivate you to change and make adjustments. For when you seek to understand a problem, it brings you closer to fixing it and closer to achieving your goals. Keeping harmony with all those around you should be a priority because harmony is one of God's priorities. He does not want you even to bring offerings to Him until there is harmony in your life. As you work toward your hope, also work to maintain harmony.

Dear God, help me to be in harmony in all of my relationships. Amen.

United for Peace

Her children arise and call her blessed; her husband also, and he praises her.

—Proverbs 31:28

Think of when you saw love modeled in life, especially the love between a husband and wife. The unity of spouses blesses people around them as their contagious love and joy overflow. The Proverbs 31 woman and her family demonstrated this type of love, primarily because of her nobility and character. She was considered to be of more value than precious jewels. Her husband was proud of her, trusting her to provide only good for him. As a housewife she was not lazy but willingly worked with her hands and made many sacrifices for her family. For example, she got up early each morning to provide food for her family. She worked in a vineyard to earn money for her family while managing everything at home. Like her husband, her children praise her and are thankful for what she does to unite the family.

Loving marriages are the heart of a community. They give hope that people can live together in peace. This kind of love seeks the best for the other person and selflessly puts the other person first. As you generously give of yourself to those you love, you will strengthen the unity and love in your family.

Dear God, thank You for my family. Keep us united in love and harmony. Amen.

Harmonious Mind

And the peace of God, which transcends all understanding, will guard your hearts and your minds in Christ Jesus.

—Philippians 4:7

As your mind stores and sorts through experiences, comments, and information, you may feel confused or overwhelmed. Modern society has saturated our senses with distractions. Today hundreds of television channels, video games, newspapers and magazines, electronic devices, and billboards compete for our attention. It is like living in the middle of Times Square in New York, where huge advertisements light up the sky at night and loud city noises fill the air. For the most part, we voluntarily open up our minds and allow much of these forces to invade our thoughts. But God calls for us to take care of our minds. Our thought life is where we connect with God in prayer. We are advised to think about those things that are noble, right, pure, lovely, and admirable. So when too much is going on inside your brain, it is time for a break.

There is peace in letting your mind unwind as you walk, write in a journal, or enjoy music. It is good to seek harmony between your thoughts and actions as you reflect on choices. Being mindful and reflective allows time to think things through and align your thoughts with your hopes.

Dear God, help me to find balance in my thought life so that my mind remains peaceful. Amen.

Embrace Harmony

And above all these put on love, which binds everything together in perfect harmony.

—Colossians 3:14 ESV

Ending a meeting with a circle where everyone holds hands and prays brings people together. Each person is linked to another person to form a group. In verse 14 of Colossians 3, Paul advised, "Above all these put on love" (ESV). But what came before the statement to quantify "above all"? Paul wanted to help his readers to daily live the Christian life. He advised that since they were Christians, they should live like Christians. He urged them to leave their former ways of life behind and take up godly attitudes and godly behavior. Primarily, Paul wanted them to be careful about how they treated one another. They should put on "compassion, kindness, humility, gentleness and patience" (v. 12 NIV). Then he said, above all of these virtues, "put on love" (v. 14 NIV).

Love holds people together and brings harmony. Love helps you overlook faults and accept quirks of individuals. Love enfolds you with joy and affirms you. Close your eyes, and think of moments when you felt the love that brings you closer to other people. As you stay in touch and support those in your circle, you will keep the chain strong and vibrant. Embrace the harmony that love brings.

Dear Father, above all else I will love and embrace harmony in my relationships. Amen.

Patchwork Quilts

There is neither Jew nor Gentile, neither slave nor free, nor is there male and female, for you are all one in Christ Jesus.

—Galatians 3:28

Patchwork quilts piece together different colors, shapes, and patterns to form a beautiful work of art. Scraps that seem different blend together within the planned design. America is similar to a patchwork quilt because of the different people from different countries who make up our own country. Since the Revolutionary War won our independence from the British, people have left their homelands to seek a better life for themselves in this country. When Heraclitus said, "The unlike is joined together, and from differences results the most beautiful harmony," he described something that is not unlike this patchwork country.

A quilt that repurposed old clothing and linens contains a special charm, linked with memories and stories from past days. Such quilts become a legacy to pass on to the next generation. Beautiful harmony can come from differences with a little thoughtful planning. Even if you share different hopes and dreams, you can join together in harmony. You will create a pattern of living that touches one another through dreams and hopes, stitched together with love.

Dear God, like a patchwork quilt, You have placed me in the midst of my relationships. Bless us to love one another and form a special bond. Amen.

Grace and Salt

Let your conversation be always full of grace, seasoned with salt.
—Colossians 4:6

It is easy to let words gush out like a waterfall, splashing into the world. The water's power and crashing sounds are reminders that sometimes a gentler flow is more soothing. However, many people carry regrets from having spoken before the thoughts in their minds are clear. The words that are spoken are harsh and hurtful, and sometimes even untrue. When this occurs, many excuse themselves, saying, "I've put my foot in my mouth." This means the remark was not intended; however, the spoken word has done its damage and cannot be reclaimed. There is no remedy for this action, only prevention so that it does not happen again.

Paul said we should use grace and salt when speaking to one another. Grace is underserved favor, and salt adds the spice or wit to a conversation. Therefore, people to whom you have spoken should leave the conversation with a sense of encouragement and hope. Allowing your words to spill out without thinking is similar to a waterfall that rushes onward. When you gush with enthusiasm and gratitude, it is exciting and reveals joy. However, when critical or sharp words pour out, they crash noisily where they fall. When you use grace and salt to guide your thinking before letting words escape your lips, your response to others will glorify God.

Dear God, guide my thoughts so that I speak words of encouragement. Amen.

Common Purpose

There are different kinds of working, but in all of them and in everyone it is the same God at work.

—1 Corinthians 12:6

Have you ever walked along a beach holding hands with someone? You move together and head in the same direction, enjoying the beauty of nature. You form a bond and are enjoying life. God has made us to work in unity with one another so that our work will bring glory to Him and help to build His kingdom. That means we are not only in partnership with people, but we are also in partnership with God. But when the partnership is disrupted because of jealousy among believers, then the work of God is hindered and relationships are damaged. Those disagreements are brought on because God has made us different and given us different skills and talents.

We must remember that God made you unique because He loves variety. Just look at the various flowers and other living things—each one is made special. We should overcome our differences and work together as God desires. There is a deeper connection when you share goals and work together to build something meaningful with another person. Your common purpose unifies you and adds depth to your relationship. As you share what is meaningful to you, may you be blessed by working with others who share your quest.

Dear Father, bless my relationships so that we can work together for a common purpose. Amen.

Powerful Memories

The memory of the righteous is a blessing.

—Proverbs 10:7 ESV

The poet William Wordsworth said, "With an eye made quiet by the power of harmony, and the deep power of joy, we see into the life of things." It seems that he may have visited a place associated with pleasant memories that shaped his inner peace. He beheld the scene in nature and rejoiced at the tranquility there. Memories embody everything that is special and sacred. Many people wonder whether they will take their precious memories with them to heaven when they pass on. The Bible is not clear on this, but in the book of Isaiah, the prophet wrote that past troubles will be hidden from our eyes (Isaiah 65:16). This could mean that when we get to heaven, our memories will be cleansed and refreshed so that we can retain only those that brought us joy or inspired our hearts.

A beautiful scene or memory can bring harmony to your mind, as you close your eyes and picture it again. Letting your senses experience the scent, sounds, and vision in your imagination recaptures the joy of past wonder. Indulge in pleasant memories to lift your spirits, and bring harmony to your mind. Such memories are blessings that rekindle the hope of harmony.

Dear God, thank You for the beautiful memories that flood my soul, giving me hope and joy. Amen.

Sweet Harmony

Live in harmony with one another.

—Romans 12:16

A barbershop quartet sings a melody with great harmony as they blend their voices, but each voice is distinct with its own pitch. They have spent time practicing together to blend their voices, and they know when one should take the lead while the other voices stay in the background and add depth to the song. The New Testament encourages us to find harmony rather than belting out our own voices over those around us. Sometimes the issue is that we are too proud to associate with others. But God wants us to put others above ourselves. That means we have to let others take the lead, and we have to work together, even if we have differences that make friendships more difficult. There is a pleasant camaraderie in people who are willing to work together. They create harmony.

As you and your friends, family members, or co-workers spend time together and join forces to work toward a common goal, you will find it is like arranging a melody or song. Rejoice when the harmony of friendship adds a depth and richness to your life and inspires your hopes. Let the melody of friendship play a song in your heart.

Dear Father, bless my relationships with others so that we can work together in harmony. Teach me how to put others above myself. Amen.

First in the Heart

God testified concerning him: "I have found David son of Jesse, a man after my own heart."

—Acts 13:22

In marriages couples who grow older and physically weaker should cling to what grows stronger, such as love for one another, memories of past pleasures, and fulfilled hopes. Your spouse occupies much of your heart and hopefully much or your time. God said David was a man after His own heart. Although David was a sinner, he was thankful to God and saw within himself an unworthiness that God forgave. This caused David to write praises to God, blessing His name. David and God had a great connection, and the Bible makes it clear that our relationship with Him should be our highest priority. If you are married, your marital bond is the second most important relationship. It should take priority over all other relationships, even including the parent-and-child relationship.

William Penn said, "In marriage do thou be wise: prefer the person before money, virtue before beauty, the mind before the body; then thou hast a wife, a friend, a companion, a second self." As you think of ways to please your loved one, you prioritize that person in your heart. Making your spouse a priority makes it easy to praise the virtues, share the hopes, and enjoy the companionship of your spouse.

Dear Father, help me keep You first in my heart and to also prioritize my marriage or other important relationships. Amen.

Living in Harmony

Live self-controlled, upright and godly lives in the present age.

—Titus 2:12

At times our lives will be chaotic, and we will have conflict with those around us. Many of us have a friendship or connection with someone who is difficult, making the relationship a constant struggle. Or we may lash out at others due to stress from a demanding job or another circumstance. These situations can bring about disharmony, but we have some level of control over the peace in our lives. We may not be able to control many things, but we have power over how we treat others and handle our circumstances. No matter what we face in life, Jesus has called us to live in love and harmony. We must focus on helping one another and putting our faith in God so that we do not become overwhelmed by our difficulties. Living in harmony is one way that we honor God and find enjoyment in life.

Many aspects of life are pleasant, and there may be moments that seem too perfect to let slip away. But if they do, you should continue to live a godly and peaceful life. Let your mind capture the beautiful moments you experience. The harmony may not last as you move forward, but you can treasure the memory. Let the anticipation of peace in heaven fill your heart with hope as you work toward harmony today.

Dear God, though harmony may be fleeting, bless me to live a godly life. Amen.

Refresh Your Hope

Satisfy us in the morning with your steadfast love, that we may rejoice and be glad all our days.

—Psalm 90:14 ESV

When your car is unattended for too long, it will likely need a tune up. It is time to give it a little extra care and attention from someone who understands and cares about cars.

If you have neglected spending time with God or have felt isolated from people, you may feel sluggish, may no longer be in tune with your hopes, and may not be performing at your best. Those signs show you might need a tune up too. Psalm 90 masterfully guides the reader to understand the brevity of life. Included in each lifetime are times of struggle and sorrow. But the psalmist understood the power of God to tune up our sad hearts. He did not want to live all of his days in a state of despair. Therefore, the psalmist called on God to bring loving satisfaction so that he could rejoice. When you are distressed, give yourself a break to refresh with God's Word, prayer, and rest. A little extra care for your soul from God is necessary. He loves you and will help you return to a better condition so that you can continue pursuing your hopes.

Dear Father, You are my hope in times of sadness. Bless me with joy when I feel out of tune with my hope. Give me strength to go on. Amen.

Little Pebbles

For though the righteous fall seven times, they rise again.

—Proverbs 24:16

When you stumble and fall, something little probably tripped you like a pebble or a little unevenness in a sidewalk. You rise up and continue on your path, perhaps a little bruised and embarrassed. Sometimes you may also fall spiritually. A little sin, such as a lie, may cause you to fall, but the book of Proverbs reveals that you will rise again. It does not matter the number of times you fall, because if your heart is sincere toward God, you will rise every time. A heart of repentance and your love for God causes you to continue moving forward.

In moving toward a dream, it is the little things that trip you and cause you to stumble. Someone once said, "Nobody trips over mountains. It is the small pebble that causes you to stumble. Pass all the pebbles in your path and you will find you have crossed the mountain." A discouraging word or unfavorable response may make it difficult to press on. You may feel bruised or even humiliated, but you can get up again and persevere. Remember, it is just a little pebble along your journey of reaching your hopes.

Dear God, forgive me when I stumble and fall because of sin. Cleanse my heart and give me strength to continue on my way. Amen.

Slow Growth

The Lord is not slow in keeping his promise, as some understand slowness.

—2 Peter 3:9

Have you ever stood beside a mighty oak tree and stared up at its height or looked at its width and leafy branches? It grew from a tiny acorn. The seed does not even resemble the tree. The little seed took quite a tumble as it dropped to the ground and slid into the dirt. It takes four or five years for an acorn to become a sapling. It continues to push down roots and shoot upward. Spiritual growth can sometimes seem slow too. Day after day, you struggle to reflect the calling that God has placed on your life. God has called you to love, but you have resentments toward someone else. God has called you to give, but you hold back some of your offering for a personal want. These and other marks of failed spirituality persist as you pray and read the Bible for insight to grow past them. Do not give up. The promises in God's Words are true, and in His time, God will give you a growth spurt.

The progress toward your dream might seem slow as well. But continue growing and learning. Let the people you admire, who seem to tower above with their success, be reminders that your hopes can grow and succeed too.

Dear God, when spiritual growth or the fulfillment of dreams slows down, give me patience to wait on You. Amen.

Tenacity

"To the one who is victorious, I will give the right to eat from the tree of life, which is in the paradise of God."

—Revelation 2:7

As a child, Albert Einstein may have seemed like a failure to some people. It took him a long time to learn to speak properly because he had to pause to consider what to say next. He received a rigid Prussian education but felt alienated. One school expelled him for being rebellious. Yet Albert Einstein went on to change the world of physics. He had great tenacity and never gave up.

Every believer who continues in their faith exhibits tenacity and will eventually be victorious. God said He will reward those in heaven who continue in their faith on earth. But there is a need for tenacity in other areas of life as well. When you become discouraged or when you grow tired, then you may want to quit pursuing your dreams. However, you must not stop. Keep exploring ideas and hopes that may take you several steps closer to your dreams. Let the promise of God be the hope that causes you to roll up your sleeves and keep striving to achieve your dreams.

Dear God, when I grow weary and feel like quitting, give me the tenacity to continue so I may fulfill the dreams that You have placed in my heart. Amen.

Include God

"Am I only a God nearby," declares the LORD, "and not a God far away?"

—Jeremiah 23:23

Some destinations seem far away as you drive for hours or even days. The odometer keeps ticking off the miles as you continue. You press on, guided by a map and a desire to reach your journey's end, and you rejoice when you arrive. The distance around the world at the equator is 24,901 miles. If you could drive that distance without stopping at an average of 60 miles an hour, you would return home in approximately 415 hours, or more than 17 days. Many people have set out to accomplish the journey around the world by various means, some with success. However, Amelia Earhart, who famously set out to fly around the world, did not succeed. Her journey ended as she mysteriously disappeared while flying over a body of water.

You may feel like there is no end in sight or that you may crash and burn as you press on toward realizing your dream. God wants you to open up your eyes and see that He is near. Although He resides in heaven, He is aware of all you are doing and wants you to include Him in your journey. So keep pressing forward toward your destination, but keep God close at all times.

Dear God, although the journey seems long and arduous, please stay near me as I continue to reach my goals. Amen.

SEPTEMBER

·•••••••••••••••••••••••••••••

Departing summer hath assumed
An aspect tenderly illumed,
The gentlest look of spring;
That calls from yonder leafy shade
Unfaded, yet prepared to fade,
A timely carolling.

—William Wordsworth

Drop by Drop

Therefore, my beloved brothers, be steadfast, immovable, always abounding in the work of the Lord, knowing that in the Lord your labor is not in vain.

—1 Corinthians 15:58 ESV

Slow, continual dripping of water onto a rock forms holes and caverns. Great underground caves grow over time and fill with amazing formations. Great canyons also grow over time and can be created by water. Located in Arizona, the Grand Canyon is the largest gorge in the United States. It was created by years of water erosion from the Colorado River. Over time the liquid persistently wears away the hard surface of rock. There is a lesson about steadfastness to be gleaned from the Grand Canyon's history. We know that one day we will spend eternity with Jesus Christ, so we should work steadily in what God wants us to do. Similarly, that for which you hope will be realized if you steadily work to accomplish it.

Do you have a busy life and feel there is little time to work toward a dream? Do you have only a few minutes a day to spare? Follow the example of dripping water, and do a little bit each day, working steadily toward the dreams you hope to achieve. Ever so slowly but steadily, your actions could make all the difference.

Dear God, strengthen me to work steadily to accomplish my dreams. Amen.

Lost Hope

"Rejoice with me; I have found my lost sheep."

—Luke 15:6

Have you ever gotten lost and so turned around that you did not know in what direction you were headed? Some people are quite directionally challenged, but thanks to global positioning systems (GPS) there is hope of heading in the right direction and reaching one's destination. Being lost can be serious if you cannot quickly find your way back onto the right path. Jesus told a story about lost sheep, which represented people who were not going to heaven. He said to imagine a shepherd caring for a hundred sheep but losing one of them. The shepherd would leave the ninety-nine sheep so he could find the one that was lost. And when the sheep was found, the shepherd would carry it home, tell all his friends, and celebrate. Jesus wanted you to know that there will be a celebration for every person who repents and goes to heaven. Jesus uses a GPS (God positioning system) to help lost people find their way to heaven.

You may know your eternal destination but still have lost the path to fulfilling your hopes. It may seem that you have had so many twists and turns in life that you are unsure of the direction to head. Prayer can be your God positioning system to help you go in the right direction. Then all you will have to do is keep moving forward, and once you find your way, you can celebrate.

Dear Father, when I lose my hope and cannot go on, reposition me toward Your path again. In Jesus' name I pray, Amen.

The Harvest

Let us not become weary in doing good, for at the proper time we will reap a harvest if we do not give up.

—Galatians 6:9

Do you ever think about how much a farmer works after planting? The seed is planted in the spring. Then the farmer nurtures the soil with fertilizer. Throughout the season, weeds are pulled, and harmful insects are sprayed. Once the plants begin to grow, they are treated for disease, and, of course, the crop is watered as needed. It takes continual observation and work, but the crop produced is worth the effort. The farmer has reaped a bountiful harvest. The food grown is good for the farmer and other people who will eat it. However, what if seeds are planted and the farmer does no work? What if plants are not nurtured or sprayed for insects and disease, and worst of all, the plants are not watered? Then the crop will be anemic, and the harvest will be small.

Similarly, Paul encouraged Christians to nurture their faith and to thirst for the water of eternal life. We are to grow by developing a relationship with God, loving one another, and removing all sins, which attack faith like a disease. If you invest in growing a strong faith in God, you will reap a bountiful harvest in heaven.

Dear God, thank You for the harvest that my faith will bring. Bless me to not grow weary in my efforts. Amen.

Focus on Your Goal

Do you not know that in a race all the runners run, but only one gets the prize? Run in such a way as to get the prize.

—1 Corinthians 9:24

Have you ever walked a five-mile trail or run a long race? If so, you took it one step at a time to reach the goal. You understood that a race requires focus. That is what Paul was trying to emphasize. He believed that you could accomplish anything once you set your mind to it. You prepare to reach your goal by training to develop strength and endurance. If you do not work hard during training runs, then you will probably not do well at the race. Then on the actual race day, you are at the starting line nervously awaiting the sound of the starting gun. When finally it is fired, off you go, running as fast as you can. As you run it may become disheartening when you look ahead and the end is far away and not in sight. However, as you draw closer, you become excited because you can see the finish line. You can reach your goal.

Reaching any goal may look daunting if you think about all the steps that have to be accomplished before the end. The key is to focus. Look at your next step, and take it today.

Dear God, bless me with focus so that I can reach my goal. Amen.

Rising Up

Forget the former things; do not dwell on the past.

—Isaiah 43:18

A fall is simply a misstep. Did you ever think about how rising up from falling is really overcoming the fall? It is a little victory. Just ask Kenyan marathon runner Hyvon Ngetich. Hyvon, who is an elite runner, set out to win a race. Once the race began, she worked her way to the front and was in the lead most of the time. Hyvon was winning. But tragically, something happened that changed that. With just two tenths of a mile left to her goal, Hyvon staggered and fell. She tried to get up but fell down again. This setback did not deter her. Although in a weakened state and with bloodied elbows and knees, she crawled the rest of the way to the finish line.

Hyvon may have fallen that day, but she rose up and still reached the finish line in third place. Though she did not win first place, the victory was in reaching the end. Do you realize that each time you try again or start over, you are taking measures to overcome a potential failure? When you rise above the problem and do not let it keep you down, you score a victory. Choose to continue your quest and believe in yourself and your hopes.

Dear Father, if I fall down while working toward my dreams, help me to rise up again in victory. Amen.

....

You Can

For I can do everything through Christ, who gives me strength.
——Philippians 4:13 NLT

When negative thoughts such as *I can't do it* enter your mind, how do you respond? Hopefully, you shout back, "Yes, I can!" You can overcome negative thinking by putting your hopes in God and His plan for you. He will strengthen you to be positive and will grant you joy. You should also be determined to succeed like the little engine in the story *The Little Engine That Could*. In the story a little train engine decided to do a job that big engines said they could not do. They could not pull a group of train cars over a hill. Although the little engine had to huff and puff, it successfully made it up the hill. It was the engine's positive attitude that helped it achieve its goal.

As you fill your mind with positive thoughts and cheerful mottos, you will find you can counter negative worries and fears. Remember that God believes in your ability and so do many of your loved ones. Merely thinking, *I can do this* is energizing and boosts confidence. Allow positive thoughts to permeate your mind so that you will be inspired to reach your goals. Smile with confidence as you think of achieving your dreams.

Dear God, when I think negative thoughts, help me to think positively and say, "I can." Amen.

Count Your Blessings

Blessed are those whose help is the God of Jacob, whose hope is in the LORD their God.

—Psalm 146:5

You may prefer warm, sunny days to gloomy, rainy ones. But rain nourishes the earth and brings forth green plants and beautiful flowers. Cloudy days also help you appreciate the days when you can bask in the sun. The biography of Johnson Oatman, Jr. does not mention many gloomy days. But he certainly encouraged others to take their cares to God when life had become difficult. As a Methodist minister Johnson wrote more than five thousand hymns, including "Count Your Blessings." The lyrics—"Count your blessings, name them one by one. Count your blessings, see what God hath done"—remind us that when we take our concerns to God, who is Lord over all, we do not have to be worried.

If you are feeling low or are experiencing many gloomy days, it may be time to stop and count your blessings. Remember the people who love you, the steps you have already taken toward a goal, and the beauty that surrounds you in this world. Be thankful for lessons learned from past frustrations. Thank God who sends blessings and is always with you. Trust that God will be with you as you continue your pursuit.

Dear Lord, help me to rise to challenges and continue my pursuit. Thanks for giving me the dream and being with me every step of the way. Amen.

Picking Up Again

Create in me a pure heart, O God, and renew a steadfast spirit within me.

—Psalm 51:10

Some people like to clean their homes or organize things when they feel frustrated. It seems that putting away clutter and removing dust settles their minds and gives them a new perspective, plus a cleaner home. Column writer Heloise has offered many tips for cleaning the home and its contents. For example, you can use bleach and water to remove dirt from grout or use a pipe cleaner to clean the slots in your knife block. These and other hints will make your home sparkle. But what about cleaning what matters most? How can you clean the clutter of sinful thoughts from your mind and heart? King David realized this was a job that was too big for him. He asked God to give him a pure or clean heart and to renew his spirit.

If you feel frustrated about a goal or seem to have lost hope, it might be time for a bit of mind and heart cleaning as well. If you cannot dust away the clutter of stray thoughts and negative comments, ask God to do it. Also, it might be time to write out your thoughts of what is really important beneath the chaos that life sometimes brings. Seek the hidden gems of wisdom among the clutter of life.

Dear God, like You did for David, create in me a clean heart and renew my mind. Amen.

A Passing Shadow

Man is like a breath; his days are like a passing shadow.

—Psalm 144:4 ESV

In long distance running an athlete may feel ready to quit until she suddenly gets a second wind. The breathing evens out, and her muscles work more smoothly as her body finds a new balance or rhythm. As a runner gets tired, slowing down for a little while helps the hormones and body recover. Slowing down also helps the runner to enjoy the sights and sounds around her. If she does not take that opportunity, she may miss something special. Life is like a race that passes very quickly because we are so busy. In the book of James, the writer said your life is "a mist that appears for a little while and then vanishes" (James 4:14). So we should take every opportunity to enjoy it, or it will seemingly fly away like "a passing shadow" (Psalm 144:4 ESV).

So slow down and catch your breath. You may need a second wind for your hopes. If you are feeling weary at pursuing your dream, it may be time to take things easier and enjoy your life. Slow your pace, and let your mind and body recover. When you bounce back, live each day like it is your last. Do not let life pass you by.

Dear God, slow me down when the days pass too quickly or I become weary. Help me to enjoy my days while I can. Amen.

Imaginative Thinking

For we are God's handiwork, created in Christ Jesus to do good works, which God prepared in advance for us to do.

—Ephesians 2:10

D r. Seuss thought outside the box. His book *Oh, the Thinks You Can Think* celebrates imagination. It encourages children to use their imagination to dream the impossible and includes the idea to think left and right, and high and low. Thinking is the process of putting ideas together to form thoughts. Unique thoughts produce creativity. Not everyone can think creatively, but creative thinking can be learned. Just like you can teach a person to draw or to paint, you can teach someone to think creatively. Creative thinking requires that you use your imagination, which is a gift from God to every human being. God, through His own imagination, created people. And God created people "to do good works" (Ephesians 2:10).

People take different approaches to developing thoughts. Some may think more analytically, and some may think more emotionally. Some may think in words and some in images. At times it is good to brainstorm and think in the opposite way of how you normally think. To help you develop in new ways, consider other people's unique ideas. You might also want to brainstorm and reflect on new ideas, even if they seem outrageous. Remember that using your imagination may help you achieve your goals in a new way.

Dear Lord, help me think creatively and open my mind to new thoughts. Amen.

Eternal Thoughts

But our citizenship is in heaven.

—Philippians 3:20

Have you thought about spiritual things lately? Do you reflect on eternity or heaven? Tragedy and death remind us that we should seek eternal hope. Our eternal hope is heaven where all believers have citizenship status. A country is made up of citizens. The country's government makes laws that protect the rights and privileges of its people, but it also makes demands. Heaven is not like that. Although heaven is a kingdom, it is not like any government on earth. In heaven Jesus will reign throughout eternity, and His kingdom is ruled by love and peace. Citizens of heaven will not have burdensome obligations. Instead, it will be a place of "no mores"—no more tears, no more pain, and no more sorrow (Revelation 21:4).

The Bible is filled with eternal thoughts and draws your mind to look forward to things beyond this world. Let such thoughts lift you above tragedy to see that life is more than you can sense or imagine. Let those thoughts help you see that today's problems are temporary, and there will be many good things to come. Let the thought of heaven be your greatest hope.

Dear God, thank You for heaven. Heaven is my real home. It is the place where I am a citizen. I look forward to spending eternity with Jesus there. In Your name I pray, Amen.

Transformed Thinking

Be made new in the attitude of your minds.

—Ephesians 4:23

Have you ever succumbed to the marketing strategy of a shopping show or ever rushed out to buy the newest fad, even though the purchase was not a wise decision? Sometimes we allow ourselves to be impressionable to commercialism. We act similar to silly putty that quickly picks up an image when pressed against it. The Bible tells us not to conform to the pattern of the world (Romans 12:2). As Christians we should be something different. Even though we live among worldly desires and temptations, God does not want us to be influenced by them. However, being different is not easy. We want to be liked, and we want some of what the world has to offer, whether good or bad. If we allow Him, the Holy Spirit will guide and strengthen us to do what is right. Choosing not to conform is a part of the growth process. We must choose to renew our minds so that day-by-day we become transformed while we are in the midst of this world.

Sometimes it helps to break away from the crowd and change your thinking. It might help to read the Bible, for it aligns with good and lofty thoughts and gives hope that will outlast all the latest styles.

Dear God, strengthen me to choose that which does not conform to the world. Help me to renew my mind. Amen.

Look Deeper

There is nothing concealed that will not be disclosed, or hidden that will not be made known.

—Luke 12:2

Snorkeling and scuba diving give people the opportunity to see beneath the surface of the ocean with its amazing array of sea life swimming about. Most people know about the life in the first two zones of the ocean. The first zone is where the water meets land, and the second zone is the upper sunlit area of the ocean. But they make up only a small portion of the ocean. The largest area of the ocean has a depth of approximately eleven thousand miles and is dark and cold. Few people have explored this part. The video *The Blue Planet: Seas of Life* reveals that a greater number of people have traveled to space than have been to the bottom of the ocean realm. However, exploration continues, and scientists hope to explore more of the deep and dark secrets of the ocean.

Looking deeper is an important quality in exploring your dreams too. It helps you see benefits of your goals that are hidden beneath the surface. When you discover something important, it raises your hopes and inspires you to achieve what might have seemed impossible. Let the intangible and hidden benefits motivate you even more to pursue your hopes.

Dear God, help me to discover what is hidden in the depths of my heart and my dreams. Amen.

Kindling a Fire

Study to shew thyself approved unto God, a workman that needeth not to be ashamed, rightly dividing the word of truth.

—2 Timothy 2:15 KJV

Have you watched how a flame flickers and shoots up high as it burns wood? It continues to burn as long as wood and oxygen are supplied. Your mind must also have fuel so that it will burn brightly. The fuel that keeps your mind burning is knowledge, and the way to obtain knowledge is to study. Studying keeps our minds stimulated and vibrant so that we can think and speak well. In the book of 2 Timothy, we are encouraged to diligently study so that we can correctly handle God's Word. Our knowledge benefits those to whom we share the truth. Therefore, one must consistently and earnestly study the Word of God.

When you are seeking to fulfill your dreams, it helps to fuel your mind. Let solid facts and ideas be like a match that sparks your thinking. When you examine and question ideas, you put your mind to work just as a fire that continues to burn. Ideas with no substance will burn away quickly, but the real truths will burn continuously, triggering good reasoning and kindling your imagination. Therefore, you should study to fuel your mind and spark new hopes.

Dear Father, my hope is to be approved by You and to reach my dreams. Bless me with all I need to study. Amen.

Blessings of Life

Always giving thanks to God the Father for everything, in the name of our Lord Jesus Christ.

—Ephesians 5:20

Breathing is natural and usually done without thinking or assistance. Enjoy a deep breath, and be thankful for your life. You did not give yourself life, nor have you placed breath within your body. God blessed you with life and gave you oxygen to breathe, and He has blessed you with so much more. Because of this, you should be continually thankful. Marcus Aurelius said, "What then remaineth but to enjoy thy life in a course and coherence of good actions?" As a child of God, blessing after blessing continues to follow you because of God's love for you and the fellowship you have with other believers. We then have the responsibility to use these blessings to do good toward others.

Your blessings include the ability to think, to be creative, to have faith, and to enjoy life. It is also a blessing to have hopes and dreams. Starting the day with gratitude for blessings by giving thanks to God through prayer reminds you of your privileges and the benefits in your life. Let gratitude for your blessings, hopes, and aspirations inspire you to take the next little step toward reaching your dreams.

Dear God my Father, thank You for all the blessings in my life. I will continually praise You for all that You do and all You provide. Amen.

Walk in the Spirit

Walk by the Spirit, and you will not gratify the desires of the flesh.
—Galatians 5:16

What happens when you let your mind wander? Do you think about a favorite book or television show, or do you worry or let jealous thoughts consume your mind? Do you know that you can choose what to reflect on and what to push out of your mind? However, it requires discipline, and discipline comes from allowing the Spirit to guide your thoughts and your actions. This is called walking in the Spirit. If you are a believer who does not walk in the Spirit, your life will not be a picture of godliness, the main character trait of a Christian. You know you are walking in the Spirit if your life produces fruit. The book of Galatians reveals the fruit of the Spirit to be "love, joy, peace, forbearance, kindness, goodness, faithfulness, gentleness and self-control" (Galatians 5:22–23).

If you want to walk in the Spirit but struggle to have positive thoughts, then think of things that are pure, good, virtuous, and lovely (Philippians 4:8). Allow the Holy Spirit to fill your mind with beauty and love, and it will be easier to make good choices and find hope.

Dear God my Father, thank You for Your Spirit that lives within me and for the thoughts that fill me with hope. Bless me to walk in the Spirit for the rest of my days. In Jesus' name I pray, Amen.

Troubleshooting

The leaves of the tree are for the healing of the nations.

—Revelation 22:2

How do you find solutions to a problem or keep from repeating mistakes? It is best to first understand what went wrong, and then try a new approach. When Adam and Eve ate fruit from the Tree of the Knowledge of Good and Evil, God's creation and all humanity became marred by sin. The world and its inhabitants were broken. But God had His own method of troubleshooting. Because humanity disobeyed, He had a plan of redemption—forgiving sins by the blood of the Lamb. Throughout the ages God's plan of redemption has been at work, and one day it will culminate in heaven. In heaven everything will be made new. No longer will there be a Tree of the Knowledge of Good and Evil. Instead, there will be a tree with special leaves for preserving health and life, and there will not be the possibility of sin.

If there is a problem in your life, it might be time to troubleshoot to find the source of the issue. Then you will know what to avoid the next time you are in this situation. Your hopes will grow as you discover new ways to overcome problems. But your greatest joy will come from knowing that our problems are temporary and will not exist in heaven.

Dear God, when I have a problem, bless me with a solution that will keep me on the path to realizing my dreams. Amen.

Hopeful Mindset

Therefore, as God's chosen people, holy and dearly loved, clothe
yourselves with compassion, kindness, humility, gentleness and patience.
—Colossians 3:12

You wake to a new day and new choices every morning. Besides grabbing a cup of java or a shower to help you wake up, how else do you prepare for your day? Do you give thanks for life and blessings with morning devotions? Or do you fret over worries? It is your choice to decide what to do. Choosing between worrying or spending time in a devotional study is not a difficult decision. Beginning the day with worry may create anxiety that lasts throughout the day. Beginning the day with a Bible study will be as if you are clothing yourself "with compassion, kindness, humility, gentleness and patience" (Colossians 3:12). Devotions are tools that you use when you meet with God. In this morning encounter, you connect to God by reflecting on Scripture, praying, and listening for His voice. God speaks to you by a still, small voice or through His Word. Your devotional time will ensure a hopeful mind-set throughout the day.

Choosing joyful thoughts by having a devotional time each morning, rather than reflecting on the worries of your life, could inspire a happier and more hopeful attitude all day. Choose to spend time with the Lord so that your hope can be renewed each morning.

Dear God, bless me with a hopeful mind-set every morning as I connect with You through devotions. Amen.

Your Story

Come and hear, all you who fear God; let me tell you what he has done for me.

—Psalm 66:16

What is your story? What has inspired, changed, or shaped your life? What struggles have you overcome? Reflect on how telling your story could inspire someone else. To share your story, begin by writing down an outline of the major events of your life. What was your life like before you became a Christian? In particular, write down your challenges and your emotional state. Then write about your encounter with Christ. What events led up to the moment you became a Christian? Where were you? Why did you choose to follow Christ? Be sure to write about how you felt in that moment. Finally, write about how Christ has changed your life and the joys you are now experiencing. Once you have finished writing your story, be ready to share it with others.

As you think about your life, and particularly your struggles, you may discover new lessons you learned. Your story is part of your legacy and can bring hope to listeners. Sharing how God has used your life and changed you is a powerful witness of your faith. Your story will especially bring hope to people who are struggling with similar problems that you have dealt with and overcome.

Dear Lord, help me to see how my life matters, and help me to share my story with people who need hope. Amen.

Analytical Thoughts

Examine yourselves to see whether you are in the faith; test yourselves.
—2 Corinthians 13:5

Do you play strategy games like chess? Do you work on solving Sudoku or crossword puzzles? Do you read and discuss books, or do you debate ideas with friends? Such skills keep your mind sharp and help you to develop analytical thinking. Analysis is the systematic dissection of components for closer study or examination. This skill is useful for discovering what needs improvement. The Bible encourages its readers to do self-examinations. We should routinely ask ourselves questions such as these: In what ways do you love your brothers and sisters? Are you consistently obeying God? How does the Spirit testify that you are a child of God? These questions and others will help us to keep our faith strong and alive. The exercise will also strengthen your analytical thinking skills.

Critical thinking helps you to make decisions and evaluate experiences. Investing a few moments in this type of thinking also stirs ideas that help you reach goals and realize hopes. It might be time to add a little analytical activity to your day to fuel your mind, stir your imagination, and continue lifelong learning. Work on a puzzle, or call a friend and start a good discussion. It may stimulate your thinking.

Dear God, thank You for analytical thinking skills. Bless me to strengthen my faith and my hope through careful analysis of myself and my dreams. Amen.

A Memory's Influence

See what great love the Father has lavished on us, that we should be called children of God!

—1 John 3:1

Smiling and thinking happy thoughts actually lifts a person's spirits. Studies have found that you can make yourself happy just by thinking about good things. Recall a joke or happy memory, and then allow your memories to influence your outlook. The apostle John, who was Jesus' beloved disciple, had happy memories that influenced his outlook. He spent three years in a close friendship with Jesus. John was chosen, along with Peter and his brother, James, to be a part of the inner circle of Jesus. This privilege allowed him to be a witness to some of Jesus' most outstanding miracles and events, such as the prayer of Christ at Gethsemane (Matthew 26:36–48). John's writings revealed an outlook that had been touched by his memories of Christ. With great faith and hope he was able to convey the love of God because of his experiences.

Remember your happiest moments and what made them special. It may not have been about possessions or success. It could have been a friendship just like John's. But whatever your memory is, allow it to influence your outlook. It will give you a positive attitude about your hopes, and you will be encouraged to achieve your dreams.

Dear God, thank You for memories, especially those that keep my outlook positive and strengthen my hope. Amen.

Captive Thoughts

We take captive every thought to make it obedient to Christ.

—2 Corinthians 10:5

Have you ever tried to diet, but could not stop thinking about chocolates or other treats? Did you give in to the temptation or overcome it with other thoughts, like an image of yourself in a new outfit? It is much easier to stay on a path of dieting if you replace your thoughts about foods with motivational thoughts and images. Our minds can be a kind of battleground as we continually wage war against thoughts that tempt us to veer off our chosen paths. The influences in the world cause some of those thoughts. Noises made by advertisements, the media, and even influential people, such as politicians and celebrities, clamor for our attention. But the apostle Paul said we can win over these influences by taking our thoughts captive. We do this by turning away from these influences and submitting our thoughts to God in prayer.

For whatever goal you have set, write down some encouraging thoughts or Bible verses that will keep your eyes on the goal and off temptations. Think of the hopes tied to your goals and the results you want. Displaying these inspiring thoughts will help you take captive every thought and stay on the path to success.

Dear Lord, I choose to submit every thought to You so that I will not lose my way to my goals. Amen.

Unexpected Thoughts

For the word of God is alive and active.

Have you had a new idea pop into your mind lately? You may not know where it came from, but if you liked the notion of it, you may have considered the idea on occasion. Do you write down these ideas in order to remember them and perhaps put them into action? The Word of the Lord, which is the Holy Bible, was written by God through men who followed the Holy Spirit's leading. Amazingly, the Bible was written by many people through thousands of years, yet its themes and truths are consistent. John Locke said, "The thoughts that come often unsought, and, as it were, drop into the mind, are commonly the most valuable of any we have." John Locke's words are a good description of the way the Bible was written.

Unexpected thoughts are often the best ones and may keep you excited for days. They may come when you are relaxed or after you puzzled over a problem. These thoughts may also open your mind to new hopes and ideas that help you to realize a dream. Rejoice at unexpected thoughts, and share them with a friend.

Dear God, help me to pay attention to these unexpected thoughts so that I might take another step toward my dream. Above all else, help me to heed the thoughts that are recorded in Your Word. Amen.

Reading for Renewal

Oh, how I love your law! I meditate on it all day long.

—Psalm 119:97

What have you read lately? Have you read any Bible passages? Reading opens your mind to ideas. Reading something uplifting helps you to experience new thoughts in your imagination, so you can renew your thinking. Reading the Bible keeps you focused and strong. Consider using a Bible reading plan, or just pick up the Bible and read daily. Many people rely on second-hand knowledge in books about the Bible. Although they are useful, they fall short in connecting you with God personally. David said he loved God's Law, which was all that had been written of the Bible to that point. Like David, we should develop a love for reading the Bible and other books as well.

Maybe it is time to take a trip to the library to spark your hopes. Or try reading Psalms. The lyrics of each psalm will give you a fresh look at the world and all God has made. Reading will inspire you when you realize that others have experienced the same struggles or pondered the same thoughts that you have. It will also encourage you to carry on during your most discouraging moments. Make reading an important part of your life, and view it as an opportunity for you to grow and strive toward your hopes.

Dear God, thank You for Your Word that gives me hope. Amen.

Kindred Spirits

So in Christ Jesus you are all children of God through faith.

—Galatians 3:26

As an orphan, Anne Shirley, the title character in the book *Anne of Green Gables*, longed for a friend who would be united with her by having a close bond. She dreamed of a friendship and time spent cherishing one another. She finally found the love and friendship that she sought in brother and sister Marilla and Matthew Cuthbert, who adopted Anne. Although Marilla and Matthew were middle-aged adults, they connected with Anne and soon grew to love her. Anne referred to Matthew as a kindred spirit because of his openheartedness toward her. A sense of belonging and acceptance is important to all of us.

As a child of God, there are many others who call God their Father. By faith they are kindred spirits in Christ. A kindred spirit shares hopes and dreams with enthusiasm. Do you have someone in your life who is a kindred spirit and truly understands you? As Anne grew up, she found more kindred spirits, people who wanted to dream and share their innermost selves. Seek a kindred spirit who will support your hopes and whose hopes you can encourage.

Dear God, thank You for the kindred spirits who are my brothers and sisters in Christ. Bless me to discover those who will connect with me as friends. Amen.

Thriving Mind

When the righteous thrive, the people rejoice.

—Proverbs 29:2

God wants you to thrive. The word *thrive* means to flourish or make progress. As a matter of fact, God wants all of His children to flourish, and when they do, there is rejoicing and celebrating among friends and family because of their success. But what does it take to be a person who thrives? One positive thought is all a person needs to overcome hardships and strive toward one's dreams. Positive thoughts can cause negative thoughts to vanish, just as light has power over darkness. And by relying on our faith in God, we can find security in His plan for us. Although life will not always go as we planned or hoped, we can cling to our hopes and think of God's goodness as inspiration to press forward.

Have you let your mind dwell on a positive thought? It is amazing how a new idea or hope can lift your spirits and fill your mind with pleasure. As you mull over the positive thought, you will let go of worries and negative thoughts. Let positive thoughts take root, and watch how they will bring growth. Knowing God's love is the most powerful of positive thoughts—hope in Him will help you thrive in following His ways.

Dear God, bless me to think positively so I can thrive. Amen.

Worry Less

Cast all your anxiety on him because he cares for you.

—1 Peter 5:7

Some people believe there is nothing wrong with worrying. They believe worry to be a thought process similar to reflection or meditation. However, for years medical doctors have expounded on the detrimental medical issues that result from worry. They contend that during the waking hours, a worrier is subject to panic attacks, and at night, a lack of sleep. Worrying can impact your daily life so much that you cannot function. One's lifestyle is interrupted as worry can cause overeating, use of tobacco, drugs, and alcohol. The doctors' major concerns are that worry can cause physical illness such as heart attack, high blood pressure, and other problems. These changes and conditions will impact your hopes and dreams as progress toward fulfilling them is thwarted.

The apostle Peter encouraged his readers to get rid of worry altogether by casting their cares on Jesus. If you hold on to worries, then you do not trust God enough to care for you. But God is your hope, and He really does care. He is able to make your life succeed, including your work, your relationships, and especially your dreams. So spend your days on accomplishing your plans and worry less. If worry breaks through, let it go by casting your concerns on Jesus.

Dear God, I give You my worries and concerns. Thank You for caring enough to take them. Amen.

Unexpected

"God is not human, that he should lie."

—Numbers 23:19

When you pray, do you tell God what to do and how to solve a problem or fulfill a hope? He loves you and knows more than you. God the Father is not a human. He does not have a body made of flesh and blood. And although God has a spirit like man, He is unlike us because He is sinless, so He cannot lie or make mistakes. Therefore, let Him take control, and talk with Him in prayer about your situation. Do not be like Ananias and his wife, Sapphira, who did not trust God. Following the ascension of Jesus, the church was made up of people at various economic levels. Many of the rich sold their land and gave the money to the apostles to be divided among the poor. Ananias and Sapphira decided to sell their land too, but they kept some of the money for themselves. They did not trust God, so they missed His blessings. It is better to let God have control and let Him surprise you with His unexpected blessings.

Andrew Murray once said, "Beware, in your prayer, above everything, of limiting God, not only by unbelief, but by fancying that you know what He can do. Expect unexpected things, above all that we ask or think." Be ready to let God shower you with surprises you never dreamed could happen.

Dear God, You are my God. Therefore, I trust You and look forward to wonderful blessings. Amen.

H.O.P.E.

"For God so loved the world that he gave his one and only Son,
that whoever believes in him shall not perish but have eternal life."
—John 3:16

Some prisoners, many with life sentences, have found a new purpose and a new reason to have hope. They have found the joy of sharing their faith, and they use *hope* as an acrostic for "Helping Other People Eternally." These prisoners share with other inmates about the joy of the future freedom they have because of God's love and about the hope they have that will last forever in heaven.

Most of us are not prisoners, but we can share the hope we have with others. Our hope is the hope of salvation. It is a promise that we are given when we first believe in God's Son, Jesus Christ. This hope is not to be kept to ourselves. It is God's desire that no person should perish but that all be saved (2 Peter 3:9). Therefore, reach out to others and talk to them about your eternal hope. And when things become increasingly difficult, let your mind dwell on your lasting future with God. Let not your heart be troubled, but let it trust in God and the freedom in Christ you always have because of your eternal hope.

Dear Father, thank You for the gift of eternal life. Lead me to share this hope with others. Amen.

Gems of Hope

"They will be my treasured possession."

—Malachi 3:17

There is the story of a hare that lived in the forest with his many friends. One day the hare was chased by a ferocious dog. The hare ran as fast as he could, but the dog was steadily gaining ground. The hare happened upon several friends as he ran, and he asked them for help. But none of his friends took time to help. They said they were too busy and used various excuses. The hare's friend, the bull, said his wife was waiting for him on the river bank. The horse said he was looking for his lost child in the forest. When the hare met his friends the buffalo, the zebra, and other animals, they all said they were busy too. The hare had to save himself.

A good friend will treat you like a treasure. If you find a rough edge on a treasure or a chip broken off, would you toss it out? No, you would try to repair the treasure. In the same way, we should try to help our friends whenever they are in need. God said we are treasures. Therefore, we should treat others as such. Your friends and loved ones are your treasures, like precious gems. If you feel the prick of an unkind word or action, such as the hare received, choose to smooth out the problem with forgiveness. After all, these are the relationships that bring hope to your life.

Dear God, thank You for friends who are my treasured possession. Amen.

OCTOBER

•••••••••••••••••••••

I'm so glad I live in a world where there are Octobers.

—L. M. Montgomery

Let God

Let your eyes look straight ahead; fix your gaze directly before you.
—Proverbs 4:25

It is difficult to let go of worries and not fixate on a problem, especially money issues and relationships. It is natural to dwell on the difficulty and try to figure out a solution. When we dwell on our issues or even on distractions, we give those things power and control over us. It is a power that belongs to only one person, and that person is God. Giving God control over everything that troubles you requires focus. The writer of Proverbs wrote that you should look straight ahead and fix your gaze in front of you. Making God your focus means that you trust Him to walk with you. Now it is time to take that trust in God one step further by taking your hands off your worries. Sometimes the answer is not in your control anyway, so letting go may be all that you can do.

You can choose to give the problem to God and to let go of worry. Thankfully, God is bigger than your worst problem, and He knows what is best for you. He also knows the perfect time to answer prayers. Listen to God's whispered answer, and place your hope in Him.

Dear Lord, help me to give my problems and worries to You. I cannot solve everything, and I want to trust You to help me. I know that You are in charge. Amen.

Let Go of Selfishness

Do nothing out of selfish ambition or vain conceit. Rather, in humility value others above yourselves.

—Philippians 2:3

Days and hours slip away quickly. Do not let a day pass without adding a little joy and hope to someone's life. Just think of the last time someone extended kindness to you. Was it a hug from a friend? Was it a kind word from a perfectly timed phone call? Do you know that God wants you to extend the same kindness to others that has been extended to you? What a privilege to love others through kindness, because in doing so, you are expressing the love of God. So do not procrastinate; tomorrow is not promised. Let go of selfishness today. A popular Quaker saying encourages this sentiment: "I shall pass through this world but once. Any good, therefore, that I can do or any kindness that I can show to any human being, let me do it now. Let me not defer or neglect it, for I shall not pass this way again."

Your little smile, friendly phone call, or helping hands may only take a few minutes, but it can make a great difference to the recipient. Choosing to make the most of your moments will bless others. The hope you offer in your actions may be just what someone needs.

Dear God, fill me with love so I can let go of selfishness and be kind to others. Amen.

Stubborn Stains

In all your ways submit to him, and he will make your paths straight.
—Proverbs 3:6

You may have used several methods and products, plus a great amount of scrubbing, to remove a stubborn stain. The key to removing a stain is to identify the type. Blood and sweat stains can be removed by rubbing a little salt into it. Stains like coffee, tea, grass, or something sticky can be removed with vinegar or lemon juice. Placing a stained item immediately in water reduces the effect of the spot. You may also favor a company that understands the quality and textures of different fabrics, so you trust their cleaning products. These are just a few examples of stain removal techniques, but they are reminders that some problems take extra effort to work out.

Like stubborn stains, your problems may require outside help. God wants to be that help. He understands you and your flaws. Submit the issue to Him, and watch Him take control. God will straighten anything that has gone awry. He can take care of the most stubborn issue. He wants to help because He is a God who cares for you and because He is able to make your paths straight. Just ask God to remove your blemishes in faith, and hope that it will make life easier and help you continue the path to your goals.

Dear God, thank You for reminding me that I can trust you to remove stubborn problems. Amen.

Building Bridges

"And besides all this, between us and you a great chasm has been set in place."

—Luke 16:26

Bridges span ravines and rivers to join land and make it possible to travel across rivers and valleys. They may be long suspension bridges, semi-circular stone arches, or even simple beams like a log across a brook. Some are engineering feats of wonder. The Golden Gate Bridge is one of those bridges and covers a chasm that separates people.

Have you noticed how negative emotions cause large gaps that separate people and destroy hopes? Take time to build a bridge to be reunited with those whom you have hurt. Do not wait until it is too late, like the rich man in one of Jesus' stories. In the story, a beggar named Lazarus sat outside of the rich man's home, begging for food. But the rich man did not provide any help. Soon they both died. The rich man, who was now in Hades, called up to Lazarus to relieve him of his agony. But there was a chasm between them that no one could cross. After death there is no option to build bridges. The rich man's actions while he was alive should teach us a lesson on how we should not treat others, especially those who are less fortunate. If hurt has created a chasm between you and someone else, build a bridge with love and forgiveness.

Dear God, help me to build a bridge of love when a chasm separates me from those I love. Amen.

The Key of Forgiveness

"I will give you the keys of the kingdom of heaven."

—Matthew 16:19

Corrie ten Boom and her family bravely aided Jews during the Holocaust. Eventually, a Dutch informant found out about the family's assisting the Jews and told the Nazis about the family's work. The family's house was soon raided, and they were captured and sent to prison camps. Corrie and her sister Betsie were sent to Ravensbrück, which was one of the most notorious concentration camps near Berlin. Although she was greatly mistreated, she never saw her parents again, and her sister became ill and died in Ravensbrück, Corrie forgave her captors. She wrote many books about the power of forgiveness to eradicate hatred and to unlock the door of love and acceptance.

You may have locked someone out of your heart because of pain, resentment, or anger. Forgiveness is the key that will help you unlock the door to let the person back in to your heart and life. Forgiveness opens your heart to free you from your pain and focus on hope again. When we choose to love and forgive, we are opening the door to the kingdom of heaven. Continue to show others the ways of the kingdom so that they can learn how to forgive rather than keep their hearts locked in hatred or isolation.

Dear God, thank You for forgiving me. May I use that same key to restore relationships in my life. Amen.

Words of Hope

Get rid of all bitterness, rage and anger, brawling and slander, along with every form of malice.

—Ephesians 4:31

The words you speak, like hope, begin in your heart. A hopeful person speaks with gentleness and love. A hopeless person often spews out cutting and angry comments or criticism. During his missionary travels, the apostle Paul tried to remedy this type of behavior. He traveled throughout Syria, Asia, and other places establishing churches and teaching Christian principles. Much of what he taught centered on helping the people to overcome attitudes of hatred and disunity. Many were new Christians who needed to understand that the way they lived and talked before Christ was not the way they should live and talk after following Christ. Paul taught that they needed to get rid of this behavior. He believed there was little hope exhibited in using hurtful and disrespectful words. Paul's lessons are important for us today.

Take time to evaluate your faith and your hope. Do you hear hurtful words, gossip, or profanity that reveal anger or little regard for God? Or are your words laced with joy, praise, and trust? If so, your hope in God is strong. Always be aware of your words, and let your words and hope match up.

Dear Father, bless my words so that people receive hope rather than hate. In Jesus' name I pray, Amen.

More and Less

A happy heart makes the face cheerful, but heartache crushes the spirit.

—Proverbs 15:13

Think of friends who always seem happy and cheerful. Did those people remember your birthday, express thanks for your actions, or overlook your faults? Happier people tend to appreciate everyone around them and forgive more easily. These actions are meaningful to people and make the bonds of friendship stronger. When you are happy, you are easy to be around as well. Your happiness is like a magnet that attracts others and causes them to appreciate you. They also want the same happiness that you have so their closeness could be their way of learning from you. However, if you are a person who forgets special days, then you cause heartache as expectations are crushed and hopes are dashed.

Think about being a "more and less" person. Choose to forgive more, and choose to be less self-absorbed. Remember to value others by giving compliments, thanking them, and spending time with them. As you cheer friends on and rejoice with them, you will find you are happier. In letting go of yourself to focus more on others, you will share hope. You will build more friendships with people who will cheer you on.

Dear Lord, please help me to be a "more and less" person, more forgiving and less forgetful. Help me to spread hope rather than heartache. Amen.

Forgiven

*Here is a trustworthy saying that deserves full acceptance: Christ
Jesus came into the world to save sinners—of whom I am the worst.*
—1 Timothy 1:15

What is the worst thing you have ever done? God forgives the worst sins, so He can forgive you for your
actions, if you ask for His forgiveness. Everyone is forgiv-
able. If God forgave Paul, then He will certainly forgive you.
Before Paul became a missionary who followed Christ, he
persecuted Christians. When Paul did this, he thought he
was doing a good service for God. Not only did Paul perse-
cute Christians, he also caused the death of many believers
and watched and approved the stoning of the devout deacon
Stephen (Acts 7:54–58; 22:19–20). But Jesus showed Paul
that he could be forgiven of the worst sins when He called
Paul to spread the Good News.

Just as God forgives us, we should forgive others. Some
pain cuts so deep that it is difficult to forgive. Some evil is so
cruel and heartless that it eats away at you and wipes away your
hope. God asks you to let go of the poison of holding on to
grudges and the wrongs done to you by others, so He can wipe
away your pain and restore your hope. Open your heart and
let God help you forgive what seems unforgivable.

Dear God, thank You for forgiving me of even the worst things I have ever done.
Amen.

Let Go of Cares

"Do not worry about your life, what you will eat or drink; or about your body, what you will wear."

—Matthew 6:25

Sprinkle each day with beauty to hold on to your sense of wonder. Jesus taught that worldly cares can easily overwhelm you, while something beautiful touches your heart and mind with hope. Therefore, He said you should not worry about your life, not even about your food and clothes. Jesus understood that anxiety is an enemy of the soul and heart. Plus your concerns are things that He promised to take care of and provide. Just let go of cares and enjoy your life. Writer Johann Wolfgang von Goethe said, "One ought, every day at least, to hear a little song, read a good poem, see a fine picture, and if it were possible, to speak a few reasonable words."

Indulging yourself each day with art, music, or nature will lift your spirits and bring your heart back to hopeful thoughts. You may want to fill a wall with pictures and sayings that reflect beauty to touch your soul, a place to pause and reflect throughout each day. Letting go of your cares will improve your health and strengthen your faith in God.

Dear God, my Father, thank You for the beauty of Your creation that is all around me. Help me to worry less and reflect more on Your wonders through art, music, and nature. Amen.

Smiles of Hope

Therefore my heart is glad and my tongue rejoices; my body also will rest secure.

—Psalm 16:9

Expressions of happiness such as smiles, grins, giggles, laughter, and chuckles bring more of the same. They are contagious expressions. Just give it a try by doing this experiment: take a walk in a park or a public place, and flash a smile at everyone you meet. The majority will return a smile; some will even stop to talk. Those who continue on their way without returning any acknowledgement will one day regretfully remember their response to you that day. And there are also those who exchange anger for your smile. When they do, smile anyway. Do not allow angry people to dictate how you feel.

So smile even through pain or trouble. Have you ever laughed or grinned at a mistake you made? Laughter makes it easier to try again, hoping you will get it right and acknowledging that mistakes happen. Joy relaxes you and triggers helpful endorphins that relieve stress. Choose to take life less seriously by looking for the bright side, especially of the absurdity of a situation or result. A smile is a gift that opens your heart to hope in spite of difficulties. As you laugh, you have the power to lighten up and move forward with your hope.

Dear God, help me to take life less seriously so that I can smile and laugh, spreading love, joy, and hope. Amen.

Aging with Hope

Therefore we do not lose heart. Though outwardly we are wasting away, yet inwardly we are being renewed day by day.

—2 Corinthians 4:16

The effects of aging are identified at an exponential rate the longer a person lives. You may notice a few wrinkles and the color of your hair changing. Your eyes may also dim, and joints may not be as flexible. But if you hold on to hope as you age, you choose to enjoy your days and make the most of your years. Paul awakened all believers to the reality that growing older and your body's deterioration is a part of life. However, Paul said it should not make any difference in the way you feel inside. As a matter of fact, your heart, your soul, and your spirit should be changing but for the better as you grow older in the Lord.

Age comes with the gift of experience and a lifetime of stories of overcoming problems. Faith in yourself and your abilities, even when you grow older, should stay alive and keep hope alive. Life continues, so it helps to laugh at your past mistakes, rejoice in successes, and lean on your experiences to build new hopes. Each day is a gift from God to continue pursuing hopes, even if you move a little slower.

Dear God, although I am getting older, thank You that my spirit is being renewed. Amen.

Hope Blooms

"Consider how the wild flowers grow. They do not labor or spin. Yet I tell you, not even Solomon in all his splendor was dressed like one of these."

—Luke 12:27

The wind blows gently on a field of flowers, and the blooms bob up and down, as though dancing and giggling with joy. It is a beautiful scene of light and color that overwhelms your senses and causes you to overflow with joy. You see with your own eyes that God's creation reflects Him and then reaches back to Him in praise. When a flower grows, it begins as a seed that forms roots, then produces a seedling, and then grows a stem. And from a stem grows leaves and then a beautiful bloom. According to the gospel of Luke, there is nothing on earth that can compare to the beauty of a flower.

A gift of fragrant flowers brings smiles and lightens a heart. They grow and bloom to fill the world with color for a little while. Their seeds reveal the promise of more joyful blooms in the future. God created a wide variety of flora that reflects a world created with great imagination. Flowers keep growing and blooming as reminders that new seeds of hope can be planted and grow too. Plant a packet of flower seeds today, and as they sprout and grow, may your hopes grow too.

Dear Father, thank You for the beauty of flowers that bloom and for the hope that they inspire. Amen.

Recycled Hope

How can a young person stay on the path of purity? By living according to your word.

—Psalm 119:9

One look at your calendar is a reminder that life is short yet full. You work, play, strive for goals, and leave a legacy. Hopefully your legacy will touch young lives. Today's youth have many struggles that we may not have experienced. The cost of higher education has skyrocketed, making it almost impossible to afford an education. Most everything on television is about sex, crime, and greed, making it difficult for youth to get a proper perspective on reality. And some youth are being caught up in alcohol and drugs as they hang with questionable characters who take advantage of the inexperience of youth. Only God's Word can sustain the heart and mind of a young person. When you share your Christian experiences and God's Word with them, you can influence them to keep their path pure.

Touching lives of young people brings hope to them. You make room for their dreams as you listen, encourage, and share your wisdom. Your time on earth is short, but it can impact many people. Consider your purpose and hopes, and think of ways to share them with a younger person who shares similar interests. You will pass on your passion as you interact with youth.

Dear Father, bless me to leave a legacy of hope for youth and others to encourage to stay on a path that leads to You. Amen.

Cheerful Heart

Remember Jesus Christ, raised from the dead, descended from David. This is my gospel.

—2 Timothy 2:8

The difference between hope and despair often lies within the heart. Your heart influences your thinking and attitude. Grief and pain tear a person up from the inside out, but a cheerful heart is open to healing. If you feel pain or sorrow today, it may be time to reflect on past joys or listen to some wholesome jokes. Better than that, it may be time to take your relationship with Christ to the next level. God did not intend for His children to keep the marvelous gift of salvation to themselves. It was intended that you share this gift with others. In sharing you not only offer the hope of salvation to people who need it but you also lift and cheer your own heart as well.

Do you have someone you can call who always sounds cheerful and can remind you of your hope in Jesus Christ? If so, give that person a call and listen to your cheerleader. Become a cheerleader, too, who looks for hope when trouble comes and remembers that Jesus Christ died for the whole world. This is the gospel that God wants you to share. This is the blessing that cheers hearts.

Dear God, when I am feeling sorrow, help me to remember the joy of my salvation. Amen.

Blissful Marriage

Husbands, love your wives, just as Christ loved the church and gave himself up for her.

—Ephesians 5:25

At one couple's wedding the little flower girl cut into their first dance and everyone laughed, including the bride and groom. The couple continued laughing throughout their long, blissful marriage. The Bible offers sound advice for husbands and wives. For example, in the book of Ephesians, wives are advised to respect their husbands, and husbands are advised to love their wives. The advice is sound and will strengthen the home as well as the bond of marriage. Friendship in marriage will also help to make your marriage healthy and blissful. As friends, you dwell on those things that you have in common while supporting each other in spite of differences. Friendship undergirds the promise to love and trust.

So strengthen the friendship that is between you and your spouse and become laugh-mates. Whether you giggle or share belly laughs, your laughter lessens stress and keeps your marriage on a more joyful note. Humor keeps fun and playfulness in your marriage. Joy creates a loving and happy atmosphere in your home. As a couple, look for the lighter side of situations to laugh and find hope together.

Dear God, bless the spouse you have given to me. May our marriage be blissful all the days of our lives. Amen.

Joy Returns

Weeping may stay for the night, but rejoicing comes in the morning.
—Psalm 30:5

Life is not all laughter and joy. Sorrow visits every heart, but there is also hope that joy will return after each tragedy passes. You can make that hope a reality, especially when the sorrow is brought on by your own doing. Sometimes the desires of our hearts are not part of God's will or plan for us. For example, God may want you to teach women in Thailand, but you decide to go to China and set up a food business. When we step outside of God's will, He will discipline us until we return. His discipline may cause weeping but only for a while. Then because of His love, joy will come back in the morning.

You have experienced various other forms of sorrow such as loss, pain, or trauma. You may have responded to each trial differently as you have worked through different stages of grief. Some hurt more than others. But just as robins return in the spring and flowers grow and bloom again, so, too, your heart will heal and find joy again. Let good memories, new memories, and gratitude for past blessings add to your healing. Let your heart be open to comfort and healing.

Dear Lord, thank You for joy that returns after I have experienced any type of sorrow. Amen.

Lasting Joy

I bring you good news that will cause great joy for all the people.
—Luke 2:10

An unexpected gift or perfect dinner while dining out may make you feel happy. It is temporary but pleasant. A lasting joy, however, gives you peace even within bad circumstances. God gave us a lasting joy when Jesus was born. Jesus is the hope of humanity. When people understand why He came, they are filled with peace and joy that can only come from God. The world cannot offer this kind of joy because it only offers temporary happiness. You may be happy because of an achievement or because you have finally been able to purchase a possession that you wanted for a long time. But once the initial impact is over, then the happiness is gone.

.God wants you to have joy so much that He made it a fruit of the Holy Spirit that grows within your heart, and God wants your joy to last. Joy flows from your relationship with God. If you hope for more joy in your life, spend time with God by reading the Bible, praying, and singing praises. Delight in planting seeds that produce the fruit of joy.

Dear God, thank You for the lasting joy I have in my heart because of Jesus. Help me to do what is necessary to cause my joy to grow more and more. Amen.

Overcoming the Fear of Laughter

"Be strong and courageous. Do not be afraid or terrified because of them, for the LORD your God goes with you; he will never leave you nor forsake you."

—Deuteronomy 31:6

Have you been embarrassed and then felt hurt when people have laughed at you? Has fear of being laughed at stopped you from pursuing a dream? There is nothing in this world that should cause you to stop hoping and working toward your dream. This is a decision you must make from the start. If you find that something or someone has sidelined you or created within you a fear of failure, remember who is with you to help you to succeed. Just be "strong and courageous" and trust Him to guide you (Deuteronomy 31:6).

No one can control opinions and reactions of other people, but you can choose how you will respond when someone laughs at your mistakes. You can laugh, too, or focus on your hopes on God and ignore the snickers. Real friends prefer to laugh with you and will feel sorry if they hurt your feelings. Let laughter strengthen your resolve and help you to push forward with your hopes.

Dear Lord, give me courage to continue to chase my hopes without fear of people laughing. Help me to trust that I will laugh with joy as my dreams come true. Amen.

Echoes of Joy

Glory in his holy name; let the hearts of those who seek the LORD rejoice.

—Psalm 105:3

Have you ever been someplace where you could yell and hear your words echo, such as between buildings or in a cave? Sound waves hit a large solid surface and bounce off, reflecting the original noise to create echoes. It is like a wave rippling across an ocean. In some places the sound ricochets against more than one surface and the echoes continue. Have you tried creating an echo with laughter instead of shouting? It sounds like many people laughing over and over again. Laughing echoes vibrate and continue for a while, filling the open space with the sound. It is an amazing feat of science.

Similarly, the presence of God in your life echoes in your heart. Joseph Marmion said, "Joy is the echo of God's life within us." When you live with the hope of eternal life, you reflect that life to others and show them lasting hope. Even more so when you seek the Lord, you reflect not only eternal life but His glory. Although God lives in your heart, He wants you to continue to seek Him on a daily basis. This causes the echoes of joy within your heart to bring glory to God.

Dear God, bless my life to echo joy so that it will be a reflection of your glory. Amen.

Choosing Joy

Now choose life, so that you and your children may live.
—Deuteronomy 30:19

Cancer patients may react to chemotherapy with a light-hearted response such as this: "I just got back my superman strength when they zapped me with kryptonite again." It is a reaction that brings laughter and hope. Actor Patrick Swayze never gave up hope and remained optimistic while he was battling pancreatic cancer. Although he was ill, he continued to work in acting roles and encouraged other cancer patients. He also raised money for cancer research and said that he dreamed of a world where cancer was cured. Choosing joy or life strengthens your ability to continue to live viably in spite of a disease like cancer. Patrick Swayze chose joy rather than sadness and defeat. He chose life even though his body was racked with pain.

The joyful attitude of someone who laughs, even when it appears life is ending, reveals a special joy like the eternal joy from Jesus that heals the soul. Holding on to hope that feeds your soul is beneficial as you look beyond pain and unfortunate circumstances. Choosing joy is a Christian response that brings hope when the world seems hopeless.

Dear Father, strengthen me, if the time comes when my body is suffering from disease, to choose joy and life. Amen.

Never Too Busy

A time to weep and a time to laugh, a time to mourn and a time to dance.

—Ecclesiastes 3:4

There should always be time to laugh and appreciate life. Days without laughter could mean you are too busy. Busyness is caused by saying yes to too many requests of your time and by being overambitious. Busyness can be draining and stressful, so it is time to stop the busyness. Set your priorities, and make a decision to say no before you are asked to do something. Saying no will not cause a natural disaster. The sun will still shine every day. Then slow down. Rome was not built in a day, and your dreams will become a reality when logically anticipated. Take care of yourself. You cannot drive a car if the tank is empty, nor can your body and soul function without fuel.

Let laughter be your test for busyness. A proverb says, "If you are too busy to laugh, you are too busy." Fueling your life with laughter recharges your body and spirit. You may want to keep a list of what makes you laugh or place funny sayings and pictures on your refrigerator. At the end of the day, reflect on absurd happenings and amusing comments; then you will find reasons to chuckle. Let laughter bring enjoyment and the hope of more laughs.

Dear God, help me to overcome busyness so I will have time to laugh. Amen.

Have Fun

Do not get drunk on wine, which leads to debauchery. Instead, be filled with the Spirit.

—Ephesians 5:18

Developing a good sense of humor and adding wit to words changes the atmosphere from dull to fun or from being tense to relaxing. As Christians we sometimes act like we are not allowed to have a good time, but God wants us to find enjoyment in life. Still, we should use discretion on how we spend our time. We should not act like people who do not know Christ. Their fun has no boundaries or restraints. Many times their atmospheres are charged with darkness and animosity as people use drugs and alcohol to fuel enjoyment. The Bible reveals this could lead to "debauchery," which means the senses are overindulged. This type of enjoyment often leads to addiction. Paul advised that instead of this type of behavior, you should be filled with the Spirit. With the Spirit in control, the fun glorifies God as it should.

Fun has many benefits. Do you still recall nursery rhymes such as "One, Two, Buckle my Shoe" or other educational rhymes? They show how playfulness benefits learning. Fun also refreshes you so that you can work on making your dreams come true.

Dear God, help me to find the joy in the fun that pleases You and strengthens my hope. Amen.

Unexpected Laughter

God has brought me laughter, and everyone who hears about this will laugh with me.

—Genesis 21:6

Sarah and Abraham's son was born when they were in their old age. They named him Isaac, meaning laughter. When they thought all hope of having a baby was gone, God surprised them and gave them a son. Sarah understood God's power, but she did not expect God's best. She laughed because, like the rest of the world, she was caught up in what she could see. But God's gift changed what she believed God would do for her. Her faith in Him became so strong that she used her life as a testimony so that others would join in with her laughter. Her life also let people know that God is a God who can do the impossible. All we have to do is allow Him to handle those things for which we hope.

So let us join in with Sarah, laughing because of God's goodness. Sarah erased her past disappointments when she laughed at herself. The first laugh was a snicker of unbelief, but that soon turned to joy. It is good to celebrate unexpected news that holds hope and joy. When something happens that seems illogical or unbelievable, laugh with hope, and rejoice that God can do the impossible in your life too.

Dear God, I believe you can do the impossible. Help me to believe you can make change in my life. Amen.

Blessings of Laughter

Our mouths were filled with laughter, our tongues with songs of joy.
—Psalm 126:2

What great blessings has God given you? What great things have you seen Him do? The answers to these questions are reasons to laugh and share hope with others. The book of Psalms records songs that were sung as the Israelites ascended the Jerusalem hill to worship God. The writings are called the Songs of Ascent. God's people had many reasons to worship God. He had done great things for them, both collectively and for different individuals. The Bible is filled with stories about God's favor that rested on His Hebrew people, from healings to provisions to conquering powerful enemies. They are stories that the Israelites have passed down from one generation to the next. They are stories filled with laughter, blessings, and hope. And all who hear them will worship God for His goodness.

You have a story too. Your story of how God has worked in your life is a blessing to share. Your testimony should fill you with joy each time you tell it, as you recall how God blessed you and did something surprisingly wonderful. Your story is a unique gift. Share your story today with someone, and do it with joy, laughter, and the hope that it will inspire their faith.

Dear God, thank You for the way You have blessed my life. I choose to share it with laughter and joy so that others will be blessed too. Amen.

Seeing Results

"But as for you, be strong and do not give up, for your work will be rewarded."

—2 Chronicles 15:7

Have you ever gotten so tired that you did not think you could do one more thing or that you could stay awake one more minute? You may have taken a deep breath or rested a few minutes and then continued on because you had to complete the task. You overcame the desire to quit. The Israelites had a desire to build a temple for God, but it was a long process. It took forty-six years for the temple of God to be built (John 2:20). The temple began with David, who first desired to build the temple, and although he was not the one to build it, it staggered the imagination with its magnificence. Among other stately features, its walls and floor were overlaid with gold, and there was a great celebration at its completion.

Have you invested a lot into a hope or dream and not seen results yet? Do you wonder if it is time to give up, time to invest a little more effort, or almost time for things to work out? The choice should be not to give up. Seeing your work to its completion will be a reward in itself. As you check your passion to continue, pray for wisdom, and focus on taking one more step forward.

Dear God, when I grow weary from working on my goal, and I am unsure if I will ever see results, help me to take one more step. Amen.

Tough Options

*"They will say to the mountains, 'Fall on us!' and to the hills,
'Cover us!'"*

—Luke 23:30

In 1917 mine workers in Arizona found themselves in a tight spot. Lack of funds for mining meant low pay for the work, but refusing to work meant poverty. This led to the phrase "between a rock and a hard place." The Bible talks about these dire moments too. When the soldiers led Jesus away to be crucified, He predicted a time when the struggles of life would be even worse than that moment. He saw a group of women who followed Him, weeping and mourning because of His suffering. He told them not to weep for Him. He said, "For if people do these things when the tree is green, what will happen when it is dry?" (Luke 23:31). Many believe that Jesus was speaking of the destruction of Jerusalem or possibly the Great Tribulation. In either event, the suffering would be so severe that women would call out for the mountains and hills to fall on them.

Harriet Beecher Stowe said, "When you get into a tight place and everything goes against you, till it seems as if you couldn't hold on a minute longer, never give up then, for that's just the place and time that the tide'll turn." Do all your options seem difficult? Think about new options. Allow your eyes and mind to find a new way.

Dear God, refresh my hope when I become stuck between a rock and a hard place. Amen.

Determination

I have fought the good fight, I have finished the race, I have kept the faith.

—2 Timothy 4:7

Johannes Gutenberg invented the printing press. He was met with many challenges, most of which were financial. To begin his print business, he borrowed money from a backer. But because he could not pay back the money, Gutenberg was sued. Gutenberg continued to work, and he eventually printed what became known as his masterpiece, a forty-two-line Bible called the Gutenberg Bible. It took determination to invent special ink, find an economical source of paper, create metal type in large quantities, and adapt the press used for making wine to printing. He persevered to fulfill his dream.

The apostle Paul had determination too. Through many struggles and near death experiences, he was able to tell Timothy that he had successfully done what God had called him to do. He had shared the Gospel to both Jews and Gentiles and throughout many cities. He kept his faith in God, even during incredible suffering. Paul's dream was to live faithfully to God, which he did from his conversion until death. What dream are you determined to fulfill? Have you considered all the steps needed to work toward fulfilling your dream and persevere, even when times get rough? Let your hope be important enough to push you on to complete the journey.

Dear God, bless me with determination to finish what I have started. Amen.

Be Your Best

And whatever you do, whether in word or deed, do it all in the name of the Lord Jesus.

—Colossians 3:17

The following is the last stanza of a poem written by Douglas Malloch:

> If you can't be a highway then just be a trail,
> If you can't be the sun be a star;
> It isn't by size that you win or you fail—
> Be the best of whatever you are!

"Be the best" is a slogan used by many organizations, including schools and military groups. Their purpose is of a competitive nature, encouraging a winning attitude. But Malloch had something different in mind when he wrote his poem. He championed those who could not win, encouraging them to be the best they could be anyway. Paul, on the other hand, taught that it did not matter whether you were winning or losing, the best or not, but he said to do whatever you do for the Lord. Our significance is found in our relationship with God and the work we dedicate to Him.

As you assess your abilities and talents, consider the best way to use them. Choose to be the best you can be for the glory of God. Look for opportunities to use your skills all in the name of Christ.

Dear God, thank You for the talents You have given me. Help me to use them for You. Amen.

Strengthened to Hope

You wearied yourself by such going about, but you would not say, "It is hopeless." You found renewal of your strength, and so you did not faint.

—Isaiah 57:10

Have you ever woken up feeling weary? Some days it may seem difficult to keep going or to renew your strength. The Israelites wearied themselves but not in the way you would think. They chose to rebel against God by worshiping the idols of foreign gods. They wearied themselves trying to find strength to continue in their perverse ways. They deceived themselves into thinking that what they had and were doing was accepted by God, but it was not. God waited for them to say that what they were looking for was hopeless. God wanted to strengthen their hope in Him.

If you are weary, first make sure it is not because you have been drawn away from your hope. Then think about developing a morning routine that strengthens you and helps you overcome the weariness. It may be good to evaluate your morning routine and add a few activities that invigorate you. A morning Bible devotion can renew your spirit. A walk or a few stretches and walking in place can renew your body. Healthy food can stimulate your mind and nourish you. With a great start, you will be ready to say, "I'm full of hope."

Dear God, strengthen me to remain true to my hope, and when I grow weary, strengthen my hope. Amen.

Future Hope

"And now, O Lord, for what do I wait? My hope is in you."

—Psalm 39:7 ESV

John Quincy Adams, who was the sixth president of the United States, was an opponent of slavery. The family into which he was born did not own slaves, and while his father's views on slavery were neutral, his mother did not support slavery. Although Adams sat through peace negotiations and many political meetings as president, he did not fight substantially against slavery until he was out of office. His patience usually worked in his favor to realize his dreams. For some of his hopes, like his desire to end slavery, he did what he could during his lifetime. He charged the next generation to continue the dream, predicting that slavery would either be abolished by civil war or by the consent of southern leaders. Adams believed it would be a slow process, saying, "Patience and perseverance have a magical effect before which difficulties disappear and obstacles vanish."

Can you wait for the right moment or for circumstances to turn in your favor? As you slow down and wait, you have time to focus on your hopes and understand why it is worth waiting. As you patiently endure, continue hoping for future blessings and believe time will make a difference.

Dear Father, help me to wait patiently for my hopes and dreams to come true. Amen.

Always Possible

"For nothing will be impossible with God."

—Luke 1:37 ESV

Do you think about possibilities along with your hopes? Optimists continue to faithfully believe everything is possible. The inventor of the masking tape, Richard Drew, was an optimist. He believed his product could meet a need. In the 1920s auto body workers used a heavy abrasive tape and butcher paper to mask parts of the car that did not need painting. However, because of the abrasiveness of the tape, some of the paint was removed along with the tape. Drew saw that they needed something less adhesive. After numerous attempts, he overcame impossible odds to develop the right glue. Although his employer, 3M, gave up on him, Drew never gave up and accomplished the impossible.

When one's hopes have been shattered, whether through a tragedy or if someone lets you down, remember that God is still with you and wants you to keep hoping. You may need to transform the dream or challenge yourself to overcome a problem. An optimistic attitude lets you sweep away hopelessness to find new ideas and new ways to realize your hopes. Through prayer and trust in God's abilities, you open up your heart and mind to listening to God. His ideas can make your seemingly impossible hope become a reality.

Dear God, help me to never give up on the possibility that my hopes can be realized through You. Amen.

NOVEMBER

•••••••••••••••••••••••••••••

*Even if something is left undone, everyone must
take time to sit still and watch the leaves turn.*

—Elizabeth Bury Lawrence

Inspired by Miracles

Your wife Elizabeth will bear you a son, and you are to call him John.

—Luke 1:13

Do you know people blessed with a miracle? Stories of unexpected healings are reminders that nothing is hopeless or impossible for God. Many miracles are recorded in the Bible, such as the birth of John the Baptist. John the Baptist's father, Zechariah, was a priest, but he still had trouble believing in a miracle. He laughed when the angel Gabriel foretold the birth of John. Because of his unbelief, the angel silenced Zechariah, and he could not speak until his baby was born.

Elizabeth, who had given up her dream of having a child, believed and received a miracle in her old age. She gave birth to her son, John the Baptist. John had a special calling on his life. He was filled with the Holy Spirit while in his mother's womb and served as the one who prepared the way for Jesus. God's miracle for Elizabeth came at the perfect time. Thank God for the miracles He has done, and let them inspire you to believe in your own miracle and your hopes.

Dear God, thank You for the miracles that are written in Your holy Word, and thank You for the inspiration I receive because of them. Bless me to believe in Your ability to perform miracles in my life. Amen.

Blessed Assurance

"On the third day he will be raised to life!"

—Matthew 20:19

After Peter and John saw Jesus speak on a mountaintop, heal many who were sick, feed thousands of people with two fish and five loaves of bread, and other miracles, Jesus told them that He would be handed over to the Sanhedrin, put to death, and rise on the third day. He mentioned His upcoming suffering and death to His close disciples, but they did not fully understand at the time. When Jesus did die, they felt hopeless and forgot about His promise until they saw Him alive again. Jesus' resurrection was the hope of not only His disciples but for all humanity. Peter and John, along with the other disciples, carried this message of hope to others. It was the assurance for the eternal life that the world needed.

God knows your future and all the conditions you will face. Some of those harsh conditions can destroy your dream. Trust that He can resurrect your dreams, even after you suffer your worst nightmares. Just have faith that God is able to do the impossible. Faith is the assurance of things hoped for (Hebrews 11:1). Rely on the assurance that God will help you to fulfill the dreams that He has placed in your heart.

Dear God, thank You for the assurance that You are able to do the impossible to help me to fulfill my dreams. Amen.

Hope Through Seeking

"You will seek me and find me when you seek me with all your heart."
—Jeremiah 29:13

A part of human nature is to have desires and seek something better for your future. How you respond to difficulties and problems reveals whether or not you still have hope. When you encounter an issue, keep seeking a solution. Seeking something better is a common theme throughout the Scriptures. God wants you to seek Him. Pursuing God shows you need Him and want what He has to offer. God told the prophet Jeremiah to tell the Israelites if they sought Him with their whole hearts, He would be found. This is essentially what Jesus told His disciples when He was teaching them to pray. He said, "Ask and it will be given to you; seek and you will find; knock and the door will be opened to you" (Matthew 7:7). Jesus knew that life would be difficult, so He wanted His disciples, and believers today, to persist in seeking God for help and for solutions.

When you cry out in pain, you are seeking something better and hoping for solutions. Your prayers for answers show that you are seeking God's help. God moves your heart to pray because He wants to answer you. God does not think you are hopeless. Persist in seeking Him, and wait for His blessings.

Dear God, help me to remain persistent in seeking You for the solutions to my problems. Amen.

The Meaning of Hope

But if we hope for what we do not yet have, we wait for it patiently.
—Romans 8:25

Some people believe the word *hope* means wishful thinking, such as hoping to receive a gift on a birthday or Christmas. But the word also means to expect something. It is a word that implies you are confident that your desire will come true. This is the kind of hope that is identified in the Bible. It is clearly exemplified in the Christian's expectation of the coming of Christ. We all wait expectantly for Christ to return for those who call Him Lord. Just like children who are sitting on the front porch on a hot summer day and waiting for the ice cream truck to turn onto their street, we hope for Jesus to return.

Think about the hopes that have already been realized and about all the blessings you have already received. Your past experiences can cause you to believe in new hopes. Journaling in a prayer diary and noting the answers to your prayers builds a strong testimony of faithful answers to fulfilled hopes. Have you received answers to your prayers lately? Have they encouraged you to pray bigger prayers and inspired bigger hopes? As you pray each day, observe how God responds. As you record your prayers, let God's responses build your confidence in Him.

Dear Father, I pray that my hopes will become real. Help me to wait expectantly. In Jesus' name I pray, Amen.

A Little More

"My food," said Jesus, "is to do the will of him who sent me and to finish his work."

—John 4:34

Have you ever been part of a fund-raising campaign that uses a chart to show its progress? It builds up little by little until the goal is reached. The line on the chart that records the progress of the campaign continues to climb and inspires everyone to keep working. Many churches use this type of chart during a fund-raising campaign. Or they may use a picture of a thermometer, marking off their progress in degrees. The key to success is the efforts of the members of the church who must donate time and work to raise money to meet the financial goal of the campaign. They must work consistently, making an effort every day to ensure the success of the campaign so the goal will be reached. While Jesus was on earth, He made an effort every day to accomplish the work that God sent Him to do.

A little more effort each day adds to the total progress to bring success. What seemed impossible is reachable, one coin or one step at a time. Rejoice over every little effort and know that little steps lead to victory.

Dear God, bless the little more work that I do to be successful. May each step lead me to accomplish the work needed to do Your will. Amen.

Wisdom to Hope

Instruct the wise and they will be wiser still; teach the righteous and they will add to their learning.

—Proverbs 9:9

Sorrow can turn to hope when there is persistence and growth. Medical researcher Louis Pasteur studied germ theory to find ways to overcome illnesses. He did not give up or consider himself hopeless when a brain stroke left him partially paralyzed in 1868. More than a decade later, he developed the vaccine to fight rabies. He also developed the process of pasteurization and helped save the silk industry, proving microbes were attacking healthy silk worms. Pasteur also developed vaccines for anthrax, chicken cholera (today called Pasteurella), and tuberculosis. He learned from studying germs and experimenting and became wiser in spite of sorrow.

What have you learned from experience and failure? Do you spend time gaining wisdom from your experiences? Take advantage of every opportunity to learn and grow, even through sorrowful experiences. Although the experience may be difficult, you will gain wisdom and knowledge. When you apply the wisdom of your lessons to new efforts, you will continue to reach your goals and have a better chance for success.

Dear God, help me to overcome sorrows so that I may gain wisdom and knowledge that can be applied to dreams. Amen.

Even More Possibilities

And we know that God causes everything to work together for the good of those who love God and are called according to his purpose for them.

—Romans 8:28 NLT

Do you ever feel like you have run out of options? You have tried everything you can think of to find a new job, get a new look, or simply figure out a new direction for your life. You have listened to your friends, read books, and even taken some more college courses, but nothing seems to open a new door. Can you really be out of possibilities? Do not despair. God may be using these situations to instruct you and move you to another place. Some of your experiences may not be good, yet none of them will ever be lost. Every difficulty has a purpose when you are a child of God and are fulfilling His purpose for your life.

You may see an end to your hope, but God sees it as an opportunity to create a new look or create a change in your life. His direction and design may not look familiar to you when He is done, but He will use your hope to make something more wonderful than you could have ever imagined. You can trust in the designer of all your hopes and your possibilities.

Dear God, sometimes things do not work out the way that I hoped, causing me to face difficulties. Thank You that You can make even my worst days work for my good. Amen.

Restoration

When Naomi realized that Ruth was determined to go with her, she stopped urging her.

—Ruth 1:18

Naomi was a woman in the Bible who lost her husband, money, and sons. As a destitute woman she had no hope. She told her daughters-in-law to leave and return to their homes with the hope that they might find new husbands. But Ruth refused to leave Naomi. Ruth told her mother-in-law, "Where you go I will go, and where you stay I will stay. Your people will be my people and your God my God. Where you die I will die, and there I will be buried" (Ruth 1:16–17). So Naomi stopped insisting that Ruth leave her. Then both women returned to Naomi's home. Ruth worked to help them survive by gleaning in fields for food and listening to Naomi's advice. God soon blessed Ruth with a husband and a child, giving both women a new family and new hope. Her child was an ancestor of Christ, who became the hope of the world.

God restores lives and dreams. In times of great loss and grief, our hope is not crushed. Just trust that God has a plan to help you in your time of need.

Dear Lord, I am thankful that You are able to restore my heart and give me new and better hopes. Bless me with hope today. Amen.

Broken Bread

While they were eating, Jesus took bread, and when he had given thanks, he broke it and gave it to his disciples, saying, "Take it; this is my body."

—Mark 14:22

On more than one occasion Jesus took bread, prayed, broke the bread, and fed a crowd of people. One occasion was the miracle of feeding the crowds with fish and loaves. On another occasion, He also took bread, broke it, and gave it to His disciples as a symbol of His broken body. This instance was symbolic because Jesus also knew that Judas Iscariot would betray Him, and then His body would be beaten, broken, and hung on the cross for us. Three days later Jesus rose from the grave so that we could have eternal life. His brokenness is our salvation.

God uses brokenness to reveal His glory. When Paul suffered from some form of affliction, He asked God to remove it from his life. But God said, "My grace is sufficient for you, for my power is made perfect in weakness" (2 Corinthians 12:9). We are not perfect, but God will use our imperfections to point to His perfect grace and love. Give God what is broken in your life and pray that He will use the brokenness to bring great hope.

Dear God, I have been broken so many times and in so many ways. Use my brokenness to bless others with hope. Amen.

Be Compassionate

Therefore, as God's chosen people, holy and dearly loved, clothe yourselves with compassion, kindness, humility, gentleness and patience.

—Colossians 3:12

Laughter and smiles transform a face. When you see others looking sad, you may ask what is wrong and try to respond with hope, a funny story, or cheerful words to lift their spirits. An act of compassion is not a lost art, but it may not be as prevalent as it once was. The culture and times have caused people to be leery of others. When once a person could receive help from strangers, today the misdeeds of others have caused innocent people to suffer rather than accept help from strangers or watch someone suffer rather than extend compassion.

Sometimes you have to take a chance and be different by being the compassionate person God has called you to be. Compassionate people ease the pain of those who are suffering. You may send cards or flowers and pray when someone you love suffers. That is showing compassion. And you have probably received sympathy and tokens of love when you have suffered. That is also compassion. Compassionate people are people God uses in our lives to give us hope.

Dear God, give me a compassionate heart so that I can be used by You to transform the lives of others. Amen.

Known by God

For you created my inmost being; you knit me together in my mother's womb.

—Psalm 139:13

God's love holds the power to change you from the inside out. It is a transforming power to make you brand new. God will not change you against your will, because God gave you free will. We are the only creatures on earth God has made who can say that we are not going to do something that He has asked us to do. He made us that way because He wants us to freely love Him back. If we refuse to love God, He will continue to love us and will remind us about His perfect ways.

God chose to create you and love you before your birth. He put you together while your mother was carrying you. He has placed part of Himself in every person, so He knows all about you and relates to you. He responds to your prayers and wants to help you to change for the better. When we accept His love, we learn more about Him and reflect His love and goodness. Then others will see His Spirit within us and will be drawn to His love. They, too, will learn that God knows them and has loved them since before they were born.

Dear God, thank You for creating me with such care. Help me to be transformed by Your love. Amen.

Stone Soup

Carry each other's burdens, and in this way you will fulfill the law of Christ.

—Galatians 6:2

The child's story *Stone Soup* shows how curiosity caused selfish people to give. In the story, weary travelers stopped in a town with an empty pot, but the villagers were unwilling to share their food with them. So on the outside of town, the travelers filled their pot with water, placed a stone in it, and put the pot over a campfire. One villager after another came by to inquire about what the travelers were doing. The travelers said they were cooking, but it was not quite ready. The villagers then each brought a food item to help build the soup. They created a bountiful celebration through sharing. The clever travelers used innovative thinking and kindness to get the people to help them, rather than responding to the villagers' selfishness with anger or disappointment. The travelers hoped for the response that they received.

Have you noticed how kindness encircles people with love and brings out the best in others? Have you seen it trigger reactions of hope where one smile elicits another smile? Have you responded to the blessing of kindness by being kinder? Start a chain reaction with a kind deed, and in doing so, you will fulfill Christ's command to love one another.

Dear Lord, bless me to be a blessing to others who need love, care, and kindness. Amen.

Good Cheer

*In the world ye shall have tribulation: but be of good cheer; I have
overcome the world.*

—John 16:33 KJV

Several times in the gospels, Jesus used the phrase, "Be of
good cheer." Some translations use "take heart" or "take
courage," but the sentiment is the same: Jesus is our hope in
troubling times. He wants us to be of good cheer. In verse 33
of John 16, Jesus offered His disciples peace. He was telling
them that He was going to leave the world, but He would send
the Comforter, the Holy Spirit, to them. Jesus knew that a
short while later Judas would come and betray Him. He knew
that He would be tortured and executed, yet He wanted His
disciples to have peace. He warned them that they would have
troubles in the world too, but He said, "Be of good cheer"
(John 16:33 KJV). Jesus knew they could have peace and be of
good cheer because of what He was about to experience. It was
the victory He had come to give the world.

Jesus showed us that He was willing to die so that we could
be of good cheer. He wanted to respond to people's needs with
forgiveness, healing, and encouragement. He knows you will
have troubles, but you can overcome them just as you have
overcome other problems. He understands the importance
of a positive attitude and the cheerful news of eternal hope.

Dear God, help me to accept the offer of Jesus to have peace and be of good
cheer. Amen.

Think Freely

All things are lawful unto me, but all things are not expedient.
—1 Corinthians 6:12 KJV

Our sense of style causes us to consider certain colors as clashing. Yet whole groups have used unusual color combinations as their peculiar symbol. For example, the Red Hat Society members don red hats and purple dresses to transform thinking about life after turning fifty. Today the organization is open to women of all ages. Their primary purpose is bonding and interaction among women. The purple and red began when founder Sue Ellen Cooper gave her friend a birthday gift of a red hat and poem that said to wear purple and red. It was an unconventional combination from a freethinking mind.

The apostle Paul was a freethinker, too, who believed that it was okay to be unconventional or without boundaries as long as you did not offend others or break God's laws. Therefore, choose to remove boundaries from your mind. Enjoy being a freethinker. Leo Tolstoy said, "Freethinkers are those who are willing to use their minds without prejudice and without fearing to understand things that clash with their own customs, privileges, or beliefs. This state of mind is not common, but it is essential for right thinking."

Dear God, thank You for a mind to think freely, so I can pave new paths to hope. Amen.

The Little Things Count

Religion that is pure and undefiled before God, the Father, is this: to visit orphans and widows in their affliction, and to keep oneself unstained from the world.

—James 1:27 ESV

Your smile, simple words, and consistent support do more than bring a single moment of joy. Caring for loved ones with meals, yard work, or laundry shows faithfulness and gives them hope that you will continue to support them. It is the little things that matter in the lives of others. You may not think it is much, but for someone who has none, a pair of shoes means a lot. There are many other needs that have not been fulfilled too. The homeless need shelter, jobs, and food, and the elderly need friendship and support. In biblical times, orphans and widows were often mistreated and taken advantage of. James explained that true religion is helping those who are oppressed and in need. A small gesture can produce hope.

Think today about all the times when some small gesture from a friend or family member made a big difference in your day or added to the hope that you carried in your heart. You do not have to make a grand gesture to give someone else hope. You simply have to offer a bit of kindness, which is a small gift of joy, and hope will blossom.

Dear God, guide me to the ones to whom I can share kindness and give hope today. Amen.

Tiny Miracles

The sun rises and the sun sets, and hurries back to where it rises.

—Ecclesiastes 1:5

The ocean carries broken pieces of glass and tosses them with the waves. These shards of glass are from broken bottles and possibly even shipwrecks. It may take twenty, thirty, or even fifty years, but eventually the water removes the sharp edges and polishes each piece until it is smooth. These pieces of glass wash up on shores where artists and children collect them and use them to create jewelry or other art pieces. The miracle of repurposing the broken glass shards continually happens, but we often do not consider the remarkable journey of the glass. Similarly, our lives are filled with miracles that often go unnoticed. Consider the birth of a baby, the rising and setting of the sun, the blooming of flowers, the flight of a bumblebee with tiny wings, and many more. These tiny miracles continue to happen every day. Without them the world would be a dull place to live.

Have you noticed little miracles that continue to happen in nature and life? If you have not, try opening up your eyes to see beyond the mundane parts of life. Note how lifeforms came into existence, where elements such as rain and snow come from, and what substances an animal like a jellyfish are made of. Also, reflect on the miracles that have happened in your own life, and hope for more miracles to be revealed in your day.

Dear God, thank You for the tiny miracles in my life. Amen.

Words of Hope

Do not let any unwholesome talk come out of your mouths.
—Ephesians 4:29

For many centuries people have looked up at the sky and called it the heavens, but many others also call it space. The word *heaven* holds so much more promise and hope than a word like *space*. *Heaven* produces feelings of wonder, optimism, and peace. The word reminds you of God and your eternal home. It is the place where angels live and where Jesus sits on a throne at the right hand of God. *Space*, on the other hand, reminds you of television shows like *Star Trek* and *Lost in Space*. Although space is a star-filled, beautiful sight for gazing, the word does not offer the kind of hope that the word *heaven* does.

Have you sometimes felt at a loss for words when you wanted to encourage someone, or have you felt that you chose the wrong words? Word choice is important. It could mean the difference between heaven and space. But it is easy to stumble and give the wrong impression, especially when you are trying to cheer up someone. Pause and think before you speak, and ask yourself, *would these words transform someone's gloom or give them hope?* Carefully choose words of hope.

Dear Lord, help me say the right words to bring joy and encouragement to people. Help me hold my tongue from being critical and rephrase thoughts to be hopeful and kind. Amen.

Joyful Example

Set an example for the believers in speech, in conduct, in love, in faith and in purity.

—1 Timothy 4:12

Do you know someone who is always kind, calm, and patient? Does that person inspire you to be more cheerful and kind? This may also be the person who generously hugs people when they need it and usually finds a reason to be thankful each day. In the book *Little Women*, the principle character, Jo, is reminded that her father set a good example. She is told, "Your father, Jo. He never loses patience, never doubts or complains, but always hopes, and works and waits so cheerfully that one is ashamed to do otherwise before him." This is in sharp contrast to Jo's personality, which was strong and willful. She had a hot temper that sometimes got her into trouble. In the book of 1 Timothy, Paul advised the young pastor Timothy to be an example of love and joy so that he could earn the respect of his elders.

People filled with joy provide an example for everyone. Do you start the day with a few minutes of calmness and prayer to fill you with peace and hope so that you will be a good example? Do you pause to transform your thoughts of complaint to kinder thoughts? Choose to go forth in peace each day.

Dear Father, help me, today and always, to be an example of love, joy, and hope. Amen.

Squeezing Lemons

Taste and see that the LORD is good.

—Psalm 34:8

Lemons must be squeezed to get the juice for making lemonade or desserts. Squeezing also helps you to select the juiciest lemons before purchase. When the lemon is cut, the aroma of the lemon quickly fills the air with a sweet citrus scent. A little sweetener, when added, turns the sour liquid into something soothing and delightful. However, sometimes lemons have been equated with something broken or in ill-repair. Lemons suggest that something is bitter and unpleasant or adverse. In this instance, the solution to overcoming the adversity and solving the problem is to make lemonade. This comes from a familiar slogan that says, "When life gives you lemons, make lemonade." The idea is that you can turn a bad situation into something pleasant.

Have you turned problems into opportunities to improve a situation? Analyzing the problem lets you discover what went wrong, and it helps you to consider possible solutions or new approaches that will bring a good change. One way this is possible is by looking to God. The psalmist acknowledged the goodness of God and encouraged us to experience His goodness by seeking Him.

Dear God, guide me to choose the right solutions for my problems so that I will not be stuck with lemons. Amen.

A New Start

Therefore, if anyone is in Christ, the new creation has come: The old has gone, the new is here.

—2 Corinthians 5:17

Starting over after failure is really an opportunity for a fresh beginning. You have moved your starting line from the past to the present. You have opted to overcome the disappointment and move on to make new plans and set new goals. By doing this you can reestablish your hope and life. Do not think of failure and starting over as an anomaly. It is part of life and success. It can even be seen in your Christian experience. The word *sin* means "to miss the mark." Whenever we choose something that does not align with God's will, we are missing the mark. However, whenever we do sin, God will forgive us and will help us begin again.

Failure has a way of waking you up to new opportunities and moving you to a new start. You have learned lessons and now know how to begin well. As you evaluate what happened, look for the skills you learned or talents that worked to apply in the future. Envision new results and make new plans to reach your hopes. May your brand-new start produce a brand-new ending.

Dear God, thank You for the new life that became mine when I became a Christian. Help me to apply this same principle when I need a new start. Amen.

Put Your House in Order

Put your house in order, because you are going to die; you will not recover.

—2 Kings 20:1

Hopefully, you enjoy your home and have made it into a place that expresses your personality and exudes love. Your love and hope make all the difference in transforming your dwelling into a home. But if your home is in disarray, it may be time to put your house in order. God used the prophet Isaiah to warn King Hezekiah that he was going to die. But first Hezekiah needed to put his house in order. God was not speaking about the king's physical dwelling. He wanted Hezekiah to say his final goodbyes, to settle disputes, and to put his spiritual life in order.

The few personal touches of mementos, choices of colors, and arrangement of furnishings are part of your style and the message you give to visitors. Cozy seating or rooms that open up for a crowd reflect your preference for intimate conversations or fun group gatherings. You have taken steps to make sure that your physical home is in order. Make sure that your spiritual life is in order as well by walking with God and obeying all He has for you to do. Take pleasure in transforming any space that does not fit your vision into a place that expresses love and hope.

Dear God, help me to get my house in order, both physically and spiritually. Amen.

The Message of Children

Children are a gift from the LORD; they are a reward from him.

—Psalm 127:3 NLT

Have you held a baby recently or watched a curious toddler explore the world? Every baby is a gift from God specially created with love. The boundless energy and curiosity of a little one shows us that exploring is exciting. At every stage babies bring joy and delight. As newborns they do not yet interact with people; however, there is a special bonding that takes place with parents. Babies learn to feel safe and secure and can recognize the touch of their moms. As toddlers, your bundles of joy transform into balls of energy. Their curiosity keeps them constantly reaching, tasting, and touching as they crawl or toddle around the house, exploring its wonders. Referring to children, the psalmist said, "Blessed is the man whose quiver is full of them" (Psalm 127:5). Often the more babies one has, the more joy and blessings that are brought to the home.

Babies remind us that God created life and wants us to live each day with hope. As you go shopping or walk through the park, notice the babies that you pass or encounter. Notice, too, how these little bundles can grab attention. Rejoice at these little lives, and receive them as a message of hope.

Dear God, thank You for babies and the blessings they are. Thank You for the hope they bring to my life. Amen.

Change the World

"Go into all the world and preach the gospel to all creation."

—Mark 16:15

Every day you bless people when you reach out to share smiles and joy. You can bring hope with every encouraging word you speak. You may not be famous, but you make a difference each day as you touch the lives of people around you. If nothing more, your smile can light up a room and transform someone's day. There are many opportunities for changing the world or making a difference. In the '60s, President John Kennedy organized the Peace Corps to give young people an opportunity to help others and make a difference in the world. President Kennedy dreamed of an army of civilian volunteers who went into various parts of the world, in particular to underdeveloped countries to make a difference. There was no set protocol, the volunteers did whatever was needed. They built and taught in schools, developed water and sewer systems, taught and helped with agriculture, and many other projects. The Peace Corps was and still is a blessing to the world.

As you prepare yourself for the day ahead, recognize that God wants to use you to bless the world and spread the gospel. Pray that God will use you as His vessel to bless others.

Dear God, guide me to make a difference in the world today. Amen.

A New Hope

He who was seated on the throne said, "I am making everything new!"

—Revelation 21:5

Have you had a dream fall apart? When one thing goes wrong, many other things may also fall apart. Have you wondered if God is trying to get your attention, so you will turn your focus to a better dream or to Him? Sometimes the old must pass away before you can take another step to accomplish your goals and fulfill your dream. Failures are like heavy bags that slow you down if you focus on these disappointments. They are reminders of drudgery and pain that you have experienced up to this point. The baggage can even make it difficult to make decisions and be creative. Wipe the slate clean, and get rid of the baggage today. That is what God will do when He creates a new heaven and a new earth. The old heaven and earth will pass away, and God will make everything new.

Your shattered dream may be a heavy weight that you have carried for long enough. It may be time to put the pieces of your talents and abilities together and create something new. Be ready for a new hope, as you wait for God to show you a new and better way.

Dear Lord, show me Your plan for my life and reveal the dreams You have for me. Help me to bring together the pieces of my talents and abilities for a new and better dream. Amen.

Wrong Way, Right Attitude

Do not provoke your children to anger, but bring them up in the discipline and instruction of the Lord.

—Ephesians 6:4 ESV

When things go wrong, how do you react? You may pray immediately and then call a loved one or friend. You may get angry, hurt, or discouraged. You may cry and feel hopeless. There are so many ways to react, but there is a right and wrong way to respond to disappointment and hurt. Today's culture instigates the wrong way. Sometimes in society, when many speak out against hurts and problems, it is the angry voices that get most of the attention. Therefore, anger is perpetuated and impacts our society, especially the younger generation. Although the message is primarily for parents, the Bible is clear, we should not provoke children to anger or cause them to be exasperated. Exasperation means they have become hardened and subject to making bad decisions about their future.

When you continue to be gracious despite facing many difficulties in life, you show your faith in your future, and you inspire future generations to be patient and have hope. Having the grace to accept adversity and still smile is not easy, but it reflects that your heart remains filled with faith and hope.

Dear God, help me to have the right attitude when things go wrong so that my actions will teach young people lessons of hope. Amen.

Passing Through

While he was blessing them, he left them and was taken up into heaven.

—Luke 24:51

Has something that you thought would be temporary lasted a long time? As life continues, you move past some problems and resolve others. If one problem has continued too long, it might be time to move past it. Moving past a stage in your life often requires that you let go of that with which you may have formed an attachment. Can you imagine what Jesus must have felt when He ascended up to heaven? He had to let go of everything on earth that He held dear for so long. He had to let go of family, including His mother, Mary; His brothers, James and Jude; and other relatives and friends. But He also had to let go of the eleven trusted people whom He had grown to love the last three years of His life—His disciples. Their time together was short as Jesus was just passing through, and it was time for Him to return to the Father.

Remind yourself that all things on earth are temporary. Sometimes transitions are necessary in life. When these changes occur, hope will help us pass through these stages of life and head toward something new. Be thankful that new days and new solutions will come.

Dear God, whenever necessary, give me strength to move on to new hope. Amen.

Restlessness

Consider it pure joy, my brothers and sisters, whenever you face trials of many kinds.

—James 1:2

Have you felt restless and yet did not know what you wanted? It may be more than a passing feeling. It may be your soul seeking a new hope. Restlessness could be a sign of impatience that needs to be overcome. When we feel restless, we should focus on our blessings because God has helped us in many ways and will help move us one step closer to our dreams. Restlessness may also be brought on by difficulty. If so, find your peace in God, who will strengthen you to persevere. Restlessness can turn into excitement because of a new path that lies ahead. You only need to step forward into the new adventure with the knowledge that God walks with you.

The unsettled and excited feelings within you may be signals to climb a new mountain. Ella Wheeler Wilcox said, "When we tire of well-worn ways, we seek for new. This restless craving in the souls of men spurs them to climb, and to seek the mountain view." As you analyze your feelings, consider what dormant passions are waiting to be called into action. Look around for needs you can fill that match your passions or an unfulfilled dream that you might want to pursue. Let your restlessness prompt you to seek new dreams.

Dear God, when I become restless, guide me to new hopes and new dreams. Amen.

Lasting Hope

You ought to live holy and godly lives as you look forward to the day of God.

—2 Peter 3:11–12

𝓘n life you have faced your share of problems and setbacks, but thankfully each one was only temporary. You can rejoice in your lasting hope that believers will experience eternal peace in heaven. Yes, life is filled with setbacks, but it is also filled with joys. No matter which you are experiencing, the Bible encourages us to live every day in light of eternity. When we focus on heaven, we lead holy and godly lives. This kind of living is determined by our attitudes toward one another, toward God, and toward all that we do. Basically, a life of love flows from a heart that is focused on God. Does that mean you should exclude yourself from the world and your work? No, God desires that we remain in the world as His representatives. We are to love others and work hard, but we must keep our focus on eternity.

Have you found it easier to face disappointment because you know it will not last? Do you thank God each night for eternity? It can be easier to accept pain and suffering if you are accustomed to looking up to God. As you keep an eternal perspective in your heart, you will find temporary drawbacks less stressful. Looking toward the future brings hope, especially when you look toward eternity.

Dear God, when I face disappointment, help me to focus on eternity. Amen.

Droplets

I thirst for you, my whole being longs for you, in a dry and parched land where there is no water.

—Psalm 63:1

Have you ever experienced drought conditions? Everything starts to dry up and turn brown. The first droplet of rain brings great hope and change to a thirsty land. Drought can occur both in the environment and in your soul. The psalmist cried out to God because He was searching for Him. An absence of God's presence had left his soul parched. He was devastated without God. Environmental drought can be devastating to the land and the people, but drought of the soul is an even greater concern. Land can overcome drought one droplet of rain at a time. Eventually the rain will bring life back to the plants. Similarly, our souls require the water of life, which is the goodness of God.

There is a familiar story of a little boy on a shore who kept tossing drying starfish into the sea. He knew he would not be able to save them all, but his actions were significant to each one he was able to rescue. His good deeds saved the lives of many parched starfish. In the same way, each kind action you perform, like a droplet of water, quenches someone's thirst and brings hope.

Dear God, use me to be a droplet of water that inspires hope in someone's soul. Amen.

Learning from One Another

As iron sharpens iron, so one person sharpens another.

—Proverbs 27:17

One persistent woman changed the world for the deaf. Anne Sullivan opened Helen Keller's mind and taught her to communicate. Helen responded with joy, and even though she could not see or hear, she added hope and inspiration to the world. The Bible refers to this as iron sharpening iron. People can change the destiny of others by pouring their lives into other people. All it takes is one person who is willing to walk with you, teaching you and demonstrating the skill or talent you are wanting to learn. By that same token, that other person can develop from you, learning about your skills and talents as well. This requires that you spend time with the people who have what you need, and that you are willing to mentor or share your life with others.

Your power to touch lives is enormous if you do not give up. As you believe in your hope and pursue it, you can change the world around you. As you wake each day, consider what you can do to touch one life that may also touch other lives. Consider who can help you learn something new so that you will achieve your goal. Like iron sharping iron, you can make a difference to yourself and others.

Dear God, help me to learn from others and use me to help others so that our hopes remain strong. Amen.

DECEMBER

·•··•••··•·••··•••·•··•••··•••·

*I wonder if the snow loves the trees and the
fields, that it kisses them so gently? And then
it covers them up snug, you know, with a
white quilt; and perhaps it says, "Go to sleep,
darlings, till the summer comes again."*

—Lewis Carroll

A Light of Hope

If I say, "Surely the darkness will hide me and the light become
night around me," even the darkness will not be dark to you.

—Psalm 139:11–12

Although hopelessness clouds the brightest life, hope brings a drastic change, like night to day. As the sun will outlast any cloud and one ray of sunshine can change a gloomy sky to glory, hope is mightier and will outlast the darkest times. Hope, like sunrays piercing the clouds, transforms and revives. It is a tool in the hand of God to strengthen your faith. Unlike our circumstances, He never changes; because He is our everlasting home, we find hope even in dark moments on earth.

Believing God is like letting a ray of light lead your way out of a pit. His strength reaches the weak. Unlike our pride, which says we should be able to work our way out of the pit, God gives hope based on His own work; He wants us to call on Him, the true Light. Hope that rests on His grace is the hope that finds daylight in a dark night.

President John F. Kennedy said, "Every area of trouble gives out a ray of hope—and the one unchangeable certainty is that nothing is certain or unchangeable." God said there is no pit so deep that He cannot find us, and His light will guide us home.

Dear God, thank You for being my everlasting hope and for being a light in the darkness. Amen.

Happy Thoughts

*Whatever is lovely, whatever is commendable, if there is any excellence,
if there is anything worthy of praise, think about these things.*

—Philippians 4:8 ESV

If you have ever hiked, you have surely come to a rough patch that forced you to climb, leap, or wade. Where the path is smooth, the journey is easy to love. Challenges, however, not only alter the scenery, but they also expose our weaknesses. Similarly, life is more difficult than we wish. But the lovely moments are no less true than the rough edges of life. We are never alone, even when we struggle or give up. God is with us, and He uses the difficulties of life for our good.

As Paul learned by thinking on what is lovely—even though imprisoned—the mind has ways of overcoming doubt and hopelessness. He knew that grace is the power that would inspire him to think in a godly way. In society this is sometimes known as "positive thinking." Paul knew from experience that thinking virtuously would strengthen faith and would even produce joy through suffering. The power is in thinking on whatever is lovely, true, and excellent—and knowing that the beauty of life in Christ is incomparably greater than the day's suffering. The rough spots of life are not the whole journey.

Dear Father, teach me to keep my inner eye focused on beauty, truth, and joy; I hope in You, the One who can lead my mind, especially when I pass through the difficult places. Amen.

Thy Will

"I lay down my life that I may take it up again."

—John 10:17 ESV

Everyone hopes God's answer to our prayers will be according to our own will. A disciple's task, however, is to identify with the prayer that Jesus taught: "Thy will be done" (Matthew 6:10 KJV). This may mean a more difficult path than what we think is best. We may ask questions like these: Will God heal me? Will God take these financial burdens away from me? God may take these problems from you, but He may not. God knows, in ways we cannot perceive, that our suffering is a participation in His redemptive work. Even as you pray and give your problems to God, ask God to use your experiences to draw others to Him.

Trust that God will be with you when you face suffering. Like Jesus, we must put God's will over our own desires. In Gethsemane Jesus prayed, "Father, if you are willing, take this cup from me; yet not my will, but yours be done" (Luke 22:42). He saw that without His suffering, mankind would be without hope. By the power of God, Jesus chose what would be both painful and best rather than what was easy and comfortable. He kept His eyes on eternity, not on the limited scope of His persecution.

Dear Father, you know my fears and weaknesses. I long for the kind of hope that my Savior demonstrates. May I love and hope in You. Amen.

Early Morning Care

There are different kinds of working, but in all of them and in everyone it is the same God at work.

—1 Corinthians 12:6

It is natural to wake up thinking about your to-do list. It feels more urgent and necessary than starting the day with praise, prayer, and songs of worship. But the true need is for each day to be handled with loving care, not anxiety. We need the Spirit to help us focus on our hope. Spiritual disciplines help you "live by faith, not by sight" (2 Corinthians 5:7). Prioritizing problems when you first wake up is a choice to put your hope in your own strength. However, hope in God's strength helps you focus on what matters for eternity.

Some keep a Bible or devotional book next to their bed, or they tune their alarm to a Christian station. Then the first thing they see and hear each morning may lead them to God. Each person has his or her own routine. A counselor may schedule a prayer walk three mornings of the week with a friend. A mother may pray and worship on her porch before dawn. A recovering addict may wake and lay his weakness at the feet of God, confessing, "I can't handle this. I need you." Whatever helps you place the day in God's care is empowering.

Dear Father, my work is Yours. My strength is Yours. And I am Yours. Amen.

Focus on the Unseen

So we fix our eyes not on what is seen, but on what is unseen, since
what is seen is temporary, but what is unseen is eternal.

—2 Corinthians 4:18

Hope is what makes the Christ-follower's world a different place from the secular person's world. Believers should not hope in this world, with all that shakes it up from generation to generation, but should hope in eternity. God said, "When the earth and all its people quake, it is I who hold its pillars firm" (Psalm 75:3 NIV). Everything on earth will pass away, including nightmares and problems, but God and His love will remain.

Focusing on God and looking beyond today's troubles are what keeps you sane when the world seems shaky. God taught His covenant people to pass the stories of God's providence to their children, testifying to His love and power. Then new generations would learn to set their hopes on God too.

It is normal to focus on your worries. That is why He reminds us to focus on His love. Your testimony is a means to hold on to your own hope, and it will also lead others to set their hope on God, who has demonstrated His power through the ages. Steadying your hope in God makes all the difference to your future and to the generations ahead.

Dear Father, because You have been faithful to all generations, our hope is firm even when the world is shaken. Amen.

God Is Bigger

For I consider that the sufferings of this present time are not worth comparing with the glory that is to be revealed to us.

—Romans 8:18 ESV

Bad news comes to all people at some point, and during this time, we need to cling to the good news. Otherwise fear, stress, or grief would overwhelm us. Only because of God's mercy, which is both deep and strong, can we escape the fate of those who are overwhelmed by trouble. God knows that times of trouble will try to overpower our hopes, so He said, "Call upon me in the day of trouble; I will deliver you, and you shall glorify me" (Psalm 50:15 ESV). The bad news that overwhelms us cannot overcome God, and His nature is to deliver those who call out to Him.

When someone close to us dies, we are still reeling from the loss years later. It shatters our world. Still, in devastating times like these, we can hope in God's goodness, which is deeper than our grief. Whenever our minds replay bad news over again, we can release these thoughts to God. The loss is intolerable. But we must anchor ourselves in the shelter of the One who is more solid than earth itself, whose goodness immeasurably exceeds any ill. He has proven Himself to be bigger than all our enemies: fear, pain, loss, and hopelessness.

Dear Father, thank You for your immeasurable goodness, despite my sufferings. Amen.

Until That Day

"Before they call I will answer; while they are still speaking I will hear."
—Isaiah 65:24

$\mathcal{I}$saiah prophesied of a day when "the wolf and the lamb shall graze together" (Isaiah 65:25 ESV). On that day, God said that He will answer the prayers of His people. But until that day comes, we must continue to put our hope in God. Today is the anniversary of Pearl Harbor, which President Franklin D. Roosevelt called "a date that will live in infamy." Since 1941 we have seen many infamous days, and we know that aggressions will continue until this prophecy is fulfilled: "For behold, I create new heavens and a new earth, and the former things shall not be remembered" (Isaiah 65:17 ESV).

The hope of a new heaven and earth is strong within our spirits. But even now, as those empowered by His Spirit await that day, we experience victory in the presence of the enemy. War is still with us, but God is working in all things to advance life. Already the faithful can point to answers sent while their prayers were only thoughts. John wrote, "The darkness is passing away and the true light is already shining" (1 John 2:8 ESV). God's presence, on a day like December 7, 1941, is like a light shining through the present darkness. Those who put faith in God do not lose hope because until that day arrives, God is with us.

Dear Father, we will hope in You, as You bring strength into the battle against darkness. Amen.

Stops Along the Way

"She has done a beautiful thing to me."

—Mark 14:6

As you look ahead at the path of your life, you may realize it is a long journey. But stopping to admire the scenery along the way will add peace to your experience. This is the kind of thing you do only if you relish the beauty of being alive in creation. This is a deeper experience of life than merely goal-reaching. God wants us to enjoy His creation and the beautiful moments of life.

Jesus lived the world's most significant journey, but He stopped to cherish children and bless them (Mark 10:16). He sent his disciples and friends away from Him so that He could commune alone with His Father. He paused to become acquainted with the man in the tree as He passed through Jericho (Luke 19:5). At a feast, Jesus appreciated the beautiful act one follower performed with her alabaster jar of perfume (Mark 14:3–9). His parables showed how observant He was of all that is fascinating in nature, the world, and the human spirit. In your journey, take time to enjoy the scenery. These are the moments that string together to create a meaningful life.

Dear God, thank You for everything You do to teach us to take time for beauty. Amen.

Navigating the Wilderness

Jesus answered, "It is written."

—Matthew 4:4

You may have trampled through wild areas and battled insects, dodged poison ivy, and cringed as a snake slithered past. Such experiences help you appreciate the comforts of home. But as Christians we know that such experiences are temporary. They are part of developing perseverance, as described in Romans 5:3–5. Jesus demonstrated an example of perseverance at the very outset of His ministry; He faced the tempter throughout His forty-day fast in the wilderness. Jesus overcame these temptations by relying on an experienced guide: God the Father, as revealed by the Scriptures.

As you navigate your way through difficulties, imitate Jesus. Just as you need a guide who is experienced in overcoming the wild when you are exploring the wilderness, you also need a spiritual guide who will help you overcome temptations. Continually feed on the Word of God as Jesus did, and during trials, the Scriptures will sustain you.

When you face a new wild territory, ask for a guide. God provides both spiritual leaders and friends who have navigated the wilderness. The Word of God within you and the guidance of fellow sojourners will help you reach the end of your journey safely.

Dear Lord, You are our hope; all guidance and sustenance come from You. Amen.

Success

Therefore God has highly exalted him.

—Philippians 2:9 ESV

Failure, one of our most feared conditions, can be a path to tremendous strength. True success can come only by a certain selfless acceptance of the failures along your way. The secret to not being destroyed by failure is to put your hope in God and His plan, not in your pride, others' approval, or success of the wrong sort.

This spiritual discipline is most evident in Jesus, as retold in Philippians 2: Christ, though He was God, agreed to be obedient as a servant. He did not grasp on to His power and take His place as King during His ministry. Instead, He agreed to be a humble servant, a failure in some people's eyes. What leader could be considered a success who is charged with capital crimes and publicly executed? Since He continuously remembered where His hope lay, He accepted failure so that He could later exhibit more strength than any other king could imagine. If we remove our pride and put our hope in whatever God calls us to, our humility will be like that of Christ's. In the right time, God exalted Him, just as He will bless us in His timing.

Dear God, save me, Lord, from fear of failure. You are the true success, and in You all my failures are redeemed. Thank You for loving me not for what I do but because Your love is unfailing. Amen.

Intentional Living

So Peter got out of the boat and walked on the water and came to Jesus.

—Matthew 14:29 ESV

As the months and years fly past, you soon recognize that life is too short. Even a day is too short to pursue all the good life lays before you, but this will foster hope to live intentionally. If you choose to spend time doing what interests you, you will begin down a path to live with zeal. Do you intentionally arrange your schedule so that there is time for those things you know would interest you? Do you make decisions to invest your hours in what feeds your hope?

Peter was the disciple most likely to act on his passions, for good or ill. If anyone was going to get out of the boat when he saw the potential of walking on water, it would be him. Some critique Peter's moment because he began to sink due to a lack of faith. But Jesus may have appreciated Peter's zeal and earnest desire to join Him in His miracle.

The apostle Paul wrote that our works were "prepared beforehand, that we should walk in them" (Ephesians 2:10 ESV). It changes the whole perspective on opportunities when we realize they have been waiting for us. They are gifts God wrapped up for us that are delivered when He calls us forth; we find them throughout life when we choose to pursue a worthy cause.

Dear God, help me to live an intentional life by walking in the works You have prepared for me. Amen.

The Heart of Hope

Whatever you do, work at it with all your heart, as working for the Lord, not for human masters.

—Colossians 3:23

As your heart beats, it keeps blood and oxygen flowing in your veins. It pumps blood to every cell in your body in less than a minute. The heart is not just significant because it sustains life; it also symbolizes the center of emotions. How long has it been since you worked at something with your whole heart? Think of how you gave the task your total effort, with passion and focus. Putting forth this kind of effort brings joy.

As you pour yourself into something you hope for, you keep your hope alive, beating steadily like your heart. We never fully comprehend how many other systems—mental, physical, and emotional—that we pump life into when our work produces joy. Wholehearted work is a godlike quality; it is like a reflection of God's work to create the universe. The Bible describes a picture of His joy in creation; personifying wisdom, King Solomon wrote, "The LORD formed me from the beginning . . . and how happy I was with the world he created; how I rejoiced with the human family" (Proverbs 8:22, 31 NLT). God delights in your wholehearted effort that produces joy.

Dear God, You created each element of the universe with wholehearted joy. Renew my hope in the life You have blessed me with. Give me a vigorous heart. Amen.

Flashes of Hope

Moses did not know that the skin of his face shone because he had been talking with God.

—Exodus 34:29 ESV

Lightning helps clear particles in the atmosphere. It turns nitrogen into a more useful state to nurture plant growth, and it helps create ozone. Lightning also led to the discovery of electricity. There is power in the flash of lightning—maybe more power than you are equipped to meet. You love to see it, yet you fear its power. When you hear thunder, you take cover. By the time lightning arrives, you can marvel at it from a safe place. Beholding its power, you are grateful to see its splendor. Seeing its dramatic performance, you are reminded of the might of God.

Moses, too, longed to see the power of God on display and said to Him, "Show me your glorious presence" (Exodus 33:18 NLT). With this reverent request, God revealed Himself to Moses, although Moses was not able to look upon God's face. Afterward, Moses returned to the Israelites as a changed man. The people could not bear even the brightness of his face, which shone brightly because he had been in God's presence. Although we cannot see God face-to-face in this life, we can see glimpses of Him through His love and power, which will produce flashes of hope.

Dear Father, I marvel at Your power and love; let them change my life. Amen.

Treausres

"He has filled the hungry with good things."

—Luke 1:53 ESV

After praying for renewed hope to energize her own project, a publicist turned to every friend who would listen, telling them how God had answered her; He had given her the word *treasures* in reference to our potential works. God let her know that her projects were treasures He had given to her. She knew then that God was cheering for her. When she passed this on, others' hopes were reborn. Do you speak encouragement to your friends? The language of hope is faith-filled. Like the language of love, hope is expressed in words, service, gifts, and time invested in someone's dreams.

Thank those who inspire you, and pass it on. Incredible things were said and enacted around Mary, an unknown girl of seemingly no significance. Each event was a marvel to Mary. She "treasured up all these things, pondering them in her heart" (Luke 2:19 ESV). Neither she nor anyone she knew imagined the treasure given to her by God, nor did she understand the universal significance of her accepting and bringing forth her treasure. Seek out and receive hope in its many forms. And when you bring forth your treasures, remember you are doing so to God's delight.

Dear Lord, thank You for creating in me a mind that dreams and a heart that believes. Amen.

Called to Hope

Having the eyes of your heart enlightened, that you may know what is the hope to which he has called you.

—Ephesians 1:18 ESV

Ephesians opens with a great prayer for enlightenment to the hope God has called us to. It is God's power at work; and that power in us is "the same as the mighty strength he exerted when he raised Christ from the dead and seated him at his right hand in the heavenly realms" (Ephesians 1:19–20). The hope God calls us to is more than the eyes can see; it takes "the eyes of your heart" (Ephesians 1:18 ESV). God enlightens our hearts, more so than our minds, to know a hope that is higher, a strength that is mightier, than anything on earth—mightier than even death. No adversary can challenge the power that is at work in you, which is the resurrection power.

Amazingly, unlike the temporal goals and good works we hope to achieve, this hope is utterly free to believers. We are not asked to work toward our hope; it is a finished work that Christ completed. He who attained the victory over every adversary has attained it for you. And until you see Him with your actual eyes, the power that raised Him from death is at work in you simply because you believe Him.

Dear God, I thank You, Father, Son, and Holy Spirit for the hope that is mine by Your power. Amen.

Advent of Hope

"I will give you a new heart, and a new spirit I will put within you."
—Ezekiel 36:26 ESV

Jesus told a skeptical crowd, who wanted to kill Him for calling God His own Father, that they had missed something obvious in the Scriptures that they held so dear: "It is [the Scriptures] that bear witness about me" (John 5:39 ESV). Even Moses wrote of the Christ who would come. Ironically, the crowd had set their hopes on Moses but did not believe his words about the coming Messiah (John 5:45).

From Genesis to Malachi, hope had centered on a coming Messiah whose advent would signify a new heart and a new spirit for everyone who would follow Him. Yes, sometimes we fail to appreciate these messianic prophesies because the identity of the Messiah isn't a mystery to us. If this Christmas season needs an infusion of hope, consider the anticipation with which our faith ancestors awaited the Messiah.

Can we recapture the hope of Simeon, who occupied the temple daily and was promised that he would live to see Christ? When baby Jesus arrived at the temple, Simeon took Him up in his arms and praised God. He said, "My eyes have seen your salvation that you have prepared in the presence of all peoples, a light for revelation to the Gentiles and glory to your people Israel" (Luke 2:30–32 ESV).

Dear God, may we hope fervently for Your advent. We long to see you. Help us recapture our awe. Amen.

Waiting Hopefully

"Blessed are those servants whom the master finds awake when he comes."

—Luke 12:37 ESV

We wait for our future with great anticipation, but the future always remains elusive. Although you only dimly guess what is the potential of your own soul, waiting on the One who calls you is the truly hopeful strategy. God knows what He will do within you and what future you will receive. Therefore, you must have discernment in your opportunities, and do not to limit yourself by small thinking. Jesus said, "What is impossible with men is possible with God" (Luke 18:27 ESV). But remember, overzealous hope can strain you if you become desperate for your hopes to be realized in your own timing. However, if you follow the Spirit's leading, you can discern His direction from your own zeal, which will produce greater joy.

The most important part of our waiting is to be a part of the work of God. Take an elderly pastor, for example. At his old age, he still has a youthful faith, and he says he will keep on evangelizing and ministering until Christ returns. His desire is to share God's Word with others for as long as he can. His eyes sparkle, and he cannot contain his enthusiasm. In the same way, let us pursue God's kingdom as we wait in hope to see the future God has for us.

Dear God, our hopes in You are true. You have our future in Your hands, and it is wonderful. Amen.

The Hope of the World

So now faith, hope, and love abide, these three.

—1 Corinthians 13:13 ESV

By giving of yourself—in shared time, talent, or gifts—you participate in the world's greatest hope: love. Consider this story: a woodworker wanted to give his nephew a special gift, so he paid attention to the boy's interests. After inspiration, he worked up his design; he started in summer and worked through fall building the piece. The enjoyment he received by turning his talents into a tangible gift for his nephew helped him feel his nephew's love throughout the year. He was never alone while in the shop; as he measured, cut, built, and carved, his beloved nephew seemed near. And when the woodworker revealed a carved airplane, the boy's gratitude and love only strengthened the bond of love.

In an address titled "The Greatest Thing in the World," evangelist Henry Drummond said, "You will find as you look back upon your life that the moments that stand out, the moments when you have really lived, are the moments when you have done things in a spirit of love." We must make an effort to share love, just as the woodworker did. If everyone were loved as well as the woodworker's nephew, much hope would be fulfilled. Every form of gift you give is a shared hope until the time comes when all hopes are realized, and love alone remains.

Dear God, we thank You, Father, for opportunities to be like You—sharing love in tangible ways. Amen.

Hope in Truth

As for us, we cannot help speaking about what we have seen and heard.
—Acts 4:20

Robert Kennedy said, "Each time a man stands up for an ideal, or acts to improve the lot of others, or strikes out against injustice, he sends forth a tiny ripple of hope." Your words and choices have an influence, and sometimes God alone knows the effects of what we do. When you study the Scriptures, you discover God's truth. Convicted by His Word, you learn how to live. As you live out the truth, you bring hope to those who see Christ in you.

The words of Peter and John brought hope to five thousand in one day. The Jewish religious leaders raged. They arrested the apostles, demanding, "By what power or by what name did you do this?" (Acts 4:7 ESV). Then they warned the disciples "to speak no more to anyone in this name" (Acts 4:17 ESV). Peter and John, even though they were uneducated men, withstood the elite: "Whether it is right in the sight of God to listen to you rather than to God, you must judge, for we cannot but speak of what we have seen and heard" (Acts 4:19–20 ESV).

Let God's Word give you wisdom and guide your heart to live out the truth.

Dear God, give me faith to uphold what You have told me, especially when truth goes against the tide. Give me the strength to stand up for what is right. Amen.

Growing Hope

And out of the ground the LORD God made to spring up every tree that is pleasant.

—Genesis 2:9 ESV

God's mercies are new every morning. Hope returns every morning, no matter what the night has inflicted and is a surprising evidence of God's continuous mercy. The heart continually finds a new seedling of hope, morning after morning. The seedling comes from God, who lets you determine what it becomes. If tended and fed, hope will send out new shoots, unfold new leaves, even bud, blossom, and flower.

Contemplation and prayer are hope's true food. In contemplation of God and His mercies, you strengthen hope. In feeding on His testimonies, His nature, and His promises, you give hope its rich soil. No amount of chemical stimulation can make hope the robust garden you covet. Hope is founded in the truth of the everlasting God and His faithfulness. Hope grows because God pursues the straying, welcomes sinners, and transforms lives. God called forth something out of nothing and conquered our enemies every day since the world's first morning, making hope vigorous. Contemplate on all these things that God has done. Then ask for more hope; seek it from the Giver of abundant life. When doubt intrudes, pray all the more.

Dear God, You who made heaven and earth, no hope is too small for You to make into a bountiful garden. Amen.

Hope Eternal

In Christ shall all be made alive.

—1 Corinthians 15:22 ESV

We who believe in the resurrected Christ are never past a youthful hope. A character in Joseph Conrad's novel *Victory* pronounced woe on one "whose heart has not learned while young to hope, to love—and to put its trust in life." However, woe cannot rob *your* heart of learning to hope, if your heart belongs to God, because "he has also set eternity in the human heart" (Ecclesiastes 3:11).

You are young and growing younger with eternity in your heart. If your bones do not show it, it is only that they still await resurrection. You underwent resurrection when you were immersed in Jesus. We can be inspired by a vigorous eighty-five-year-old who is passionate whenever he reminds his friends to lay hold of God's promises and whenever he attests to the authority given to anyone covered by the blood of Jesus. When you lay hold of the power and promises, he says, enemies must fall. Despair falls back. With the Lord, your strength is renewed, and hope is part of it. Seeing life brimming from his face, you know you are young in God, with a heart still learning all the ways of hope.

Dear God, I have not learned hope perfectly, but in You I am a child; teach my heart to hope. Amen.

Hope of Love

In the image of God he created him; male and female.

—Genesis 1:27 ESV

The triune God, prototype of all loving relationships, has wired us for love and companionship. The reason why the longing to share life with someone is one of life's greatest desires is because God longs for you to share the intimacy of His own eternal communion: Father, Son, and Holy Spirit. The feeling of loneliness is an effect of not having a perfect loving relationship. When we are in heaven with Christ, we will experience the fulfillment that comes from a perfect relationship. Until then we will develop lasting relationships that reflect God's love and that will be made complete in heaven. Let us follow the words of the author of Hebrews: "Consider how we may spur one another on toward love and good deeds, not giving up meeting together, as some are in the habit of doing, but encouraging one another—and all the more as you see the Day approaching" (Hebrews 10:24–25).

Recognize the sanctity of your relationships by committing them to God and nurturing your love for Him as your primary companion. God brings into your life the right people at the right time. Those with the potential to remain are those who treasure your heart as God's own beloved. Companions who reciprocate God's love reinforce our hope.

Dear God, let me know love as You do. Entrusting my heart to You, I have everything I long for. Amen.

The Birth of Hope

"For God so loved the world, that he gave his only Son, that whoever believes in him should not perish but have eternal life."

—John 3:16 ESV

Christmas celebrations centering anywhere other than on the hope born to the world drown out the good news of Christ's birth. It was a silent, holy night when our Savior was born. The birth prophesied for generations had silently shaken the powers of hell. No one but His parents heard the newborn King's cries; the Hope born to generations is now heralded in the silence of a heart that worships, realizing Jesus "has caused us to be born again to a living hope" (1 Peter 1:3 ESV). Much of the world was unaware of Christ's coming. Similarly, those who are caught up in Christmas traditions today but do not celebrate the hope that Christ's birth gave to the world are unaware of the true power of Christmas.

The writer of Hebrews said that everyone was enslaved by the fear of death before God revealed His salvation in the life of Christ. If the idea of Christmas sets you free—your hope in Christ genuinely releases you from slavery—then you celebrate the birth of Christ. Because of His birth, we can have a new birth: "You have been born again, not of perishable seed, but of imperishable, through the living and abiding word of God" (1 Peter 1:23 ESV).

Dear God, thank You for becoming flesh. I thank You with my whole heart that I am Yours forever. Amen.

One Star

When they saw the star, they were overjoyed.

—Matthew 2:10

The Christmas lights now in the neighborhoods have no rival at any other season. We put up lights to celebrate the Light of the world who was born, but the very first Christmas light was a distant star. Almost every soul on earth missed it. No one knew to look for it except the wise men who were entrusted with the secret. When they traveled across the hemisphere following a star, even God's covenant nation was unaware. People longed to see a great light. Prophets of Israel had foretold of the Messiah, but few hoped to see Him in their time. Times were not ideal. A foreign oppressor held power over God's people. Soldiers dominated the streets, and taxes were harsh. God's temple stood amid infidels. Who kept the Law, in its essence? Did any of God's people love Him with their whole hearts and souls? The people longed for the Messiah, but they did not see the signs of His coming.

Then the child came in an unknown fashion. Those star-following wise men were of the first to seek Him out: "The star that they had seen when it rose went before them until it came to rest over the place where the child was" (Matthew 2:9 ESV). Each of us sees hope that no one else may see. Share your hope and your light with someone who needs it.

Dear God, You are the Life and the Light of the world. Thank You for revealing Yourself to me. Amen.

The Hope of Ages

But when the set time had fully come, God sent his Son, born of a woman, born under the law.

—Galatians 4:4

It was a very long wait from the Garden of Eden to the stable where Jesus was born. But God told His people about the One who would bring salvation. The first messianic prophecy said this: "He shall bruise your head, and you shall bruise his heel" (Genesis 3:15 ESV). Abraham's promise came next: through his offspring, everyone on earth would be blessed. Christ's coming was also foretold at Jacob's death. Moses foretold it when he delivered the Law. Even Balaam foretold of a star coming out of Jacob and a scepter to crush the enemies. Throughout the Psalms and the Prophets, messianic references become more explicit—and heartrending, in context of the nation's rebellion, their sorrows, and the sorrows of their Father.

All throughout the ages, as people had waited for the advent of the Hope of Israel, God was working in ways we did not know. "When the set time had fully come, God sent his Son" (Galatians 4:4). Waiting is demanded of every age of His people. Even now, we have waited thousands of years for His final return and for the fulfillment of everyone's hopes. We cannot comprehend his timing, but we know the One we believe in.

Dear God, I rejoice in Your coming, I trust in Your promises; I long for Your return! Come, Lord Jesus! Amen.

Reason for Hope

Let your unfailing love surround us, LORD, for our hope is in you alone.

—Psalm 33:22 NLT

Jesus was sent to suffer, die, and rise to bring great hope to all. Before His advent here, in heaven He accepted the assignment, the unfathomable love of God that was being enacted on our behalf. It came at a cost we are slow to see. We are so loved; how could we not hope in such a loving God? At His birth, becoming fully human yet divine, did the boy still know the full sacrifice He had agreed to? By examining His recorded words, we see that Jesus as a man had to agree all over again to do the job He had agreed to before the Father sent Him: resisting all temptation, learning obedience with much suffering, laying down His life, bearing all the sin of mankind, and lying forsaken in a tomb—to reconcile all things to God.

Is Jesus the reason for your hope? If you see Him with the eyes of your heart, you know the reason for your hope. If you cannot see Him, ask Him to reveal Himself to you. You are surrounded by the love of Jesus, who wants the best for you. He sent His Spirit to guide you and enlighten your mind and help you pursue your hopes. Let Jesus be the reason you continue to persevere and believe in your hopes.

Dear God, thank You for Jesus, who is the reason for my hope. Amen.

Faithful Hope

Blessed is she who has believed that the Lord would fulfill his promises to her!

—Luke 1:45

When you listen to God and learn at His feet daily, you will receive certain promises. Through Spirit-given affirmations, you recognize promises that came not from your own will but from your Father, who cherishes your desires. You must believe in God's promises and have faith that He will keep them.

Imagine what kind of faith Mary, the mother of Jesus, must have cultivated beforehand that enabled her to trust God's plan. So it was that from the lips of an unremarkable girl came a soaring piece of poetry, prophetic and memorialized:

> My soul magnifies the Lord,
> and my spirit rejoices in God my Savior,
> for he has looked on the humble estate of his servant.
> For behold, from now on all generations will call me blessed;
> for he who is mighty has done great things for me,
> and holy is his name.

LUKE 1:46–49 ESV

As you aspire to something God has promised you, pray in faith as He leads you toward the new blessings.

Dear God, keep me believing your promises as I hope, especially when my faith is tested. Amen.

Boundless

*And this is the testimony: God has given us eternal life, and this life
is in his Son.*

—1 John 5:11

When you contemplate the redemption story, from the Fall to the days when thunder, quakes, and empty tombs revealed Jesus' death and resurrection, you get an inkling of the imagination of God. He is glorified when His children imitate Him, using the boundless imagination He gave us. Imagination is far from childish, but rather it is strenuous, demanding work. It is a work of God. He loves bigger thinking, freer imagining. Trust Him and ask for more.

One practice to help you develop your boundless imagination is to keep a list. As you go through the Scriptures each day, write everything God says you are. For example, from John 3:18 you can claim this identity: I am not condemned. From Romans 3:24, you can say this: I am justified by His grace. Keep adding to your list daily, and repeat those truths to yourself. You will not succumb to your doubts if you believe what God says about you in His Word. God says that your life is in Christ. When remembering and claiming this truth, you knock down invisible fences that limit you. Let your imagination work for you in freeing your mind from false boundaries, and grow into a boundless hope!

Dear God, my life is in You. Inspire me to join with You in Your creativity. Amen.

Exploring the Future

I felt sure of all of you, that my joy would be the joy of you all.
—2 Corinthians 2:3 ESV

Have you ever desired the close bond of the first disciples? The depth of their shared life surpasses modern practices. When Paul told the Corinthians he was sure his joy would bring joy to them, it was in the context of extreme suffering. They had suffered vicariously when Paul was "so utterly burdened beyond [his] strength that [he] despaired of life itself" (2 Corinthians 1:8 ESV). Only such friends care to feel each other's suffering and joys.

It is rare to replicate that community, but we need to try. Continually seek from God what you need in terms of communal life among creative thinkers. Be sensitive and follow as He leads you into a close-knit community. Invite some people to walk, talk, have lunch, or even to start a group. Ask the Spirit for opportunities to meet regularly with those few. Inspiring people are too valuable to shy away from. Even if you are an introvert, your best thinking is enhanced by community. Some need one-on-one friend time; some need a book club or Bible class, and some need a setting like a coffee shop where people are near but not intruding. Your future is wide open as you enter a new year with new hopes among encouraging people.

Dear God, bring me into fellowship with friends who bring You joy and who can share mine. Amen.

Beautiful Dreams

"Your old men shall dream dreams, and your young men shall see visions."

—Joel 2:28 ESV

As God's sons and daughters, we have His Spirit pouring out on us. He began to pour it out at Pentecost, but the Spirit is like a river that flows on and on. Ezekiel records a prophecy in which believers are pictured like trees that grow on either side of the river, whose leaves are always green; they keep bearing fruit month after month. The fruit of the tree "will serve for food and their leaves for healing" (Ezekiel 47:12). This is a dream that inspires confidence. Not because of your own spirit, but because God's Spirit is poured out on you. God equips you so that He can use you to fulfill His purposes.

The dreams He gives to you are to be taken seriously. You are meant to be fruitful, to nourish, and to heal. Your dreams take part in God's grand plan to heal and bring beauty throughout the generations, to the very end of the age. God's prophets have always warned about a time of trials unlike any before. But He also has promised that when darkness increases, the light will increase even more. For this reason He distributes His gifts: your dreams, your spirit, your nourishing, and your healing. These are sustained by His flowing River.

Dear God, I am Yours with dreams You gave to me to bless others. I am overwhelmed by Your grace. Keep my hope fresh. Amen.

A New View

Will not the ministry of the Spirit have even more glory?
—2 Corinthians 3:8 ESV

With Jesus one last time, the eleven stood atop Mount Olivet. They were at the end of an era for both themselves and their nation. Having apprenticed as Jewish disciples of the Messiah, they would descend the mountain as apostles and would usher in a new era. They naively believed that Christ would return in their lifetime, but this contrasted with the grand hope of God's plan. They asked him, "Lord, will you at this time restore the kingdom to Israel?" (Acts 1:6 ESV). He said to them, "It is not for you to know times or seasons that the Father has fixed by his own authority. But you will receive power when the Holy Spirit has come upon you, and you will be my witnesses in Jerusalem and in all Judea and Samaria, and to the end of the earth" (Acts 1:7–8 ESV).

His emphasis was on the power they would receive. But the timing was not for them to know. As a servant of Christ, there are two things you can assuredly hope in: you have God's power, and you are His witness. On the last day of the year, you stand at the end of an era and on the edge of your new hopes. Although much of the path is hidden, you can count on the calling and power of God. May your journey be blessed.

Dear Lord, as I enter a new year, I ask Your blessing on my hopes and dreams. Amen.

Notes

Scripture Index

Scripture Index

Scripture Index

Scripture Index

Scripture Index

Scripture Index

Scripture Index

Scripture Index

Scripture Index